Designing with Models

A Studio Guide to Architectural Process Models
Third Edition

CRISS B. MILLS

WILEY

John Wiley & Sons, Inc.

Library of Congress Cataloging-in-Publication Data:

Mills, Criss.

 Designing with models : a studio guide to architectural process models / Criss B. Mills. – 3rd ed.

  p. cm.

 Includes bibliographical references and index.

 ISBN 978-0-470-49885-9 (pbk. : alk. paper); ISBN 978-0-470-94739-5 (ebk); ISBN 978-0-470-94740-1 (ebk); ISBN 978-0-470-94741-8 (ebk); ISBN 978-0-470-95067-8 (ebk); ISBN 978-0-470-95080-7 (ebk)

1. Architectural models--Handbooks, manuals, etc. I. Title.

 NA2790.M5 2011

 720.22'8–dc22 2010036844

CONTENTS

ACKNOWLEDGMENTS

Many of the examples in this book were submitted by students, professors, and architectural offices. Their examples have imparted far greater depth to the text, and I wish to express my full appreciation for their efforts. I would also like to thank Tonya Beach and Sara Baxter for their valuable contributions ith editing, support, and technical advice.

FOREWORD

This book is about using the architectural model as a tool for discovery. When used as an integral part of the design process, study models are capable of generating information in time comparable to drawing and offer one of the strongest exploration methods available. The strategies and techniques presented here provide a broad range of options. However, because this book is primarily concerned with the design process, elaborate presentation models are not stressed. Instead, work is explored with quick-sketch constructions and simple finish models that can be built with materials suitable for studio or in-house construction. Although most of the projects are approached from an architectural perspective, the techniques apply equally well to three-dimensional artwork and industrial design.

There are several reasons why models should be part of every design process. Perhaps the most important one is the understanding to be gained by seeing form in physical space. This physical presence allows the designer to interact directly with the model and obtain instant feedback. Another benefit inherent to physical models, as opposed to computer drawings, is the relationship they share with buildings by existing in the world of dynamic forces. While the correspondence is not an exact analog, physical models can be used to predict structural behavior. This role is traditional in the case of models made for wind tunnels and ship design. Finally, the communicative power of the physical model overcomes problems inherent in conveying three-dimensional computer drawings to a gathering of clients.

INTRODUCTION

In this third edition of the book, a stronger emphasis has been placed on the design process and the study model investigations that contribute to its development. To this end, a number of new examples from design firms and academic programs serve to further this emphasis. In concert with new work, the contents have also been ordered to reinforce the design bias by positioning technical topics as support material.

As many are aware, the use of rapid prototyping model techniques such as laser cutters and powder printers has grown exponentially over the past five years. In recognition of their proliferation, many new examples stemming from this type of production have also been added. However, this is not intended to change the original focus of the book, which takes the position that hand-built analog models still hold a valuable place in the design process.

For an illustration of how both investigative methods, analog and digital models, continue to be utilized in design practices to great advantage, one has only to look to design in Denmark or Spain. In these practices, the advantages of hand-built model production are exploited as always, but every opportunity to employ rapid prototyping is incorporated as well. This represents the best form of practice in which both old and new design methods are used based on how each can best contribute to the design exploration.

MODEL HISTORY

During Egyptian and Greco-Roman times, architectural models were made primarily as symbols. In the Middle Ages, with the advent of the cathedrals, masons would move through the countryside carrying models of their particular expertise such as arch building. During the Renaissance, models were used as a means to attract the support of patrons (as in the case of the Duomo in Florence, Italy). As architectural education became dominated by Beaux-Arts training, models became supplanted almost completely by drawing. Architecture was conceived in large part as elevation and plan studies, with three-dimensional media having little relevance. However, by the late 1800s, architects such as Antonio Gaudi began using models as a means to explore structural ideas and develop an architectural language. By the turn of the century, the seeds of modern architecture had begun to take root. With it came a perspective that looked at architecture as the experience of movement through space. Orthographic and perspective drawing were recognized to be limited exploration methods, giving rise to the model as a design tool. In the 1920s and 1930s, the Bauhaus and architects like Le Corbusier elevated the use of modeling to an integral component of architectural education and practice. During the 1950s, modernism embodied form by translating highly reductive designs into one or two simple platonic solids (cube, cylinder, etc). With this shift, beyond providing a means of apprehending scale and massing, the model's role began to wane. As the hegemony of corporate modernism was fractured in the late 1970s, spatial exploration followed a number of new branches, and the model regained its position as a powerful tool for exploration. In the early 1990s, the model's role was challenged by a shift in technology. At this point, it was suggested that computer-assisted design (CAD) and modeling programs could substitute digital simulations for all experiences.

While many of the advantages offered by digital media did prove to offer positive benefits, the condition of removal inherent to the virtual experience could not be easily overcome. In reaction to the problem of removal, Ben Damon, an architect with Morphosis (a pioneering office in rapid prototyping), responds to the idea of a completely digital modeling environment by stating: "… physical models will never go away." He goes on to add that the immediacy and direct relationship offered by the physical model plays a vital role in design development. Similar sentiments are echoed by James Glymph with Frank Gehry and Partners, LLP. In regards to digital modeling, Mr. Glymph points out that "it would be a serious mistake to think it could replace models and drawing entirely." With these realizations has come a resurgence of interest in traditional physical models and the introduction of rapid prototype models, aimed at reconnecting digital and physical design methods.

MODEL TYPES
Typical Model Types Employed in the Design Process

This chapter sets out the terminology for models as to their use in the development sequence and typology. The models are classified in a way that describes their common usage in architectural settings with examples of each.

Model Types

Models are referred to in a variety of ways, and terms may be used interchangeably in different settings. Although there is no standard, the definitions in the following lists are commonly used. All of the model types discussed (sketch, massing, development, etc.) are considered to be study models, including those used for formal presentations. As such, their purpose is to generate design ideas and serve as vehicles for refinement. They can range from quick, rough constructions to resolved models. Whatever state they are in, the term *study model* implies that they are always open to investigation and refinement.

Study models can be considered to belong to two different groups: *primary models* and *secondary models*. The primary set has to do with the level or stage of design evolution, and the secondary set refers to particular sections or aspects of the project under focus. A secondary model may be built as a primary model type, depending on the level of focus. For example, a model used to develop interior spaces would be thought of as an interior model but would also be a sketch model, development model, or presentation model, depending on its level of focus.

Primary Models

Primary models are abstract in concept and are employed to explore different stages of focus.

Sketch

Diagram

Concept

Massing

Solid/Void

Development

Presentation/Finish

Secondary Models

Secondary models are used to look at particular building or site components.

Site Contour

Site Context/Urban

Entourage/Site Foliage

Interior

Section

Façade

Framing/Structure

Detail/Connections

Sketch Models

Sketch models constitute the initial phase of study models. They are like three-dimensional drawing and sketching—a medium for speed and spontaneity.

Sketch models generally are not overly concerned with craft but with providing a quick way to visualize space. They are intended to be cut into and modified as exploration proceeds. These models may also be produced as a quick series to explore variations on a general design direction. Although many of the models shown throughout the book are produced as expressive explorations, sketch models are also valuable when built with greater precision and used to explore qualities of alignment, proportion, and spatial definition.

Sketch models are generally built at relatively small scales from inexpensive materials such as chipboard or poster board.

Several examples of sketch models are shown, ranging from small building propositions to ideas of space and site relationships.

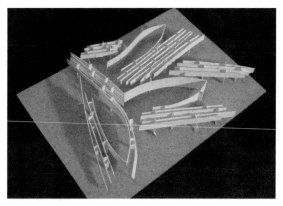

Sketch model
Small sketches can be made early in the design phase to explore basic building organizations and reflect general relationships of program circulation and architectural concerns.

Sketch model
Sketch models can explore basic relationships among a number of program components (actual size, 11").

Sketch model
Sketch models can carry genetic information about the way building spaces will flow and read. In this case, the model was a translation of drawing exercises that began incorporating the program (actual size, 6").

Sketch model
Sketch models can explore conceptual ideas to translate ideas. In this case, the model explores ideas about program spaces and light.

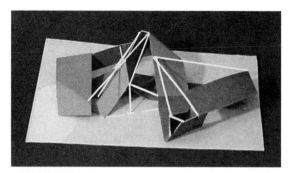

Sketch model

Sketch models can look at ideas of path and movement. Pictured is a small model using folding as a formal means to establish space.

Sketch model

Sketch models can articulate base drawings and diagrams. Beginning sketch designs look at a scheme of crossing paths. Variations are explored to refine the initial direction.

Sketch model

Sketch models can explore basic organizational principles. Above is a small sketch of a circular scheme that looks at the way layers can be used to define the space.

Sketch model

Sketch models can explore gestures and continuity. Pictured is an initial folded gesture that establishes the relationships on which subsequent design development will be based.

Sketch model

Sketch models can explore the 3D relationship between overlapping spaces. Above, alternate sketch models that look at variations in a basic scheme of cross-paths.

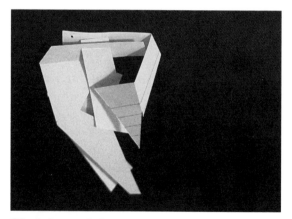

Sketch model

Sketch models can look at layers and site relationships. A small folded study from cardstock made to explore sectional relationships and respond to a triangular site is pictured above.

Diagram Models

Diagram models are related to sketch models and conceptual models. However, like their two-dimensional counterparts, they map out abstract issues of program, structure, circulation, and site relationships.

Although they are similar to drawn forms, the three-dimensional quality of diagram models can begin to describe space as it relates to architectural issues and suggest ideas for further exploration.

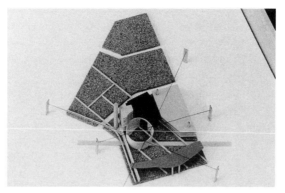

Diagram model
A small model used to map out abstract site relationships and establish initial tectonic elements such as the circular element.

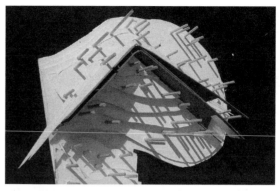

Diagram model
A small diagram model of two converging lines that set out the path the project will take to cut through the landscape.

Diagram model
Diagrams can be used to explore the basic organization of site schemes.

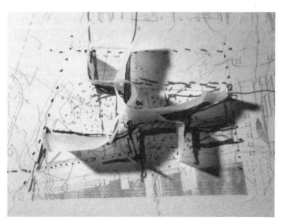

Diagram model
A diagram that maps the points between site relationships setting out key organizational concepts.

Diagram model
Another simple diagram used to describe contrasting relationships between the indirect processional element and the axial component.

Concept Models

Concept models are built at the initial stages of a project to explore abstract qualities such as materiality, site relationships, and interpretive themes. These models can be thought of as a specialized form of the sketch models and are used as the "genetic coding" to inform architectural directions.

Translations can be made by a variety of means, such as dissecting the model with drawings, using suggested geometries, producing readings based on formal qualities, or interpreting literary themes. The following concept models were established at the outset of several different projects. Although their use as genetic information is similar, their conceptual bases are quite different and illustrate the degree to which conceptual approaches can vary. Several other examples of concept models and architectural interpretations have been derived from these models. See "Interpreting" in Chapter 2.

Concept model
A model made to explore ideas about shade, light, and shadow.

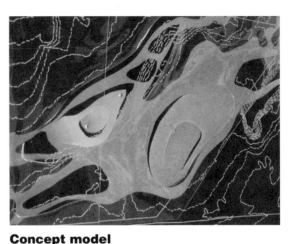

Concept model
A model that attempts to translate the abstract properties of water into fixed materials.

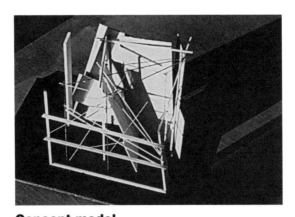

Concept model
A model exploring abstract qualities of light and material relationships.

Concept model
A model of interrelated components to form a "machine" that can in turn generate a secondary reading.

Massing Models

Massing models are simple models that depict volume and are typically devoid of openings. These models can be constructed at small scales due to their lack of detail and will quickly reflect a building's size and proportion at an early stage.

Massing models are used in a similar manner to sketch models and solid/void models. At times, they may be built as partial solid/void models.

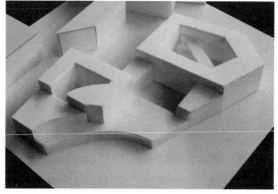

Massing model
A massing model that sets out only the limits and extent of the external space but leaves issues of spatial voids and internal relations unaddressed.

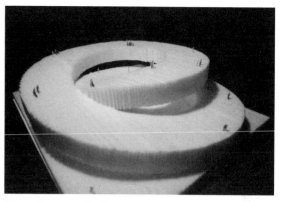

Massing model
A massing model built from sections of foam core to describe the basic formal space of a spiral.

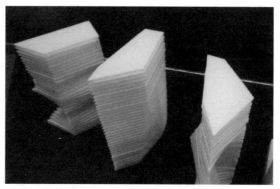

Massing model
A set of massing models made to look at alternatives to the scheme. The forms speak to subtractive methods of space and achieve their form through stacked sections of foam core.

Massing model
Massing models can be made in any number of forms, but their defining characteristic is the absence of openings.

Solid/Void Models

Solid/void models can be built as development or sketch models, but unlike massing models, they display the relationship between the open and closed areas of the building. Generally, these models are more useful for understanding a building's character than simple massing models. A comparison with massing models reveals the potential misreading of character conveyed by massing models, particularly in less conventional designs.

The examples primarily reflect models that have reached the stage of development models; however, any of these studies could have been made at very small sizes and still have displayed the differences between open space and solid mass. The main difference imposed by size is that smaller openings can be omitted as the model is decreased in size.

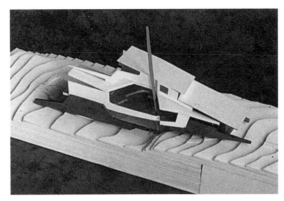

Solid/void model
The central void and linear nature of wall and roof planes is easily read in this solid/void study.

Solid/void model
This model type is somewhere between a development model and a refined sketch model. *Note:* All major voids have been incorporated to reflect the light and open quality of the building.

Solid/void model
This model represents an extreme case where the voids are all important and use of pure massing would offer very little comprehension of the space.

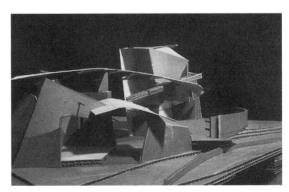

Solid/void model
Complex geometric patterns have been established at this stage, but the model has not been taken to the level of defining glass planes and material hierarchies.

Solid/void model

Rather than simple massing, the open and closed relationships of the project can be explored early on in the design sequence.

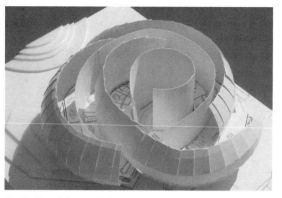

Solid/void model

This model works to keep the internal space open so that the relationship between shell and volume can be managed during development.

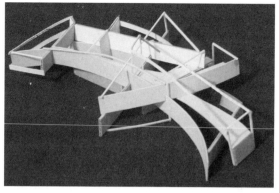

Solid/void model

This model reverses the relationship between solid/void and emphasizes the void space over the solid space.

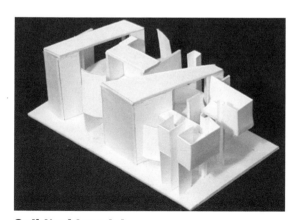

Solid/void model

This model represents a careful balance between solid mass and open void and is very suggestive in the type of spatial relationships that can be seen in its space.

Solid/void model

This model lets the path through its central body maintain clarity without reverting to pure massing.

Solid/void model

Voids can be established as a series of layers that are open as in these floor plates, but at the same time describe the general mass of the building.

Development Models

Use of development models implies that some initial decisions have been made and a second or third level of exploration is being conducted. It also implies that the overall geometry remains fixed, and at least one intermediate stage of exploration will be executed before proceeding to the presentation model. This stage may involve looking at alternate wall treatments, refining proportions, or developing alternate elements.

Development models are typically increased in scale from the previous sketch studies to allow the designer to focus on the next level of design.

The examples can, in some instances, be considered to be finish models. The main difference is that they are essentially abstract representations of building relationships and are still open to modification and refinement. Moreover, they have not been detailed to reflect such aspects as material thickness and glazing.

In a number of cases, after further exploration, the building design may end with a development model or with drawing as a means to communicate the final level of details.

For more on development models and their place in the progression of building design, see "Development" in Chapter 2.

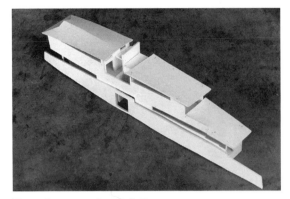

Development model
After several studies, the model was built to reflect basic decisions accurately. At this stage, relationships in the middle section of the building were refined as well as wall and roof configurations.

Development model
A typical level of design resolution at the development model stage. General building relationships have been established, but window openings and other details are undergoing design development consideration.

Development model
Once all the basic schematic relationships were established in the project, the model was increased in scale to address design decisions for its interior space.

Development model
This was a refined study of materials and proportions. At this stage, the designer is ready to begin overlaying a second layer of architectural detail.

Development model
This project has established all basic relationships and has begun to look at the design of secondary components.

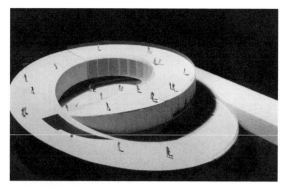

Development model
The massing model for this project established the simple spiral action. In this study, the development of entrance, roof conditions, and skin was explored.

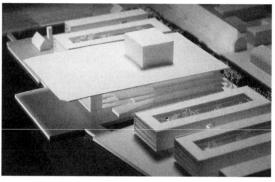

Development model
After some basic schematic studies, several development models were made that explored relationships between roof and plaza space.

Development model
Basic sketch relationships have been established, and the developmental model has proceeded from the implications of these sketch studies.

Development model
After initial solid/void studies, the model is increased in scale and internal/external relationships are developed.

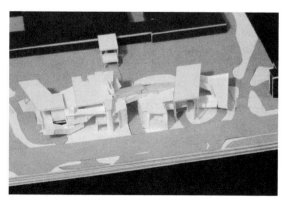

Development model
This model illustrates the exception that models move up in scale as development proceeds. While this model is very small, it is able to articulate all of the basic project relationships needed.

Presentation/Finish Models

The terms *presentation model* and *finish model* are used interchangeably to describe models that represent a completed design and are built with attention to craftsmanship.

They are used to confirm design decisions and communicate with clients who may not fully appreciate the implications of rougher studies.

Finish models are typically built as monochromatic constructions made from one material, such as foam core or museum board. This blank, abstract treatment allows the model to be read in many ways without the potential distractions of material simulations. White or light-colored materials such as balsa wood are also used because shadow lines, voids, and planes are well articulated by light.

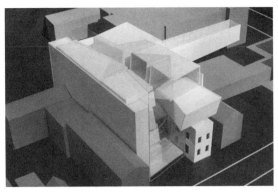

Finish model

A wood finish model is shown in the space of a site context model. *Note:* The context model is treated as a massing model to focus attention on the new building.

Finish model

A well-detailed finish model at this scale of study. It can be compared to the development model for the same project on the preceding page (lower right).

Finish model

This finish model delineates the structure and glass mullions. It also carefully conveys the reading of the roof thickness as it slims to a knife edge to cantilever over the plaza.

Finish model

For this finish model, all the details of skin have been modeled and an accurate reading of texture and light relationships is conveyed.

Finish model
The finish model includes furnishings and complete development of the façade in terms of light/dark.

Finish model
A simple wood finish model conveys refined spatial relationships and the texture of the roof detailing.

Finish model
This model is highly detailed and includes all the readings of interior and exterior space.

Finish model
A simple model that includes the skin design for the parking deck below the units. This is a paper model but conveys all the essentials of the project.

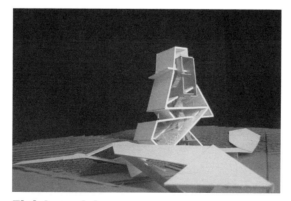

Finish model
Another simple paper finish model that conveys the project space. The wall thickness of the fold has been carefully controlled by layering material and capping the edges.

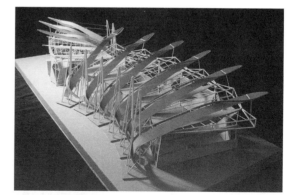

Finish model
A finish model with the detail of structure provided. It is a highly intricate construction made by hand from chipboard and bass wood sticks.

Site Contour Models

Site models, or contour models, are built to study topography and the building's relationship to the site. They typically reproduce the slope of the land, or *grade,* by employing a series of scaled layers that represent increments of rise and fall in the landscape.

As study constructions, they can be modified to fit the building to the site, control water, and implement landscape design.

Site contour
A typical contour model displays site grades at regular intervals. Grade increments may represent anywhere from 6″ to 5 ft., depending on the size of the site and the size of the model.

Site contour
A steeply sloped site is modeled with faceted, corrugated cardboard planes.

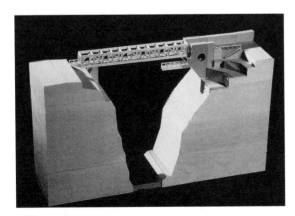

Site contour
Steep site contours may be modeled as a section of property limited to the area of focus.

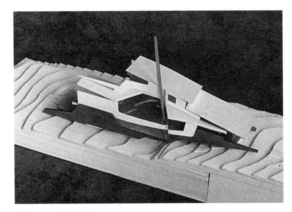

Site contour
A site model is often limited to the property lines and appears as a section of the landscape.

Site contour
In modeling relatively large, flat areas, such as urban blocks, contours may only reflect the character of the urban street grid.

Context Models

Context models are models that show the surrounding buildings. They are built to study the building's relationship to the mass and character of existing architecture. Context models can be used to show an existing building on the property or the neighboring area, or expand to include an entire urban section. Context models are incorporated into contour models and allow issues of grading and landscape design to be explored in relation to the building. It is typical to treat the existing buildings of a context model as mass models, using neutral coloring to allow the new work to read as contrasting construction. Context models can be built to accommodate different projects by leaving a blank hole to fit various buildings into the site. In the example on the bottom right, the ground plane has been built over a hollow void. Context buildings are then inserted into the hole left in the surface material.

Urban models look at an entire urban condition from sectors of the city to the entire urban settlement. They are used like other study models to explore relationships, only on a much larger scale. They usually depict all built elements as massing blocks.

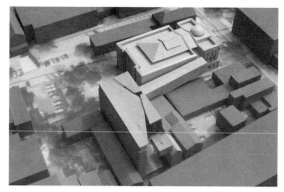

Site context
This project uses an existing building as the site for a building addition. The context building is needed as a basis for reaction and scaling the addition. The completed project is shown with finish models.

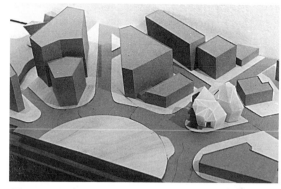

Site context
The immediate context has been expanded to include buildings in a portion of an urban area. Although the buildings do not directly touch the site, they set the overall scale relationships between the existing and new.

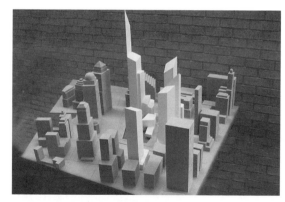

Site context/urban model
An example of a context model with a large area of study. The scale relationships between new and existing buildings is critical. The model also functions as an urban model, looking at issues concerning the development of several city blocks.

Urban model
This urban model includes the detail massing of a large section of Copenhagen to set the context for the Opera House in the center.

Urban Models

Urban models are used as design tools in the same way as other design models. The shift in perception is primarily one of scale. These models move from studies that show the context of adjacent blocks to neighborhoods, districts, and entire cities. Unlike context models that depict only existing buildings, they are made to design sections of the city. While these models could be made with computer programs and often are, the large size of real estate they represent is much easier to comprehend with large physical models rather than relatively small computer screens.

The two models on the bottom are from the Charleston Civic Design Center (UDC). The models are under active consideration in the planning of different redevelopment efforts within the city. They provide valuable illustrations of how models can convey a three-dimensional understanding of urban proposals.

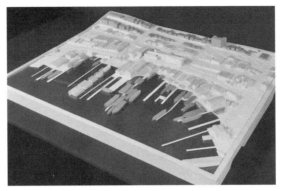

Urban study model
This model served as an urban design exploration and set the context for a new exhibition hall.

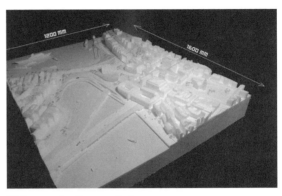

Urban study model
The model was made to set out the conditions for an urban design project along the waterfront.

Cooper River Bridge neighborhood
This model was made to study the area around the old and new bridge locations in order to reconnect the neighborhood. Revitalization goals look at ways to provide places for new homes, public spaces, and businesses.

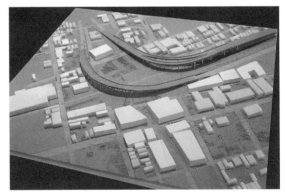

Charleston Gateway
Arrival into Charleston is via three ragged traffic interchanges. This model is an active study model used to explore design options to recast this approach and create a considered gateway experience.

Entourage/Site Foliage

Entourage refers to the modeling of people, trees, and site furnishings. Scaled figures are modeled during the investigative stages, to give a sense of the scale of the building. Trees are included at the presentation stage (usually without people). Site furnishings, such as benches, lamps, and so forth, are typically reserved for elaborate model simulations.

For design studies and simple finish models, it is best to treat foliage and entourage simply and abstractly. Elaborate simulations can easily overshadow the building both in terms of its psychological importance and by physically obscuring the project itself.

The examples offer several simple but effective methods used to provide unobtrusive site foliage. For more information on site foliage, see Chapter 10.

Entourage
Trees have been made by stacking layers of cut paper on wooden sticks. This method lends itself to larger-scale foliage.

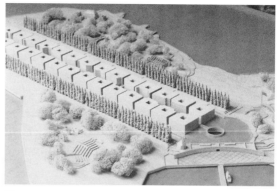

Entourage
Lichen and rolled paper trees have been used for small-scale foliage.

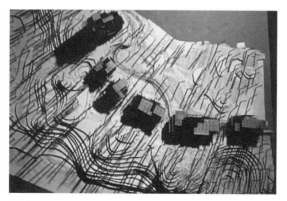

Entourage
Trees have been treated abstractly by using bare plastic rods. This gives a sense of wooded density without interfering with the perception of the building.

Entourage
Yarrow trees or dried plants can be used for larger-scale models.

Interior Models

Interior models generally function as development models and are constructed to study interior architectural spaces and furnishings. They are built at scales starting at 1/4″ = 1′0″ but are more useful at 1/2″ = 1′0″ and larger. These models need to define the borders of the space but remain open for viewing and accessibility.

The design of interior spaces is approached much the same as the building itself. A designer should realize that a building contains internal space worthy of the same consideration given to the exterior form. By opening up the building and "walking through" the space, observing it in three dimensions, many ideas can be generated.

Interior models typically employ various means to gain visual access to internal space. Rooftops can be removed to look down into the model, sides may be removed to gain horizontal access (as in section models), and holes can be cut into the underside to allow the viewer to look up into the space. In large models, very large openings in the bottom can permit total visual access.

1/2″ House interiors study
This 1/2″ = 1′0″ scale foam core model employs a removable roof for viewing. The scale is large enough to permit reading of details as small as 1 in. and allows components to be developed inside the model.

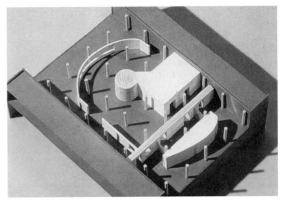

Interior model
This is a case where the entire design is an interiors project, and the architecture is worked out in much the same way as external building design.

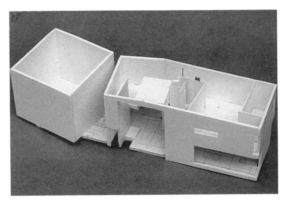

1/4″ House interiors study
Existing 1/4″ = 1′0″ scale models such as this are often large enough to develop interior partitions and circulation elements.

Interior space
The model has been built solely to explore the internal space of the project. The scale is small at 1/8th but carefully modeled so that all the spaces can be clearly apprehended.

Interior model

The 1/8th scale model was large enough to allow the designer to develop the interior atrium space.

Interior model

A larger model at 1/4″ gives a full reading of the interior space.

Interior model

A cutaway section doubles as an interior model and in some respects can be considered the equivalent of interior models.

Interior model

The interior space of the project has been made accessible by removing the exterior skin.

Interior model

With the ability to look deeply into the interior space with the camera lens, an accurate reading of the spatial experience can be obtained.

Interior model

The interior space of this model at 1/2″ scale is large enough to put the viewer's perception directly in the space.

Section Models

Section models are built to study relationships between vertical spaces. They are produced by slicing the building at a revealing location. The cut is usually made at the point where a number of complex relationships interact and can be jogged or sliced on an angle if needed. The use of section models as study models can be most effective in working out the complexities of relationships, which are often difficult to visualize in two dimensions.

Section models are related to interior models in that they reveal interior spaces. One of the key differences lies in their vertical orientation, in contrast to the plan or top view typically offered by interior models.

Section models are also closely related to façade models and are sometimes referred to as *cutaway elevations* or *section/elevations*.

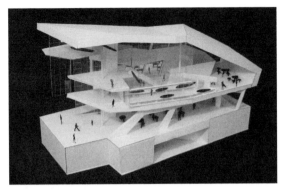

Section model
The section model at 1/8" is large enough to reveal the interior relationships between floor levels and partitions.

Section model
This section model was built to explore relationships between internal floors and vertical spaces. It can be thought of as an interior model as well.

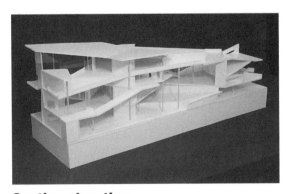

Section elevation
The section of a larger project can provide a transitional shift, allowing the relationships to reveal another reading of the space.

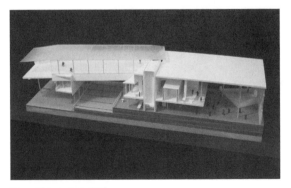

Section model
Section models such as this one are key in understanding the intersection between two types of space.

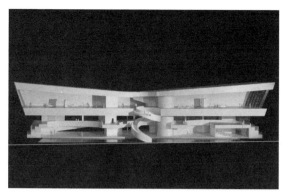

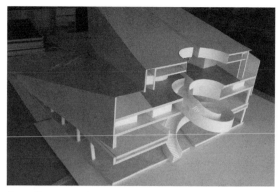

Section model

A classic section model cut in the longitudinal direction and revealing all of the vertical relationships in the building.

Section model

A transverse section cut through the project on the left reveals a different set of relationships.

Section model

This section through the Copenhagen Opera House reveals the different nature of the spaces from backstage, fly space, lobby, and plaza.

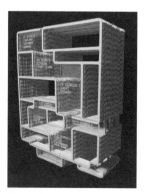

Section model

This large section model of the Ohio State Architecture School was built to develop the linear atrium space of the ramps.

Section model

In contrast to typical cuts that divide the project into sectors, a section can be cut as a discrete "plug" out of the larger set of spatial relationships.

Section model

Sectional approaches to design can be carried out by developing all relationships in section rather than in plan.

Façade Models

Façade models are built when isolated elevations are needed for study and refinement. This situation typically occurs with infill buildings where the street elevation is the primary building image. In other cases, façades may be created to serve as context for additions to exterior elevations.

In the context of the urban street fabric, the manipulation of relatively shallow depths is used to create the illusion of greater spatial volumes. This can be taken further to look at the negative space produced by the façade and to generate new readings.

Although façade models are ideal study vehicles for flat, orthogonal elevations, they may not prove as useful in determining the character of nonorthogonal geometries.

Façade model
A classic example of a façade as it might occur in an infill situation. Relatively flat elevations like this are well suited to façade model exploration.

Façade model
The façade was built to serve as a background to develop the deck and entry canopies.
Note: The windows have been drawn on rather than cut out as in a solid/void study.

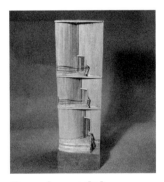

Façade model
A façade model built to work out the design for an infill project.

Façade model
Details of the façade have been developed at full scale in a mock-up that conveys complete understanding of its elements.

Façade study
This image of a mountain was used to inform the design of the façade panel to the right. Mapping images on to façades has become a common theme in design and is facilitated by digital technology.

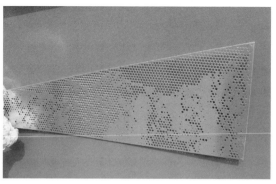

Façade model component
The image of the mountain has been rasterized and cut into the scale façade material. The resultant screen was used to mask the interior of a parking garage.

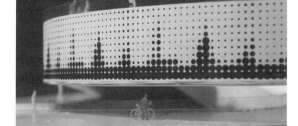

Façade model surface
In a similar idea to above, images of the city have been abstracted and mapped on a surface to create the façade design.

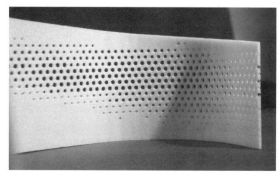

Façade model component
Openings have been cut into model material with a laser to gauge the effect of light inside the building.

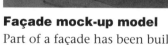

Façade mock-up model
Part of a façade has been built at full scale using foam core. This model allows complete understanding of each component and their attachment to substructure.

Framing/Structural Models

A framing/structural model is related to a detailing model in that its primary use is to visualize the relationship between framing and structural systems in space. The exact location of beams, load transfers, and other technical considerations can be determined. When built to large scales, framing models can be used to study the detailing of complex connections.

This model type also can also be used to explore creative designs for structures such as bridges and trusses, to convey details to builders and to test loading characteristics.

Framing models are built at relatively large scales (1/4″ = 1′0″ minimum) in order to show the relationship between members.

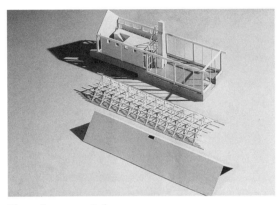

Framing model
Framing models are used to work out the design and location of all structural members and can be extremely useful in working with complex geometries.

Structural model
The lower section of Frank Gehry's *Experience Music Project* has been modeled to understand the structural system used to support undulating exterior panels.

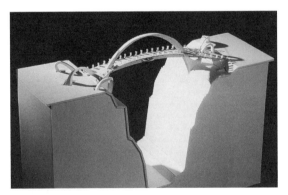

Bridge model
The usefulness of the model in designing structural elements should be apparent when working out innovative solutions to architecturally designed structures such as this bridge.

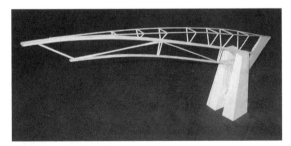

Structural test
A single cantilever truss is made at 1/4″ scale to refine the design and test its structural integrity. A simple application of pressure at its end can quickly determine weak points.

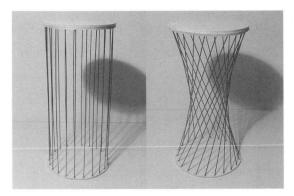

Form-generating structure
A model of a hyperbolic tension structure creates a direct link between form and the logic that generates a change in form through mechanical actions.

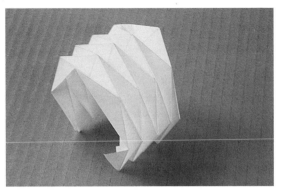

Folded structure
Structural models using folded panels to create a series of arches can lead to a number or structurally driven designs.

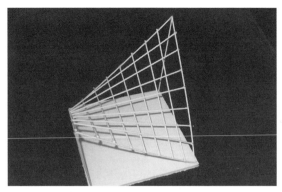

Hyperbolic roof arch
The hyperbolic roof form or saddle is flexible and has become the basis of many architectural projects. This model demonstrates the way in which the curving saddle is created by a grid of straight lines.

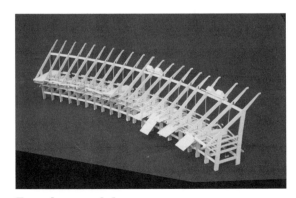

Framing model
Framing is typically thought of as a repetitive system for wood or steel, but this model of concrete stadium frames shows that the system can operate at very large scales.

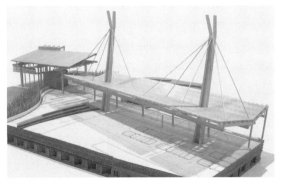

Suspension frame model
This modeling of a masted suspension system points out the strong relationship between structural strategy and the resultant architectural language.

Connection/Detail Models

Connection and detail models are built to develop interior and exterior details such as structural joints, window treatments, railings, and fascias.

These models are treated in a similar manner as models of complete buildings but are built at much larger scales to allow the finer readings of form articulation and connections.

Connection models are closely related to structural and framing models, as they provide a closer look at critical joints and intersections.

Scales typically range from 1/2″ = 1′0″ to 3″ = 1′0″. Detail models can be helpful in resolving design ideas and construction details and in facilitating client communication.

The examples demonstrate various ways models can be used to develop building details or furnishings.

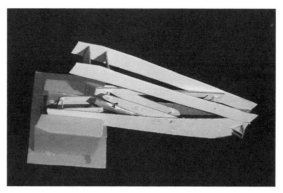

Connection model
This study of ramp supports used modeled components to explore the joint action of members as they were folded together.

Building detail model
This window surround was built at 3″ = 1′0″ (a relatively large scale) to study relationships between corner connections and wall depth. This is typical of the way models can be used to develop and refine building details.

Connection model
This model has been built to focus on the design of a specific connection. The way in which the joint is expressed and the mechanical action have been worked out on the model.

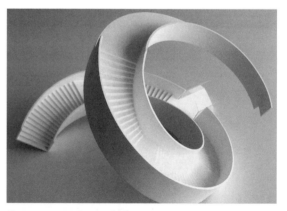

Component model
This model of a spiral stair carries all the detail needed to understand both the exact path of the stair and its full reading as an element.

Industrial Design Models

Another area where models are widely used is industrial design. In fact, rapid prototyping was first developed for the engineering and industrial design industry to make research tests. The physical models play several roles and work in concert with computer models. Traditionally, models were used to develop rough ideas, create prototypes, and test ergonomic properties (the way in which the body interfaces with the object). Today, models still play an active role, but computers and rapid prototyping are used extensively to test versions of the actual product.

The project examples show several important aspects of industrial design modeling studies.

Industrial design model
Models made from painted foam and 3D printers are used to work out the design for an electric planar.

Rapid prototype model
A stereo lithography model shows all the working parts through a translucent cover material. This allows the actual parts to be tested for fit and operation.

Industrial design model
This model of a carburetor is typical of the kind of industrial models initially made by 3D printers.

EXPLORATION

A Framework for Conceiving and Using Models in the Design Process

The chapter sets out methods and examples for design exploration and discovery. The design sequence proceeds in evolutionary stages, with each stage containing a range of studies to explore design alternatives.

An Overview of Section Concepts

The following outline presents an overview of the typical stages in the design process for models. The considerations are similar to those of drawn projects, but most of the required information is derived directly from the model. *Note:* The linear form of the outline is one of convention, as many of the steps may be combined or used interactively.

SCALE
Determining appropriate scale based on:

Project Size
Fitting the building and site to the available work space

Type of Study
Adjusting for the stage of development

Level of Detail
Scaling for the size of details being explored

Assigned Scale
Determining scale, after making concept and sketch models without using a fixed scale

IDEAS
Generating initial information through:

Drawing with the Model
Sketching ideas exclusively with the model using expressive and carefully proportioned approaches

Working with Two-Dimensional Drawings
Working back and forth between drawn and modeled information

ALTERNATIVES
Exploring design directions by:

Multiple Approaches
Building multiple solutions or testing multiple treatments on a single model

Adjustable Models
Using movable parts to explore alternative relationships

SITE
Integrating site concerns with other design information:

Contour Models
Including site information as an integral part of the initial driving forces for design direction

Context Models
Responding to environment as it affects initial design direction

MANIPULATION
Working with models to visualize options:

Modifying and Editing
Cutting and adding parts to design directly on the model

Modifying Site Contours
Integrating the building with the site

Digression
Using the unexpected and unintentional to inform design ideas

Interpreting
Making a fundamental shift in the physical form or perception of the model

DEVELOPMENT
Developing the project by:

Project Development
Exploring an evolutionary path from initial concepts to a complete project

Increasing Scale
Building larger models as the investigation moves from general concerns of site and scheme to focused concerns of elevations, interior space, and detailing

Coding and Hierarchy
Establishing hierarchy and coding to define a range of contrasting elements and code conceptual layers

Converting
Renovation of existing models versus entirely rebuilding

Focusing
Moving studies through successive stages of refinement

Scale
Key Scaling Issues

Models can be built at various scales. The size of the model may not be indicative of the scale, as physically large models may be built at small scales and vice versa. Determining the appropriate scale depends on several considerations, as discussed in the following paragraphs.

Project Size

The size of the model depends on how large the actual building and/or site will be, and is governed by the availability of work space.

Level of Study

The scale and size of the model depends on the level of detail that is needed, such as sketch, development, presentation, interior, or detail.

Level of Detail

The scale of the model depends on the level of detail that is needed. A prime reason to increase a model's scale is to include more detail. A scaled-up model without additional detail may appear ungainly. Accordingly, it can be more convincing and practical to imagine fine details on smaller models rather than to construct large models with insufficient detail.

Assigned Scale

By maintaining the relative proportions between components, models may be initiated without using a particular scale. A scale can be assigned to a model after it is built. This technique is useful on small sketch studies. In this case, a small model of a human figure can then be made to a size that is correctly proportioned to the building model in relation to how the designer envisions the actual size of the building. The full-scale height of the figure (assumed to be approximately 6 ft.), can then be compared to various scales on a scale ruler to find the one that matches the 6-ft. dimension of the model figure. This scale can then be assigned to the building model and used to determine its actual "full-scale" dimensions. This can also be done by assuming a typical floor-to-floor height of 12–14 ft. on a multistory building (or as appropriate to the project such as 9–11 ft. for a typical residential model). The designer then can compare various scales on the ruler to find the one that matches the floor-to-floor heights on the model at the assumed "full-scale" dimension. For small models, it will probably be necessary to use an engineering scale rule, where scales between 1″ = 20′ and 1″ = 200′ are available. For an example of this technique at work see Chapter 9, "Case Study B."

EXAMPLES: SCALE DECISIONS AND CONSIDERATIONS

- A typical model of a house might be scaled at a maximum of 1/4″=1′0″ so that an actual length of 96 ft. would occupy 2 ft. of desk space.

- For a larger building involving several hundred feet, a scale of 1/8″ = 1′0″ might be used effectively.

- Large sites usually use engineering scales of 1″ = 50′, 100′, or 200′ to make the model manageable.

- Sketch models typically start at very small scales such as 1/32″, 1/16″, or 1/8″ = 1′0″, and focus on general relationships. As the design direction is further developed, models can be increased in scale to study detailed issues.

- Models needed for context only may be scaled at smaller sizes such as 1″ = 20′ or 1/16″ = 1′0″.

- Presentation models are generally effective if they are built large enough to be detailed. For a house, this could be 1/4″ = 1′0″ or larger. For a large building, 1/8″ = 1′0″ might be an appropriate size.

- Modeling details must be constructed to scale. This consideration makes it very difficult to simulate dimensions such as 2 or 3″ at a scale of 1/8″ = 1′0″ or smaller.

- For studies such as window mullions, roof fascia and connections, larger scales such as 1/2″ or 1″ = 1′0″ are needed.

- For smaller scales, fine details should be implied.

Scale Relationships

Another aspect of scale that is important to consider is the scale relationship between different elements. This can range from very small things like a detail or a connection, to very large things like a city or a landscape. In all cases, it is important to understand and control the scale of the space and its elements by placing them in direct context with scale human figures and context buildings.

Understanding scale does not mean that every judgment revolves around the body. Spatial experience may be unaccommodating and completely outside this perspective. However, space should still be understood in terms of human perception when exploring it.

Examples encountered include:

- The scale of the human body to the scale of a room
- The scale of an element of a building to the entire building
- The scale of a building to a city block

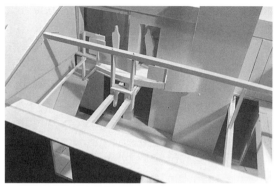

Scale figures
Scale figures can be cut as model parts or inserted with montage techniques. They should be included at every stage of development.

The body in space
The scale of a room should be explored in relation to its inhabitants. Large public spaces are particularly instructive.

Scale of entry
The entry to the Chrysler Building is typical of an opening scaled to fit the building. The actual entry door is one small element inserted into the opening.

Scale of context
All scale issues do not center on the human body. Buildings should be considered in context with other buildings and at an urban scale.

Ideas
Expressive Model Drawing

Strategy

Models assembled with the speed of two-dimensional sketching can be effectively used as the prime generator of information without the aid of drawings or exact scales. To facilitate this, begin by becoming familiar with the basic program, site requirements, and structural options until they become part of the designer's internal knowledge of the project parameters. These can then be put aside to approach the model from another perspective. It may be difficult at first to reconcile practical concerns with your discoveries; however, with experience, they can be intuitively approximated and later used to inform design moves.

Although the model need not be built to a predetermined scale, it should employ relatively proportioned relationships between its parts, such as floor-to-floor heights. These heights can be measured later and assigned a scale to fit the project. For more information on assigning scale, see "Scale" in this chapter.

Illustration

Sketch models are shown from the beginning phases of two different projects. Although specific project requirements were in mind, sketch models were constructed without exact scales or drawings to generate initial ideas.

Sketch model—exposition center
A small strip of foam serves to test initial gestures about space that knots back on itself.

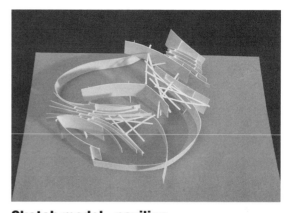

Sketch model—pavilion
At the beginning stages of a project, a small paper sketch model helps define path, moments of intensity, and a range of scales.

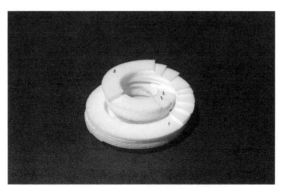

Sketch model—exposition center
The foam spiral above has been resolved into a small sketch model that explores the same type of internal "knot" but now responds to conventions of gravity, pedestrian circulation, and site context.

Sketch model—pavilion
The paper model shown at the top of the page begins to take shape as a set of internal and external spaces to "sketch out" the initial relationships of the project.

Additive/Subtractive Drawing

Strategy

One way of approaching three-dimensional forms is in terms of additive and subtractive operations. In additive operations, individual components are joined together to form a construction. In subtractive operations, models are initiated with a block of material and pieces are subtracted to arrive at the design. Additive processes are more often associated with solid/void models, and subtractive models and mass models are closer in conception. In practice, a combination of additive and subtractive approaches is employed.

Illustration

The projects employ additive and subtractive processes as labeled.

Formal Proportioning

Strategy

Another important approach is to use the model as a device for refining proportions and making exacting spatial alignments. This approach requires tighter control and greater attention to crafting the model and focuses on placement and adjustment as its primary concerns.

Illustration

The example on the far right illustrates space developed through rational alignment.

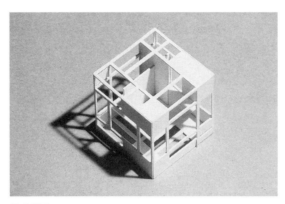

Additive space
Individual planes and sticks have been joined together in an additive process to define space. The reverse perception of the cube might see it as a solid, carved away to leave the voids.

Additive and subtractive space
Both subtractive and additive spatial operations are explored in this model. The model has been conceived through digital modeling and built as a hand model to realize its elements.

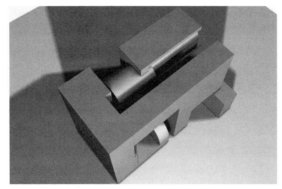

Subtractive space
This massing model can be perceived as having been carved away from a solid block. The model started as a rectangular block of space with subtractions made using Boolean operations in a digital modeling program.

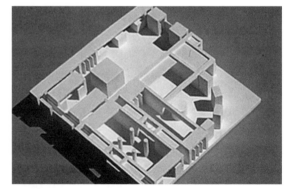

Alignment development model
Modeling as an exercise in aligning objects is the focus of this study. The idea of drawing as an exercise in fine-tuning proportion and alignment becomes well defined.

Working with Plan and Elevation Drawings

Strategy

The sketch model can be used in concert with simple scaled drawings to set a general direction. Once the building begins to emerge, the model can be used as a focal point to help visualize additional design decisions. Conversely, design elements carried out on the model can be used to refine drawings such as elevation studies, which in turn can be used to inform the model. The key to using each effectively is to decide which medium offers more efficiency and at the same time provides useful information in relation to the investigation at hand. For example, at the development stage, elevation drawings of flat walls can be more effective in refining compositions than a model. Conversely, elevations of a sculptural building geometry may offer little useful information about the building as compared with a model. This type of dialogue between drawn information and modeled information can be one of the most efficient means for project development.

Illustration

The projects to the right were initially generated from scaled schematic plans and sketches.

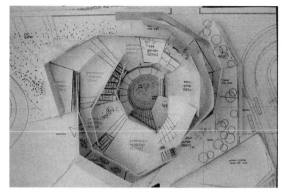

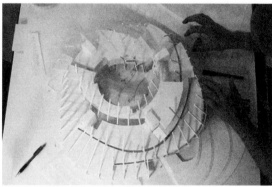

Schematic drawings

Schematic plan drawings above have been used to establish the initial placement of the walls of the labyrinth below. Once the direction has been set by the drawing, the space of the model begins to be informed by the model itself.

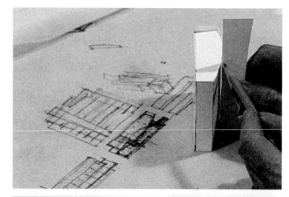

Schematic drawings

Small-scaled plan and section studies were used to produce initial model information. Curved pieces are measured directly off the actual model radiuses. *Note:* For step-by-step illustration of the model assembly, see Case Studies in Chapter 9.

Working with Concept Drawings

Strategy

Another way of approaching the relationship between two-dimensional drawings and three-dimensional constructions is to exploit the conceptual dialogue between the two mediums. In this process, drawings such as collages and paintings can be interpreted to produce three-dimensional forms, and, conversely, models can be interpreted as drawings to set up orthogonal plan and section relationships.

This process is usually carried out in the early stages of a project, and the constructions typically require further interpretation to move them forward into architectural propositions.

Once the basic operation is understood, this relationship can be transferred back and forth a number of times to develop an evolving process. For related examples, see "Interpreting" later in this chapter.

Illustration

The following projects show examples of drawing and model strategies used to work with drawings in this way. In the first three projects, the model preceded the drawing and was interpreted to generate it. In the last two projects, the two-dimensional drawing was interpreted to generate the three-dimensional forms.

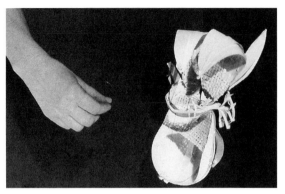

Project 1 pattern model

The model was developed using pattern pieces through the process described under "Manipulation" in the section called "Interpreting" in this chapter.

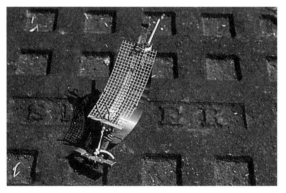

Project 2 transformer model

This model explored the idea of change and transformation. The potential unfolding of its components was analyzed in the accompanying drawings.

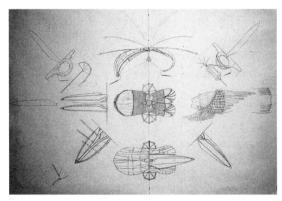

Project 1—pattern drawing

The object was carefully dissected with elevations and section drawing studies and reduced to a set of two-dimensional diagrams.

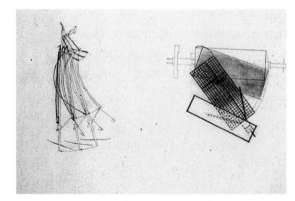

Project 2—transformer drawing

Drawings of the model in motion were subsequently used as abstract generative information to begin plan and section studies.

Project 4—collage drawing
The collage was designed as an abstract composition from a series of overlays. Once experience is gained with the process, elements can be controlled to help facilitate specific program needs.

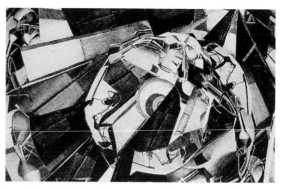

Project 5—Duchamp collage drawing
A collage drawing created from Marcel Duchamp's *Nude Descending a Staircase* served as the initial design move.

Project 3—site overlay
The model was extracted from overlay drawings developed as integral studies of site geometries, histories, and traces. Although not a two-dimensional drawing in the conventional sense, at this scale the model reads like one and makes clear the interwoven plan geometries used to form it.

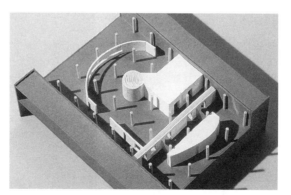

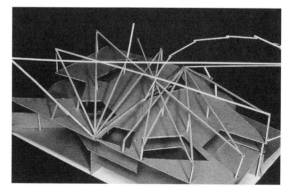

Project 4—collage space
The model was interpreted as space for a gallery from the collage drawing above. This particular translation moved the project directly into the articulation of programmed spaces.

Project 5—Duchamp collage space
An interpretive concept model was made from the collage.

Alternatives
Multiple Approaches
Strategy

Whatever stage of development the project is investigating, distinctly different approaches should be explored to generate ideas and potential directions. In studies, this implies the construction of multiple sketch models. Models can in turn be selected from the alternative approaches and used for further study. As the project develops, alternatives might include ways to handle certain sections or building details. Composite models can also be made that incorporate ideas from different explorations.

Illustrations

In the following seven projects, multiple sketch models were constructed to explore several directions.

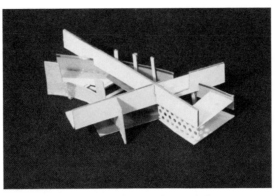

Project 1—first alternative: axis
The model establishes the design from small drawings as one anchored by a strong crossing point with space flowing counter to it.

Project 1—third alternative: fold
The initial project draws on folding as an alternative means of establishing form and employs a simple bipolar relationship.

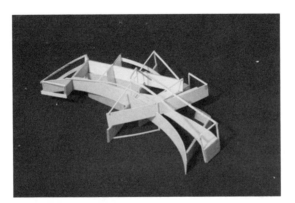

Project 1—second alternative: flow
The project was extruded from small overlay drawings and emphasizes the flow of space.

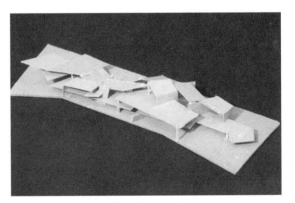

Project 1—fourth alternative: program
Another alternative looks at reading the underlying project information as a scattering of interwoven program spaces.

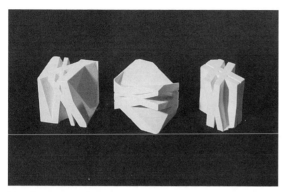

Project 2—three schemes

The models illustrate three different but related studies produced to explore formal proportioning and alignment of space.

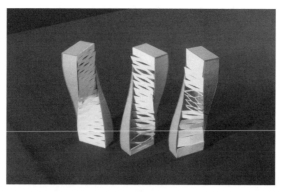

Project 3—three schemes

Three very related schemes have been produced to look at alternative façade treatments.

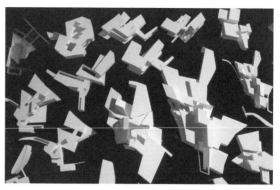

Project 4—alternative variations

A large array of alternative design models for the same project is shown. This type of exhaustive study underlines the need for exploration during the design phase.

Project 5—alternate schemes

An evolutionary array of solutions to a courtyard scheme illustrates the type of quick exercises that are carried out in examining a range of possibilities.

Project 6—development model alternatives

A large array of models for the Natural Gas Building in Barcelona illustrates the kind of attention required to adequately test design alternatives.

Project 7—alternative variations

A series of possible variations on a central theme demonstrate the range of alternatives available simply by looking at path and proportion.

Adjustable Model

Strategy

Another method for exploring alternative approaches is to construct models with components that can be adjusted to test various arrangements. Changes to the models may be recorded with a camera. This method of recording alternatives can also work well when making significant changes to a conventional sketch or development model. Adjustable models are set up so that each component can be repositioned. This model type is built with a deep, open base to allow columns to be pushed or pulled through the base. The holes for columns should be cut tightly so that friction will arrest the movement at the desired points. By moving the columns up and down, it is possible to examine the elements in a variety of different attitudes.

Illustration

The models depict an alternative exploration method that allows components such as roof planes and spaces to be varied in relationship to each other without the designers having to build multiple models.

Roof relationships

This 1/8" = 1'0" scale model was built to study and fine-tune the relationship between a series of intersecting roof planes.

The model is turned up to expose the tails of controlling sticks beneath. Pulling or pushing on the sticks changes the attitude of the roof and can be set and considered in an infinite number of increments. *Note:* It can be helpful when fine-tuning roof attitudes to include perimeter walls, but in some cases, this may inhibit the ability to alter relationships.

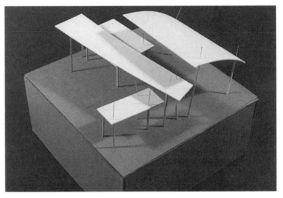

Roof relationships

The initial setting of roof planes.
Note: Straight pins have been used to attach museum board to the balsa sticks. If pins interfere with adjustments, they can be trimmed with side cutting pliers or electrical dykes.

Spatial relationships

Program space is suspended in space using wire hung from a frame to help determine the XYZ positioning of elements. This method allows the designer to go beyond ideas of stacking floors when thinking vertically.

Site Models
Contour Models

Strategy

Exploration should include the impact of the site on design decisions from the earliest stages. The construction of a site model is essential considering alternative site relationships.

Sketch contour models can be built out of chipboard, scrap corrugated cardboard, and other inexpensive materials, and should be assembled with the idea that their reason for existence is to be cut into and modified in a number of ways. Presentation contour models are constructed with the use of similar methods but differ in their use of materials.

Site models can be made from other materials such as plaster and foam. Sitework can be designed versus simply modeling existing grades and modifying them.

Typical studies employing the contour model include exploring:

- The building's scale in relation to the land mass
- How the building will knit into the site through devices such as grade changes and retaining walls
- Landscaping issues such as drives, walks, and other outdoor spaces

Illustration

The examples show common types of site models employed.

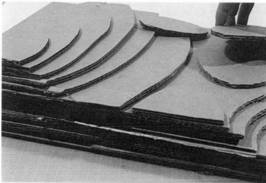

Solid contour models

Solid constructions are versatile and stable. One of their main advantages is that they can easily be cut on and patched. This makes them ideal for experimenting with grades and site designs as the project evolves.

Because the layers go all the way across their grade level, any cut into the grades will pass through the layers below. This makes it very easy to keep track of the effects of changes by counting contours.

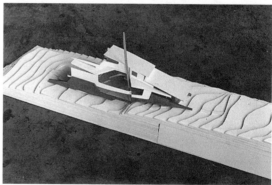

Hollow contour models

Hollow models use less material and can be added to existing models. They can be difficult to modify, as any cut through the contours reveals the space below and must be patched. They are also less durable than solid models.

The lower model has been built as a partial solid/hollow model. As the site gets progressively steep, solid sections can be stepped up to include only those areas where alterations are likely to occur. *Note:* Panels at rear of model reveal the hollow section.

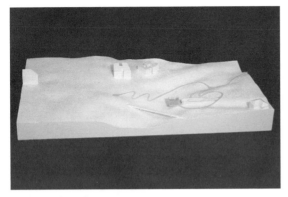

Foam contour model

A foam contour model can be made when smooth grades are desired. The surface can be modified with relative ease. Models like this can also be cut with computer numerically controlled (CNC) milling equipment.

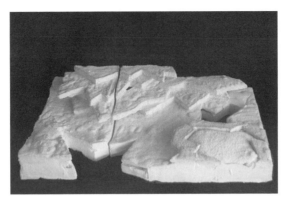

Designed plaster contour models

Sites can be designed as plaster castings by stacking up objects and sand in layers to make a negative mold. The casting can be poured in layers to create undercuts, etc. (see Chapter 8 for more information).

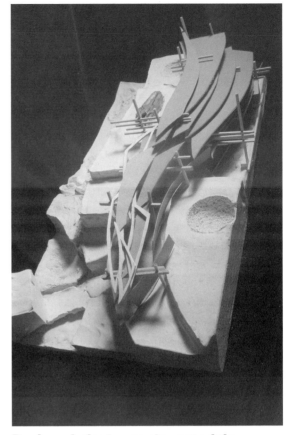

Designed plaster contour models

The site was cast as a designed project to engage the idea of terrain. The site can be further worked by carving in the plaster. The project built on the site takes its direction from the site.

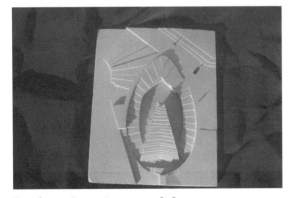

Designed contour models

Sites made out of corrugated cardboard can be designed as works of their own. This site used the plans for a building as beginning information for its design.

Designed contour models

The site for this project was designed first, then additions were made based on responses to the site.

Context Models

Strategy

For all projects, especially sites in urban environment, it is necessary to construct at least the neighboring context buildings early on in the investigation. By representing them in some form, the scale of the project and relation between buildings can begin to be understood.

Illustration

Models ranging from a large urban area to the immediate site are shown. *Note:* The context is treated as an abstract mass to allow the new work to be easily apprehended.

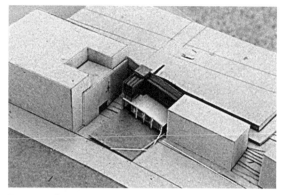

Immediate building context
The adjacent buildings on this site are critical to understanding the nature of the project as they actually define the space of the site.

Large urban context
Buildings have been cut from laminated layers of particle board and painted flat gray as a noncompeting background.

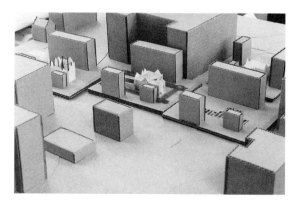

Neighboring context
Neighboring structures have been built from neutral corrugated cardboard as simple mass models in order to understand the new building's relationship with the existing fabric.

Immediate building context
Adjacent buildings have been built with less detail to serve as context for the new addition (light wood), and gray paint helps code and downplay them.

Context model in progress
An urban context model in the process of construction is shown. Massing models of surrounding buildings have been cut from wood blocks and placed on the topographic map over their respective footprints.

Manipulation
Modifying and Editing

Strategy

Equally important to creating the model is the act of operating on it to discover and refine ideas. Modifications are most effective if the model is cut into and explored without becoming unduly concerned about its appearance or original configuration. If design operations appear to be difficult to implement, rough cutting will help establish the initial idea, and the resulting jagged surfaces can then be "cleaned up" once the idea is developed.

This type of investigation is important since many of the design decisions cannot be visualized until the model is established. A number of ideas will be suggested by the model itself, and the new readings may prove more interesting than the original construction.

Illustration

Two projects have been modified and illustrate the kind of investigations that might be carried out at two different stages of model evolution. The sketch model is still in the process of formation and can undergo radical transformations before moving on to the development model stage. The development model has reached the point where major relationships have been established and individual sections of the model can be modified and reformed.

Modifying sketch models
A sketch model has been used as a working site and is radically altered to discover other relationships. The process was initiated by cutting completely through the model along a selected bias.

Modifying development models
One of the development models shown in Chapter 1, "Model Types/Development Models," was used to refine the exterior wall relationship. At this point the previous wall components have been taken off and new cuts have been made directly on the model.

Modifying a sketch model
The resultant halves were reassembled in a new relationship. This assemblage was used to visualize new components that were then quickly cut and tested for successful integration.

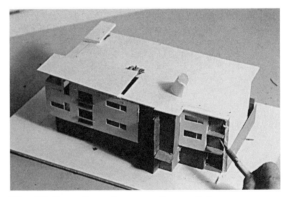

Modifying development models
The wall area has been rebuilt in a new but related configuration to refine this section of the design.

Modifying Site Contours

Strategy

Experiments should be carried out on the site in a similar manner to the building. Solid contour models made from inexpensive materials such as chipboard or corrugated cardboard are ideal for these studies. Grades can be cut out or added to accommodate a variety of conditions. As you experiment with various landscape treatments, it is helpful to save removed contour material so it can be replaced for alternative solutions.

Modifications also can be made to hollow models, but new contours must be attached to fill the holes left by cutting into the model.

TYPICAL MODIFICATIONS

- Creating a level grade for the building
- Creating drives and walks that cut into or rise above existing grades
- Creating cuts through several grades where soil must be retained (This typically occurs along property lines where changes are made.)
- Create terraces, berms, and drainage swales

Illustration

The images on the right show cardboard study models used to explore grade changes for drives, walks, and buildings. The images on the far right are of sites made from malleable materials that can be molded as desired.

Contour model changes
Contours are cut for an entry drive in the model. Slopes can be calculated by counting contours and the distance to the next level. The model is 1/8" scale. Each contour = 1'0", so 10 ft. forward produces a 1-in-10 slope.

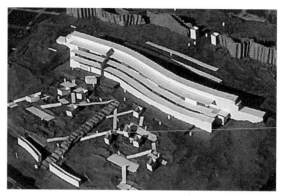

Plasticine site model
Grades and leveled areas for building footprints can easily be molded from this claylike material. Grades have the advantage of smooth appearance, but it is difficult to transfer the contours to drawings.

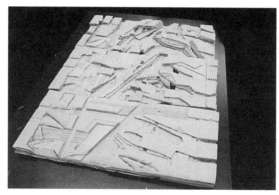

Study model with grade changes
The initial set of contours has been modified to design the landscape and accommodate site requirements such as road access, walls, and building footprints.

Plastic clay study for a park
This material can be quickly formed and is conducive to exploring alternatives. *Note:* As in the preceding example, it can be difficult to transfer grades accurately to drawings, and achieving crisp edge definition is challenging.

Digression

Strategy

Many times in the course of exploration, new directions emerge that do not follow the original intention. Instead of ignoring these and steering the design along preconceived paths, it can be profitable to let go of earlier ideas and follow implications suggested by the model. This may involve following the design through a strong shift in direction or even returning to an earlier generation in favor of later versions. Readings that emerge from rough modeling craft such as warped, off-center, or overlapping materials can be adopted as a discovered event and are many times more interesting than the intended readings.

Illustration

The sketch model and second-stage interpretations on the right demonstrate the tendency to regularize anomalies in the model in keeping with intended readings. This is a case where it can be argued that the earlier exploration was potentially more interesting than the "tightened-up" finish model and interpretation of the sketch model.

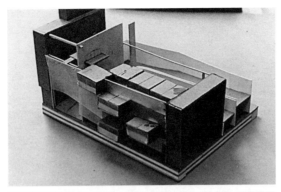

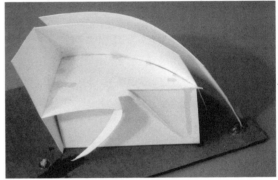

Using accidents

The thin acetate wall on the front of this sketch model displays a degree of unintentional warping and curvature that is potentially interesting. Although not the actual second stage for the project, the lower model is typical of the regularization applied to make the model conform to preconceptions. The results can be less interesting than the "accidents" suggested by the rough sketch. For this reason, it can be useful to let the project evolve on its own and take advantage of unintended discoveries.

Maintaining discovery

A form of reverse digression can occur in which model discoveries are lost in the translation to a higher level of refinement. In this example, many ideas developed in earlier stages have been "normalized" when moving to the refined version. The loss of discovery is similar in effect to a failure to use accidents. In both cases, regularizing tendencies and an unwillingness to let the model guide the evolution of the project have displaced some interesting ideas.

Interpreting

Strategy

Sometimes manipulation can be a matter of making a fundamental shift in either the model or the designer's perception of the model. This can be accomplished by using a number of processes. Processes can be combined or modified to generate other approaches based on your own exploration.

Illustration

The examples represent several typical strategies. They are similar in nature to concept models and are offered as experimental approaches to stimulate ideas.

The study models typically used to explore various strategies employ quick assembly techniques and offer the designer freedom to experiment without becoming unduly attached to the product.

The final set of projects are concept models pared with models made to extract a reading from them to create an architectural space. These models provide a link between the abstract, conceptual nature of models used to generate ideas and models that begin translating ideas into integrated building designs.

Fragment

A section of a large model has been severed from its original context and placed in a new attitude. This fragment is then reinterpreted as a complete building. By exploring new attitudes, several different solutions to the project are suggested.

Recycling

Another example that expands on the idea of fragments is to treat parts from previous models as found objects. By building a large inventory of cast-off project pieces, you can rethink and cross-assemble them. With modifications and the introduction of new elements, a number of ideas can be produced in short order.

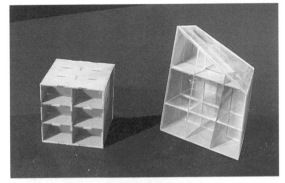

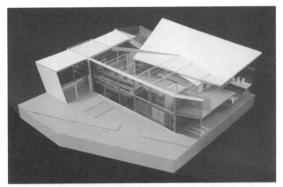

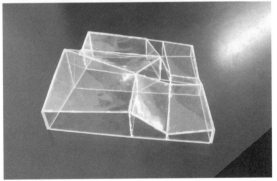

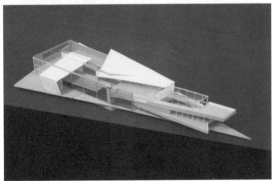

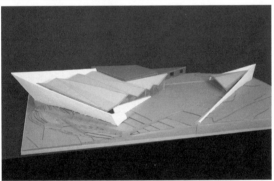

Distortion

Distortion relies on the premise that a standard prototype exists. The standard is then manipulated by pulling, twisting, and warping to create a new reading but is governed by its initial logic.

In the example above, an orthogonal box on the left has been distorted by elongating one side at an angle.

In the lower example, an orthogonal form has been pushed and pulled at points to create the form. Digital models are particularly adept at distortional manipulations.

Scale shift

This process allows the generation of a derivative project by operating on a previously completed project.

A section of the 1/16″ = 1′0″ scale model (lower model) has been identified with particularly interesting relationships. This section was isolated and reinterpreted at two times its original size.

The new model is now taken to represent the same square footage as the original project, and the program is reinserted into it.

Scale shift

In another example of the same strategy, a section of the 1/8″ = 1′0″ scale model (lower model) has been identified with particularly interesting relationships. This section was isolated and reinterpreted at four times its original size.

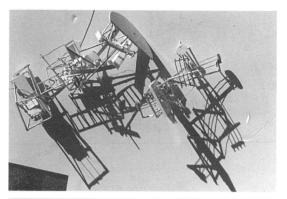

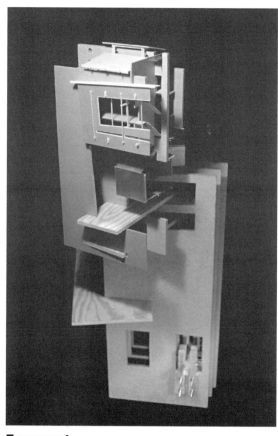

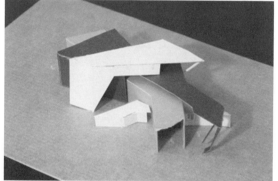

Fragment

This project derived an intricate acoustic universe by analyzing the structure of Giorgio de Chirco's paintings and making a number of machine studies. A fragment of the proposed building was constructed to examine the physical structure, building systems, and spatial and auditory environments.

Projecting

An interesting exercise for generating new ideas involves the use of three-dimensional forms to produce two-dimensional images. The shadows thrown off by the objects are best experimented with at lower sun or artificial light angles. The models can be turned in many directions to explore various types of shadow patterns. The patterns can be interpreted to create new models and models can in turn generate successive two-dimensional patterns through a reflexive interchange of information.

Axonometric

The process involves a dialogue between drawing and the model and is related to the topics discussed in "Working with Drawings" in this chapter. It is initiated by overlaying several outline drawings and extruding selected elements upward at varying heights to create a three-dimensional axonometric drawing. The drawing is then interpreted as a building and invested with program, site considerations, and structure to produce the model. The process becomes more controllable after experimenting several times.

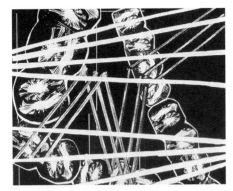

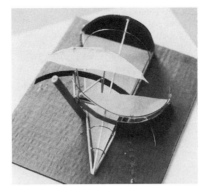

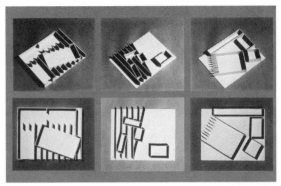

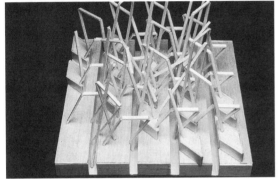

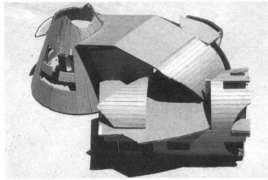

Collage

To begin, a collage is created by manipulating a set of base images from any number of sources. A model is then made based on the collage. The models will most likely become a concept model, but interpretations can convert the ideas directly into a building scheme. Part of this is controlled by the nature of the drawing. Repetitive images are less likely to lend themselves to the hierarchy of programmatic issues. For possible variations on the collage approach, see "Working with Concept Drawings" earlier in the chapter.

Collision

Two strategies employing the idea of collision are shown. Both are initiated in model form. The model above was started by building two open "wire frame" forms of contrasting size and shapes and engaging the two parts. The resultant collision can be used to make decisions about what is solid and open and how programming might be accommodated.

The model below uses a similar approach, but the three forms used for collision were solid masses carved away to create the voids. Intersections offer the most potential.

Intervention/rotation

Intervention is similar in concept to collision. A regular field such as a grid or other repetitive pattern is established as the ground or regular field. An "alien" in size and shape is then imposed in the body of the pattern at some disruptive or rotated angle. The resultant space is interpreted to accommodate architectural considerations. The diagram above illustrates the basic idea. The lower model is a building developed from imposing a curved gesture on an existing grid structure.

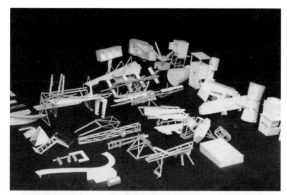

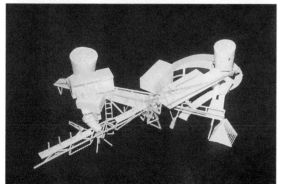

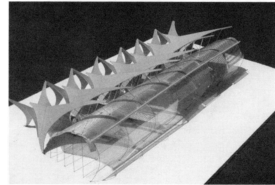

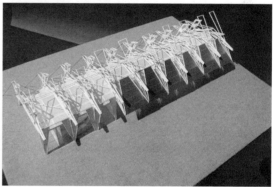

Lexicon

This process is related to recycling elements; however, rather than using existing elements, a vocabulary (or lexicon) of new parts is generated. The elements can be created as a number of platonic forms with variations. The parts for this example were generated by designing seven kiosks, then disassembling them. Many elements were used to create critical mass capable of producing unpredictable combinations. The model below was one of dozens made from combining the various elements.

Repetitive frames

This process involves the use of a repeated element to form an architecturally designed armature. To begin, a single frame is designed with a height and span in mind. The frame is stressed by pressing on key points, and ideas for modifications are incorporated to reinforce structural weak points. The frame is repeated to enclose a generic volume of space and becomes the structural frame for a building. In the example, the frames have been roofed and glazed to develop a small airport terminal.

Repetitive frames

Like the previous example, schematic models and development studies can be seen with the single frame. In the first example, the material is intended to be concrete shell construction, and for this one, steel members are employed. Designs were developed by looking at the body and tectonic structures such as bridges and cranes, as well as work by other architects.

Oblique Folding

Folding as a generative process can be used to discover a number of spatial relationships. Depending on the direction taken, the folds can be used to build enclosure or explore oblique space, producing internal layers and relationships.

The project on this page explores space on the oblique or angle. Initial moves were developed in three dimensions by means of folding and cutting a single 12″ × 12″ sheet of chipboard to produce spaces in relation to a site. The spaces responded to program and the highly sectional qualities of the site. The flowing sheet created an internal logic that carried through the components.

The models show the various stages from the initial folding to development and final model on the site.

Folding—study model stage 1
The initial fold made from a 12″ × 12″ sheet.

Folding—study model stage 2
The sheet is folded on itself to create layers and define spatial enclosure.

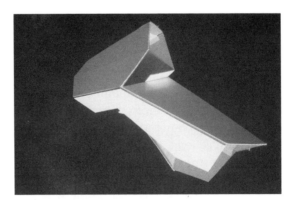

Folding—study model stage 3
The space of the building comes together as the fold closes. The fold itself takes its direction from the site as it works to negotiate between upper and lower elevations of the site.

Folding—final model stage 4
The study model is developed in context with the site model.

Orthogonal folding

Folding can proceed along conventional lines without the complications of oblique space.

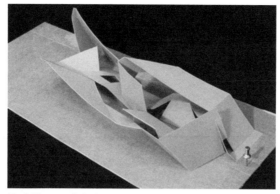

Folding with layers

Creating internal layers with sectional relationships is one of the strengths of the folding process.

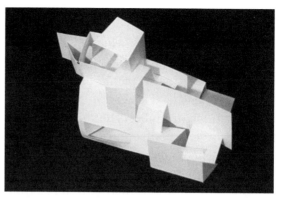

Folding continuous space

Folding can be used to explore continuous space.

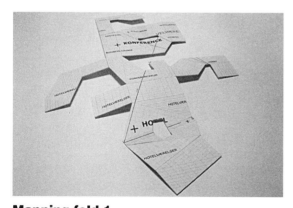

Mapping fold 1

Instead of folding with the idea of creating certain types of space, the initial plan to be folded can be derived from mapping another set of relationships.

Mapping fold 2

The edges must be planned in a way that will allow for assembly. In this case, a solid form is the result of the process.

Mapping fold 3

The final model has come about from folding two different sheets and putting them together. See the Scala project by Henning Larsen in Chapter 4.

Material Studies

Exploration of material behavior constitutes a rethinking of architectural formation. Studies include reaction to planar materials such as cloth and metal deformation, draping, folding, and light studies. The language established by the investigation is developed to translate into building propositions. This approach is in contrast to conventional methods that conceive of form as skin or cladding supported by framework.

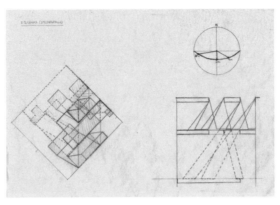

Light mapping project

In this project, light from two specific times of the year is tracked as it enters through precut openings created in response to a set of rules. The light path is drawn as an axonometric and section study.

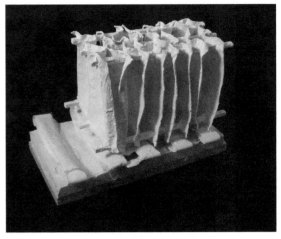

Plaster material study

In this example, sheets of gauze have been dipped in plaster and compressed into folds on a framework. The plastic quality of the space is a direct result of the coalition of material constraints.

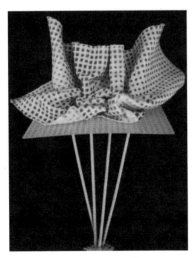

Folded cloth mapping

This study looks at the folding properties of cloth and begins to establish spatial interpretation by mapping the points of intensity.

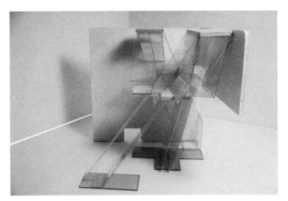

Light model

The light mapping from the project above is built as a physical manifestation of the light. The intersections between different projections are some of the most interesting aspects of the study.

Light mapping project

Spatial intensities have been mapped using colored line. The framework that gives space to the mapping becomes part of the dialogue.

Water/light mapping project 1

The quality of light through water becomes the basis for investigation in this study.

Water/light mapping project 2

The levels of intensity are flattened into layers in this interpretation.

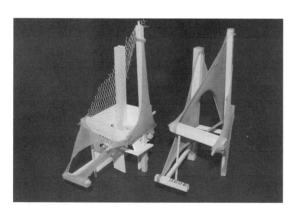

Elastic mapping project

This material study is based on the elastic properties of stretched cloth and the dialogue between the apparatus created to hold the material in tension.

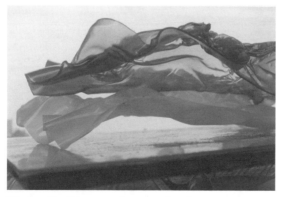

Water/light mapping project 3

Water and light are translated into space by bending layers of plexiglass. This attempt uses the transparent qualities of the plastic to make direct connections with the way light passes though the liquid medium.

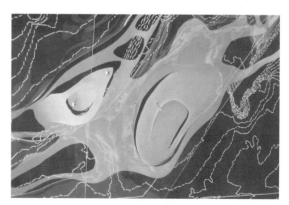

Water/light mapping project 4

In this iteration of investigations, the contour lines produced on the ocean floor are used as starting points. Mylar sheets are cut and elevated over and around each other to emulate the flowing properties of water.

Development
Project Development

The development process is central to use of the model as a design tool. The approaches discussed in the sections "Ideas" and "Manip-ulation" are applied using study models in a chain of evolutionary stages. This process is similar to two-dimensional design evolution in that concepts are used to develop schemes and are integrated with structure, site, and programming issues to produce a complete architecture. The process relies on the inter-related concepts of "Increasing Scale" and "Focusing" (discussed later in this chapter) as methods for advancement and is reinforced by "Coding and Hierarchy of Materials" and the "Converting" techniques also discussed later in the chapter.

Illustration

An abbreviated model progression with four stages of refinement bridges the gap between the single-stage interpretations of concept models (shown previously) and the expanded set of model stages in "Focusing" presented later in this chapter.

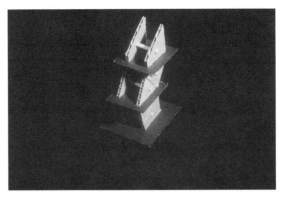

Retreat stage 1
The project explores themes from the play *Eleemosynary* to design a retreat for Echo, a primary character in the play. The study employs a simple harmonica as its initial design generator.

Retreat stage 2
A sketch model is used to develop spatial organizations and site engagement using the conceptual tectonic system as a basis for decisions.

Retreat stage 3
The concept model is used to develop basic tectonic systems.

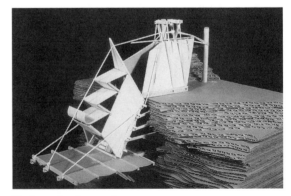

Retreat stage 4
The study is increased in scale and focus to develop the ideas into the retreat for Echo. The final project can be seen to effectively integrate ideas from the isolated study models.

Increasing Scale: Sketch–Development–Finish Models

Strategy

As a model evolves, it is typical to increase its size, moving from general relationships to greater levels of detail. This process of starting small and moving up in scale is analogous to focusing a lens. At low powers, the lens sees only general shapes and gestures. As greater focal powers are applied, elements become increasingly defined until details are clearly apprehended. See "Scale" in this chapter.

Illustration

In the examples to the right, the initial sketch models were established at small scales. As the direction became more focused, the scale was increased to develop more detailed readings.

Project A—initial 1/32″ scale model
A project investigation looking at overall issues of scale, massing and mechanics of the scheme with a small 1/32″ = 1′0″ sketch model.

Project B—initial 1/32″ scale model
A project investigation looking at overall issues of program, scale, light, and relationship to urban context.

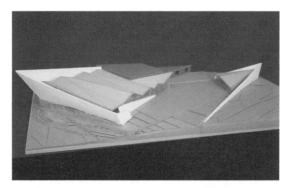

Project A—1/8″ development model
With the direction of overall issues established, the model is enlarged by a factor of four to 1/8″ = 1′0″ to facilitate a higher level of focus.

Project B—1/4″ scale development model
With an increase of scale, further development addresses elements such as the façade and roof section.

Project C—initial small study models

These small models were used to explore and refine the basic relationships for the project below.

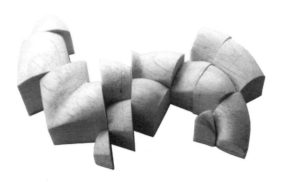

Project D—initial 1/32F″ scale study model

This model was used to explore the form and program relationships of the project.

Project E—initial small study models

A number of small subtractive models were made from stacked sections to explore initial directions.

Project C—1/8″ development/finish model

With the direction of overall issues established, the model is enlarged to 1/8″ = 1′0″ to facilitate a much higher level of focus.

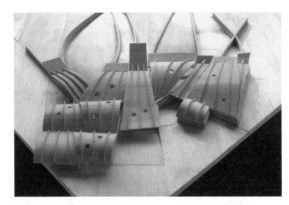

Project D—1/8″ development model

Once a direction was set by the model above, a set of site relationships was integrated and interpreted at a larger scale.

Project E—1/8″ development model

From the models above, one was selected to make a very large development model that could reflect the internal light conditions and serve as a platform to develop the large hole in the center.

Increasing Scale: Sketch–Development–Finish Models

Illustration

The development models to the right take the idea of scaling to the next level of focus by increasing the scale. In some cases, the scale increase may involve selected sections of the project; in others, the entire project may be built at a much larger size. The larger scale is important not only in facilitating better understanding of the internal experience, but in representing the next level of detail. Through exploration and refinement of this next generation of models, the project continues to evolve.

Project F—1/16″ scale development model

The project model at 1/16″ = 1′0″ is large enough to understand the space but demands a closer look to understand more about the interior relationships.

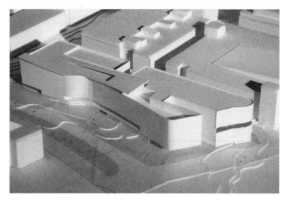

Project G—1/32F″ scale development model

The project model at 1/32″ = 1′0″ is large enough to understand the full implications of the project and indicate the major openings on the building façade.

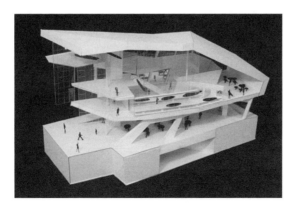

Project F—overall 1/8″ scale section model

This 1/8″ scale section model, at twice the size of the preceding project, is large enough to work out interior relationships.

Project G—section/development model

To fully understand the interior space, a much larger model is built at eight times the size of the smaller study.

Increasing Scale: Building Interior Models

Strategy

Part of the process of increasing scale involves enlarging the model to be able to focus on and develop interior components. Such models typically function as development models and are constructed to study interior architectural spaces and millwork.

Interior models are typically built at scales starting at 1/4″= 1′0″ and larger if possible. These models must define the borders of the space but remain open for viewing and working room.

Illustration

The models demonstrate typical scales and treatments for interior models.

1/8″ Atrium interiors study

This 1/8″ scale model is as small as interior models should be made. However, if carefully executed, they can provide a large range of information.

Digital model interior rendering

This digital rendering of the interior space of the project to the left can be used to compare the two methods of working. While the digital model offers a more realistic sense of the space, it can be difficult to alter in the design stage.

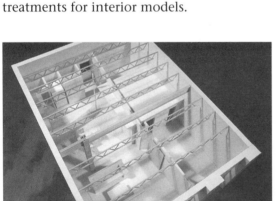

1/2″ Interior unit model

This model was built to convey the interior space of a typical loft unit. At this scale, it carries the detailing of every truss member and includes furnishings for scale comparison.

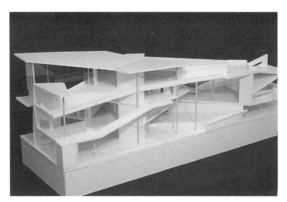

1/4″ Scale section study

An isolated section study taken at the core of a project can give a clear understanding of complicated floor-to-floor relationships. Primary elements such as library stacks and desks are included to convey scale.

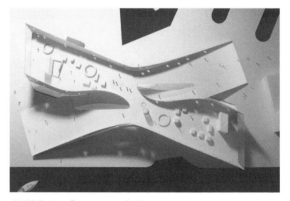

1/4″ Interiors model

By building only the interior space of this scheme, designers obtained a clear understanding of the spatial continuity at the crossover point. Providing furnishings also helped anchor the space.

Increasing Scale: Detail Models

Strategy

As project development proceeds, models are built at even larger scales to develop details such as window treatments, railings, fascias, and so forth.

These models are treated in a similar manner as building models but are built at much larger scales to study the finer readings of form articulation and connections.

Scales typically range from 1/2″ = 1′0″ to 3″ = 1′0″. Detail models can be helpful in resolving design ideas and construction details and in facilitating client communication.

Illustration

The models on the right demonstrate ways in which the models can be used to develop details or special furnishings.

A window surround
This museum board and foam core model was built at relatively large 3″ = 1′0″ scale to study relationships between corner connections and wall depth. *Note:* Test angles have been cut to fit the curved corners together.

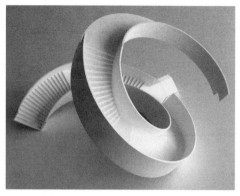

Spiral stairs
The set of spiral stairs is built out in detail and conveys a full sense of what the exact experience of this element will be like as well as defining the path of the spiral.

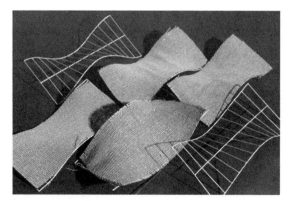

Shanghai panels
These models of the panels for the Spanish Pavilion at the Shanghai exposition were worked out in small-scale studies using soldered wire and fabric. A language for the full-scale panels was developed through them.

Façade detail
This study for façade openings has been rendered at a very large scale to explore the subtleties of the layers.

Coding and Hierarchy of Materials

Strategy

It is effective to use different materials based on classifications of building elements such as interior/exterior wall elements, program and structure. This type of coding reinforces the ability to "read," or understand the project's defining elements and geometries. It also begins to convey the sense of weight the various elements will project in terms of both their relative importance and physical heaviness. As projects become more resolved, components should reflect the actual scale thickness of walls, roofs, slabs, beams, and the like. This hierarchical range imparts a level of contrasting elements to make the model convincing as an architectural representation.

Illustration

The following projects use a range of scales and color to reflect different component types.

The two illustrations at the bottom of the page demonstrate the practice of detailing edges to reflect their true scaled thickness. *Note:* As a model is scaled up, it will not present a contrasting range of elements and can appear unconvincing if the thicknesses of modeling sheets do not accurately reflect the true scale of the elements.

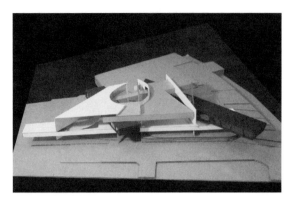

Coded program

The program elements of this 1/16″ scale model were color coded and used to read the interlocking nature of the spaces as they penetrated each other.

Coded materials and concept

The coding of this model can be read in two ways. The material of the central datum wall, dark box behind it, and translucent screen wall in front all convey a sense of contrasts both in color, weight, and material. Alternately, the conceptual organization anchored by the central wall with adjoining components is clearly delineated.

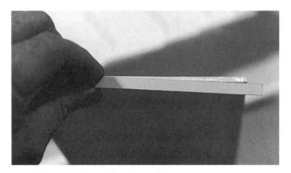

1/4″ Scale fascia detail

A 1/8″ foam core roof plane is edged with a 10″ scaled strip of museum board.

1/4″ Scale fascia detail

The edge of the roof now reflects the true 10″ depth of the fascia.

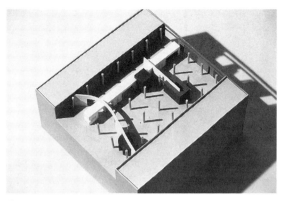

Coded program components

A clear delineation is made between the program components by coding the interior of the space gray, circulation elements in white, and program spaces in dark board.

Coded buildings and addition

The model components for an addition use coding to differentiate between the dark-colored existing building and the new elements.

Coding planning elements

In this model, buildings, site elements, and tectonic constructions such as the unifying trellis work have all been coded with a range of materials to clearly differentiate the complex.

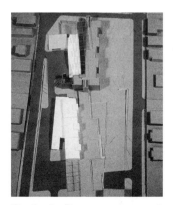

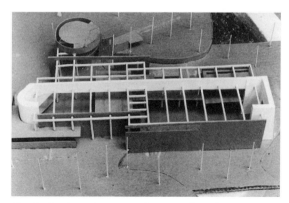

Coded site components

The site is coded to differentiate the ground plane, roads, existing buildings, and new structures (in white). *Note:* The site and existing buildings are in darker neutral tones and allow the new work to stand out.

Coded addition elements

The contrast between the dark walls of the existing building and the new components, intervening through its space, can be clearly read because of the contrasting materials.

Coded structure and organization

White anchor and circulation elements, gray board walls, and a wood structural grid have been used to reinforce structural systems and program organization.

Converting: Renovating Models

Strategy

Although there is a point when many decisions have been made and a model has to be recrafted, models are often needlessly rebuilt every time a few elements are changed. This can consume a lot of time. Instead, renovation techniques can be used to effectively clean up the model. In many cases, the results of these techniques are entirely adequate for more formal presentations.

Illustration

The sketch model on the right is refaced to upgrade its level of finish. For complete step-by-step illustration of this project, see "Case Study B" in Chapter 9.

Models on the far right have been covered in paper to code and upgrade their level of finish.

Project A—renovation

A typical refacing begins by cutting openings in an overlay sheet. This method is more practical than cutting holes through the model. Transfer tape is used for large surfaces likely to warp if glue is applied.

Project B—covering with paper

Colored paper can be used to renovate or code the model's surface. Paper can be attached with Spray Mount or double-face transfer tape. Glue sticks can be used on the edges.

Project A—renovation

The resultant understated shadow lines generally read better on small models as visual layers. Additional facings can be cut and applied over all the original cuts to continue elevating the model's finish.

Project C—site renovation

Site surfaces can be covered with paper to smooth out contours on rough models. The paper helps visually reduce the large change in contours on the initial model and serves to elevate the level of finish.

PROJECT DEVELOPMENT

Academic Examples in Support of Exploration

In academic work, modeling offers one of the strongest ways to understand the impact of design decisions on the design and is of particular value when working with complex geometries. The following projects present examples of models from several architecture programs. Many of the strategies discussed in Chapters 1 and 2 can be seen at work.

Focusing

Strategy

Focusing refers to the application of evolutionary stages of development. It draws on all the ideas presented in the previous chapter and is central to the process of moving a project from a germ of an idea through successive stages of development. The process may begin with alternatives and digression, but as it evolves, each new model builds on the generalized relationships of the previous stage to arrive at an integrated building design.

Typical Evolutionary Stages

Proceeding from initial information:

- To alternate concept and sketch studies
- To fixed geometry and relationships
- To exploring alternative treatments
- To looking at alternative detailing
- To a resolved project design

Illustration

The projects on the following pages show an array of development stages typical of a project designed with the model as a primary study tool.

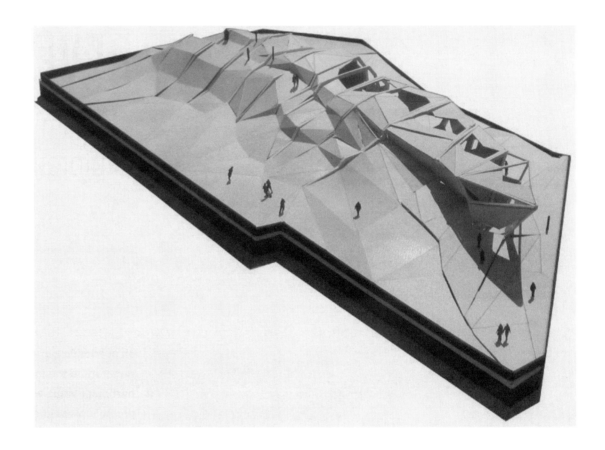

College Complex

This project presents several strong aspects of modeling. They include development of conceptual ideas through successive stages and the use of the model to develop the façade and elevations. See "Increasing Scale" in Chapter 2.

College complex stage 1

The development of dormitories, galleries, and art studios is initiated with a concept/gesture model to interpret the dichotomy between the suburban and urban landscapes.

College complex stage 2

The relationship suggested by the concept model is engaged with the site. This sketch model serves to translate gestures into a building construct.

College complex stage 3

Growing out of the earlier discoveries, the program and other organizational issues are engaged for possible occupations on the site.

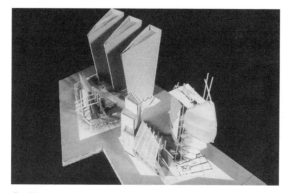

College complex stage 4

The overall organization and general form of the complex has been developed, and attention turns to refining individual elements.

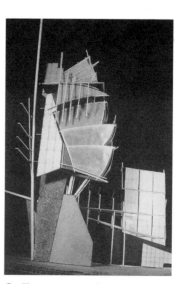

College complex stage 5

The tower is developed as a finish model. A section of the tower is then scaled up for more study. See Chapter 2, "Increasing Scale: Development–Finish Models."

Courthouse

This project is for a new courthouse in Charlotte, North Carolina. The courthouse proposal included a plaza on the north side of the site. An overarching concern for the development of the architectural forms was to respond to daylight in ways that would not block the sun in the plaza. The unconventional form was determined using physical and computer models to carve away mass in response to a pragmatic set of criteria and tests.

The process worked back and forth between physical and computer models. The physical models were used to simulate light projections and shadows on the plaza at different sun angles.

The studies clearly illustrate the movement from early sketch models to a developed and crafted final version.

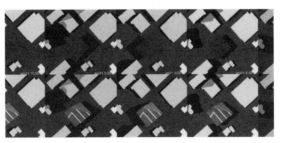

Office building stage 1—concept drawing
The initial project information is derived from a two-dimensional pattern drawing. Although a lot of interpretive space is left by the drawing, it provides direction and is fully exploited by the three-dimensional studies.

Office building stage 2—sketch model
The drawing is interpreted as a three-dimensional construction that begins to respond to the shadows cast on the plaza.

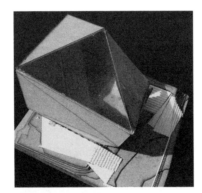

Office building stage 3—development model
The conceptual model is developed into a spatial proposition that reacts to program and site response.

Office building stage 4—finish model
The final model has developed readings of skin, structure, and layering as a refinement of the development study. Although the glazed structure transmits maximum light, it would have been instructive to take photographs with the light source behind the building.

Chapel Addition

This project was a competition proposal for the addition of a chapel to an existing health care facility. The chapel was conceived as the intersection between building and landscape. As such, it sought to blur the distinction between them, using gardens, walls, and water in a scattered occupation of the site.

The project development relied heavily on models, and the progression from early studies to final design display a classic use of general studies that progress to refined iterations.

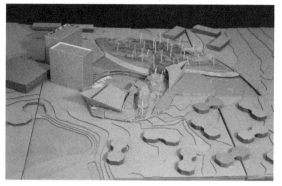

Study model—stage 2

The project was first defined with some definite relationships to the existing building. In the process, the site has been redesigned to respond to the new proposition for the addition.

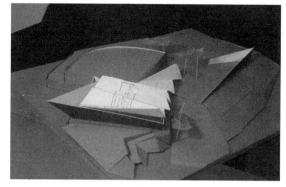

Development model—stage 3

With the basic organization of the project in place, the project is developed including walls and roofscape. The folded planes of the roof add structural strength, allowing the roof to float over the wall so light can pass through.

Initial study model—stage 1

In the formative stage of the project, a number of ideas are tested out for scale and their relationship to the existing building. Even at this early stage, embryonic ideas for the folded roof idea are present.

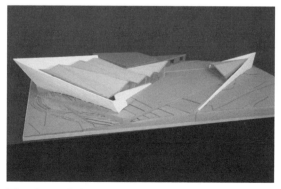

Final model—stage 4

The completed design is articulated on a large site model and conveys the dual character of light/heavy, with the roof floating over masonry walls.

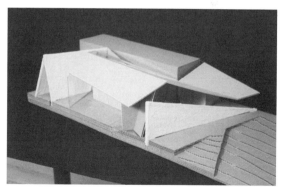

Building section—stage 5

In order to explore the design more thoroughly, a portion of the project has been built out at 1/2" scale. At this scale, the materials and support for the building can be developed and clearly delineated.

BiblioTierra Library

This project was for a library and conceived of the site as a park in a dense urban area that became a topographic space for the library.

The project began by analyzing sun angles and establishing the program in sections that were integrated into the landscape. By connecting the sectional stages, the library spaces began to form in plan. As the topography of the section was connected, the landscape for the park also began to take shape.

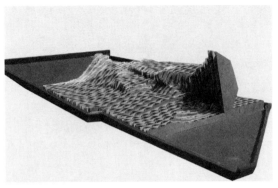

Section infill—stage 2
The sectional information established by a mapping of the profiles is rendered as a solid construction of mass, translating the work into topography.

Section development—stage 3
The space between each section is connected to establish the crossing plan for the library. Key program components such as the tower are developed.

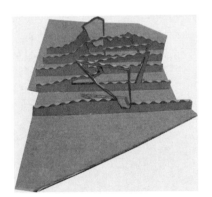

Section study—stage 1
The project is initiated through the study of program and terrain sections established at regular intervals. The program element of the tower is suggested by the final breakout of the profiles.

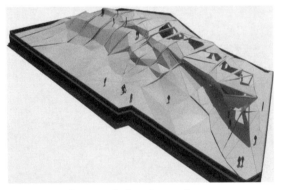

Topography model—stage 4
The project evolves into architecture as landscape with fissures in the surface providing light.

Entry tower study—stage 5
The tower on the topography model is isolated and increased in scale to develop a reading of this element.

Observatory

The project consists of an observatory for the Clemson University campus. The program is intentionally vertical, with sectional relationships to tie the architecture to the earth and sky. The project investigation is transformational in that conceptual drawings have been used to produce images with overlapping readings. The drawing was then interpreted as a three-dimensional apparatus. The physical construct of the apparatus was used to derive a set of architectural relationships that in this instance relied on the language of the continuous Möbius strip.

Ribbon study—stage 1
The initial translation of relationships drawn from the apparatus can be seen in this model. At this stage, basic program blocks have been incorporated as integral to the study.

Ribbon development—stage 2
The space of the ribbon is refined and placed into the context of site. Once in the site, it spreads out to interweave its path with the earth.

Apparatus study—stage 1
The base drawing has been used to produce this apparatus or machine and establishes a set of interactive relationships.

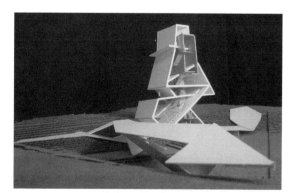

Ribbon development—stage 4
The project is refined to address circulation, enclosure, and material thickness.

Final ribbon model—stage 5
The model is increased in scale to develop interior relationships as well as the conditions of entry and connections to earth.

Piranesi's Labyrinth Museum

This project consisted of a small museum for display of Piranesi's work in the three-level space of an abandoned infill building in downtown Anderson, South Carolina. The concept revolved around the exploration of interior space as labyrinth using the base information of Piranesi's Carcel etchings. This was combined with the distortional world of Dr. Calgary and the nature of ice to inform subsequent development.

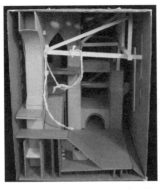

Space of the labyrinth—stage 1
The initial design work was carried out as an exercise aimed at interpreting the space of Piranesi's Carcel etchings. This exercise provided a base understanding of the qualities of the labyrinth.

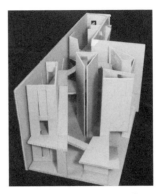

Spatial interpretation—stage 2
The spatial understandings from the previous study were applied to the program to create a similar experience. This first reading misses the distortional space of Dr. Calgary.

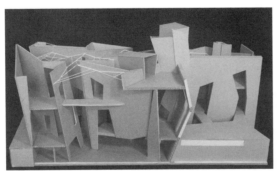

Final museum—stage 3
A second attempt to understand the space captures the labyrinthic, distortional space of Dr. Calgary.

Roof plan
The massing of the space as an enclosed experience, with openings for light, can be appreciated in the context of the infill walls it occupies.

Southern Culture Complex

This project consisted of a large cultural complex set into the strip culture of Anderson, South Carolina. The program for the project was developed as a response to southern culture. The program components were meant to be a social mixer and became a strong driver of the project.

Along with the program forces, a set of four different exercises were undertaken to explore various means to translate ideas and images into architectural form. As a base for the exercises, site information was used to produce a drawing with potential interpretive possibilities.

This particular project employed axonometric extrusions from the site drawing coupled with careful program distribution to arrive at the project conclusion.

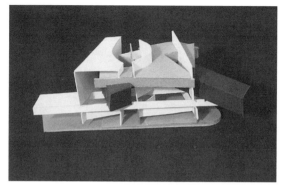

Initial axon model—stage 1
This model was made from an axonometric drawing without concern for exact scale. It did, however, concern itself with program and site, using color-coded materials to delineate major program changes.

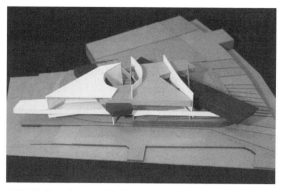

1/16″ Scale model on site—stage 2
The model to the left was adjusted to an exact scale and begins to come into dialogue with the site.

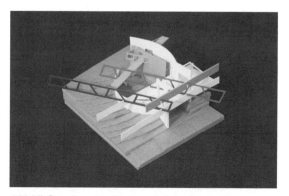

1/16″ Scale study model—stage 3
The center section on the previous model was isolated and built as a skeletal construction to study site relationship in this area.

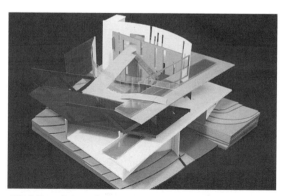

1/8″ Scale section model—stage 4
The same central area, along with a greater portion of the surrounding space, was increased in scale to develop the space and its interface.

Design/Build Project

The project was the result of a six-week design/build exercise. The project was developed around *The Man Who Was Thursday,* a play based on G. K. Chesterton's 1908 book and used by the Russian constructivists in building their stage sets.

The work was designed using a large array of study models. The final constructed artifact was located as a temporary structure in the courtyard of the Lee Hall architecture building. As this was a team project, the initial studies ranged across a broad spectrum of ideas centered around the play and constructivist language. After making a number of small studies at 1/8″ scale, design teams begin narrowing the focus of design along a select path by passing the models to other teams for refinement. The model scale was moved progressively up from 1/8″ = 1′0″ scale to 1/4″ = 1′0″ and finally to 1/2″ = 1′0″. At this stage, drawings begin to play a large role in refining the project.

The models shown represent a continuous thread that can be followed through a particular design direction that led to the final design. An image is included of the complete collection of study models in order to convey the extent of exploration employed in the design sequence.

Full study model array
This jumbled pile of models gives an idea of how many different studies were explored during the three-week design phase of the project.

Initial gesture model—stage 1
This model was one of the initial abstract studies that influenced much of the ultimate project direction.

Final constructed work

Initial 1/8″ = 1′0″ study model—stage 2

This model along with the model on the previous page became the two seminal drivers of the project.

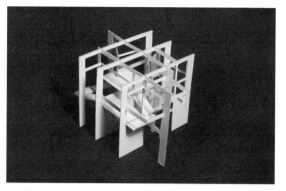

1/4″ = 1′0″ Frame scheme model—stage 3

As a continuation of the frame scheme from the model on the left, this scheme explored a constrained version of serial geometry with moveable partitions.

Merged 1/8″ = 1′0″ study—stage 4

This small model was the first attempt to merge the previous models. It served as a clear guide for refinement.

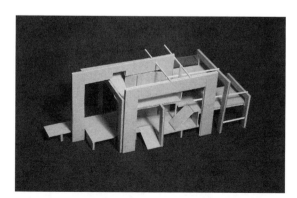

1/4″ = 1′0″ Study of the smaller model—stage 5

This model is a larger version of the 1/8″ = 1′0″ merged model and served to transmit a reading of its space at increased scale.

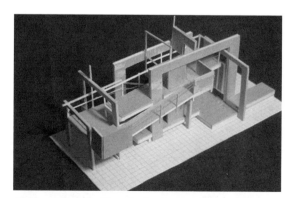

1/4″ = 1′0″ Refined study model—stage 6

This was the final design study in the chain of exploration and was used to refine the circulation path as well as the language of the frames. Construction drawings were made using this model as a basis.

1/2″ = 1′0″ Finish model—stage 7

This model wa s made to study details of the project at a larger, more refined scale. As the project was temporary in nature, this model serves as its representational memory.

Urban Museum/Plaza

This was a large urban project located in Barcelona, Spain. The project looked at redesigning an intersection in the city to create a greater sense of place. In addition to an urban park, a museum was developed from the intersections of the space.

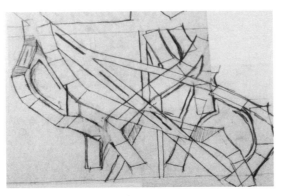

Flow plan—stage 2
The plan above was made to analyze and develop a new reading of the urban spaces.

Site layout—stage 3
The new site design has been studied in three dimensions and begins to suggest the way in which public spaces and a building can be derived from them.

Site information—stage 1
The drawing of existing conditions gives a clear indication of the strong cross axis that anchors the site as well as the network of roads around it.

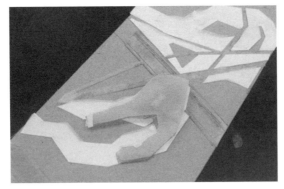

Site development—stage 4
The three-dimensional investigation of the site has been expanded to develop public spaces and the museum space.

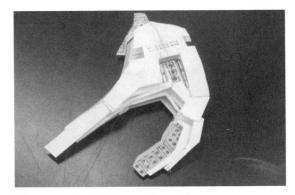

Museum building—stage 5
The museum building emerges directly out of the nexus of site information. It has been built up in layers and studied at a larger scale.

PROJECT DEVELOPMENT IN PRACTICE

Design Firm Examples in Support of Exploration

In practice, modeling offers one of the strongest ways to understand the impact of design decisions on the built work and is of particular value when working with complex geometries. The following projects present examples of models from several types of practices. Many of the strategies discussed in Chapters 1 and 2 can be seen at work, as well as the connection between built work and the model exploration that helped form it.

Mack Scogin Merrill Elam Architects (Formerly Scogin Elam and Bray)

This office makes extensive use of the model in the development of every project. A cross-section of work reveals many of the strategies in Chapter 2 applied in response to a particular need or situation. Whereas the structure of one project may be difficult to understand without the aid of a detail model, another may require a scaled-up section to study the spatial experience. The role of the model is also seen to vary depending on the design direction. In some cases, a combination of models and drawings has been used; in others, multiple alternates or exclusive reliance on the model formed the rule.

Examples drawn from 10 different projects are used to illustrate the diverse role of the model in the daily course of this firm's practice.

Buckhead Library, Atlanta, Georgia

The models from the project demonstrate two primary ways they are treated. First, because the project was initially developed with the drawings, a small 1/8″ = 1′0″ scale model was built to confirm decisions. In the second instance, in order to develop the entry sequence and canopy elements, the front section was increased in size to a 1/4″ = 1′0″ scale. At this scale, the model was large enough to convey the experience of the space. The image of the completed building confirms the ability of the scaled-up model to predict a reality.

Buckhead Library—1/8 scale
This small development/finish model was made after the overall design relationships were established and depicts a three-dimensional sketch of the entry canopies at the front of the building.

Buckhead Library—1/4″ = 1′0″ elevation
The front section of the building has been doubled in scale in order to develop the design of the entry canopies. The model and elevation drawings were used in concert to compose its elements.

Buckhead Library—completed building
The completed building, in a view similar to that taken of the 1/4″ scale model, reflects the quality of space projected in the design studies.

Knowlton Hall, Knowlton School of Architecture, The Ohio State University, Columbus, Ohio

The design for the new school of architecture took its initial direction from a previous project for the Laban Dance Center shown below. With similar concerns and program responses, the various alternate schemes evolved, as shown in this sequence to produce the realized building. While the form of the building can be seen to undergo various shifts, the strategy for its internal space remains constant with a large social mixer in the form of a ramp system, energizing the perimeter program spaces.

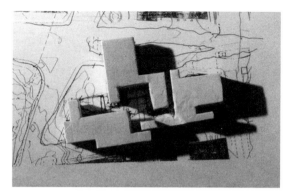

Massing model
With the idea of a centralized space at the core, the building perimeter is pushed out to the edges of the site with sections of it out over the street.

Conceptual flow study
In another study of the site, the flow of activity and influences on the site was analyzed with this conceptual model. Many of the later spatial voids relate to this study.

Laban Dance Center design models
With similar program requirements such as a large, centralized space and internal light, the site context is used as in Laban to arrive at a stacked section with a ramp to activate it.

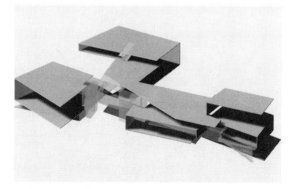

Folded model with ramp system
As in Laban, the interior events are pushed to the exterior of the building to form a folded container. Digital and physical models are made to develop the ramping system at the core of building.

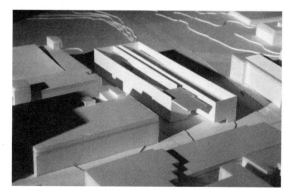

Box scheme
Originally budgeted as an addition, the desire for a new building brought about a radical simplification of the folded scheme as a simple box in order to conform to the budget.

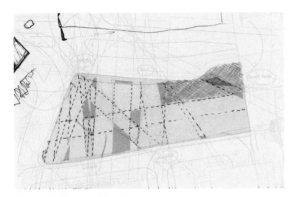

Regulating site lines

With a change to the project direction, another series of site lines was studied. These generated a similar internal experience while resisting the grid as the sole regulating device.

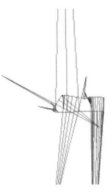

Regulating building lines

To discover other means to produce specific regulating information, the site perimeter is used to generate a series of tangent lines to a projected center for each arc. These lines are used to lay out the structural system.

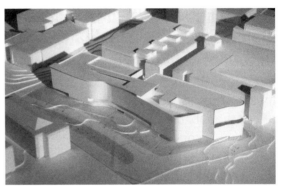

Modified box scheme

In order to move beyond the constraints of the box scheme, the building envelope becomes an extrusion of the site with projections, cuts, and slices that bring the interior to the exterior and the exterior to the interior.

Development model

A larger model is made to explore issues of the skin, openings, and site development.

Interior model of inclined planes

The project is now carried largely by the section. The all-important ramping internal system, referred to as a mixing apparatus, is modeled at a large scale to study its trajectory and relationship to the staggered floor levels.

Large development study model

A very large study model was made to fully develop and confirm the experience of the interior spaces.

Yale University Health Services Building, Yale University, New Haven, Connecticut

This collection of wood study models for the Health Services building illustrates the type of exhaustive search that is typically carried out by the firm in model form. In this case, the triangular siting dictates a compact form, which is manipulated to introduce light into the interior spaces. There was also a conscious decision to respond to Eero Saarinen's buildings on site, such as Morse College, and "ease" the form to create a sensuous building.

Compact wood block model

This scheme explores an irregular breakup of spaces that adheres to an overall compact perimeter.

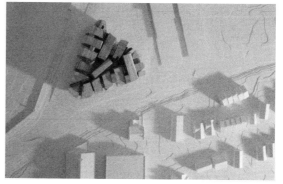

Modulated wood block model

A series of units regulated by the two street axes and infilled with program in the gap is used to define the triangular space. The introduction of light deep into the building space is most aggressive in this scheme.

Program-driven wood block model

Various program blocks are assembled with gaps to flesh out the triangular site.

Regularized wood block model

This model divides the mass of the triangle into regular quadrants while softening the edges.

Final model

In the final scheme, the block has become one continuous sculpted mass with cuts and depressions in its surface guided by the other studies.

Gates Center for Computer Science, Carnegie Mellon University, Pittsburg, Pennsylvania

In this project, a complex set of program spaces competed for maximum exposure to light. The initial studies may appear to be formal exercises but were rational mappings of the quantity of exterior wall demanded by the project for each program space. This strategy was taken to extremes and refined through a number of studies to yield the final set of forms for the building. There was also a large change in elevation across the site and the building is used to mediate this shift.

Sketch conceptual study model

This model was made from a drawing as an extrusion of all the perimeter wall surfaces that the program brief called for.

Stacked conceptual model

The program "puzzle" pieces were stacked as floor-to-floor sections in this model to provide interior light wells.

Project development model

The ideas for introducing light into the building have been regularized by the major program blocks but still retain some of the deep wells into the building section.

Final scheme

The final model, while rationalized to some degree, can be seen to be clearly connected to the early studies and is still close to the design from the development stage.

Callas, Shortridge Associates

Seagrove House, Santa Rosa Beach, Florida

Among other projects, this firm has designed many outstanding houses and uses the study model as a site for exploration throughout the process.

The model is a key element in understanding the dynamic space of the Seagrove House. Of special interest is the evolution of model refinement, particularly in the development stage, and the use of the model on the site as a tool for construction visualization. The images on this page compare views of the on-site model and the project as it nears completion. All roofs are constructed so that they can be removed from the models to reveal interior spaces and framing systems.

Seagrove House—finish model
North elevation of the final model was used during construction to understand overall relationships and framing. The model has been increased in scale from the last development model on the following page and detailed.

Seagrove House—finish model
South elevation of the final model. When compared with a similar view of the built work, it becomes clear that the model space carries strong predictive powers.

Seagrove House—built work
As it nears completion, the active space of the built work reflects the model's ability to orchestrate the composition. On entering, the space exceeds the promise of the model.

Seagrove House—built work
The built work offers two different readings from front to back. Whereas the north elevation breaks apart to perform a dance in space, this elevation engages the southern horizon.

Seagrove House Study/ Development Models

These models represent explorations used to define various sections of the building. At this point, a rough general scheme has been established and study begins by orchestrating the overall building. As sections are generally resolved, focus can be seen to shift to alternate solutions for individual elements.

The study culminates in a development model with relationships similar to the finish model but less detailed.

Seagrove House—stage 1

At this point, the house appears related to its final form, but the walls have yet to be defined. Individual elements are only suggested, and other forms of expression are explored.

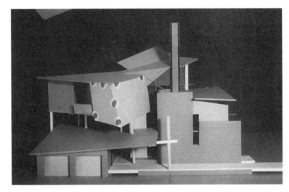

Seagrove House—stage 2, front

The major elements on the north elevation appear to be formed at this stage, and alternate elements such as the angled box (with taped corners on the second story) are experimented with.

Seagrove House—stage 3, lakeside

The south elevation of the development model appears generally formed. Study has been focused on the tower and the spaces directly below it.

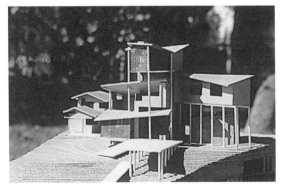

Seagrove House—stage 4, lakeside

At this point, most of the spaces on the south elevation have been established, and final refinement can take place.

Seagrove House—stage 5, front

This development model is similar to the final model, except less attention has been given to detailing openings and intersections.

Roto Architects Inc.

This firm employs a flexible improvisational working style that adapts itself to the inevitable and unique aspects of each project. Much of the work has been designed and built through collaborative relationships with clients. In the course of this collaboration, various design methods have been explored, with modeling playing a key role in the development of new systems.

Sinte Gleska University (SGU), Antelope, South Dakota

Sinte Gleska University is the first and oldest tribal university in the Americas. Roto Architects was asked to plan and build an entirely new campus for the university. The project used models to develop highly refined readings of the spatial and diagrammatic structures of the Lakota traditional systems of movement and rest. The detailed model of the multipurpose building displays many of the aspects in respect to focusing and hierarchy.

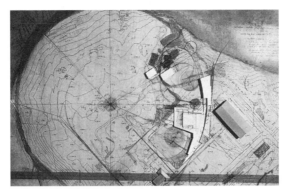

SGU master plan
Models and drawings have been used in concert to map out site relationships that reflect traditional Lakota spatial systems.

SGU Multipurpose Building
Modeling elements were used to develop and detail every structural member and incorporate traditional Lakote beliefs and a layering of ordering systems.

SGU Technology Building and Student Center
The ribbed roof structure, moving from left to right, employs modeling to describe the form of mythological star formation bridging between the two buildings.

SGU Multipurpose Building
A highly developed detail of the Kapemni, or universal model (center), considers every structural element in relation to scale and hierarchy extending attention down to the 27 symbolic ribs of the buffalo as shown in the center of the roof structure.

Dorland Mountain Arts Colony, Temecula, California

The project replaces a small retreat building for an arts colony. The building reflects the way that indigenous structures form unique volumes based on the constraints of time and materials. The models are an exercise in three-dimensional drawing. By placing key members to shape the volume, a structural frame is developed, which springs from unique construction and bracing systems.

Carlson-Reges Residence, Los Angeles, California

This residence was built as a series of additions grafted onto an existing industrial building. Materials were primarily brought into the project from a scrap yard adjacent to the building. As much of the work was developed as an ongoing work in progress, models were used to direct overall moves on each section and evolve expression during construction.

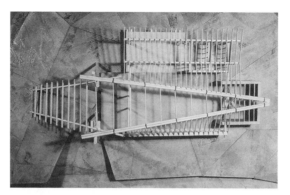

Dorland Mountain Arts Colony
The diagram of the triangulated frame and its subsystems can be clearly read in plan view.

Dorland Mountain Arts Colony
The volume generated by filling in the spaces demonstrates the effectiveness of using a three-dimensional diagram to establish the skeletal outline. The model also facilitates the rethinking of triangulated bracing systems.

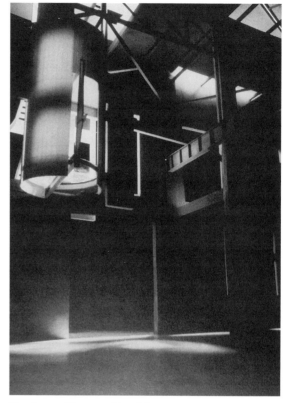

Carlson-Reges Residence
The quality of the existing space is reflected in this interior model, and the effects of the new light monitor can be experienced just as it might read in the space.

Enric Miralles and Benedetta Tagliabue (EMBT) Architects

This firm is internationally famous for its innovative work and has a number of built works. Three-dimensional design tools in the form of the physical model play a large role in their design process. The models range from early conceptual studies to large full-scale mock-ups, with exhaustive studies carried out at every stage. The site plays a large role in developing the design as a manipulated topography, and the model studies reflect this orientation.

Examples are drawn from six of their projects to illustrate the role of the model.

Palafolls Library, Palafolls, Spain

The models from this project are typical of EMBT's process. Initiated as a drawing of an embryo, a dream, the drawing has been manipulated and adapted to the landscape. In this case, the landscape contributes its own response to the project, and the two directions are used to inform each other.

Concept drawing and model
The drawing on the left is based around an embryo, and this drawing is interpreted as a three-dimensional model.

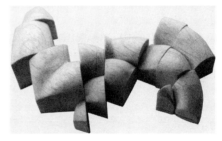

Model manipulation
The model is then manipulated by slicing it into sections and shifting the parts to bring light into all sections of the space.

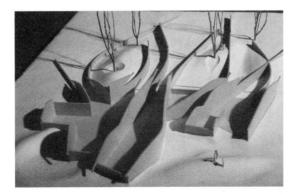

Landscape "hairs"
Extensions of the landscape "grow" from the site. These conceptual "hairs" bind the site and project together.

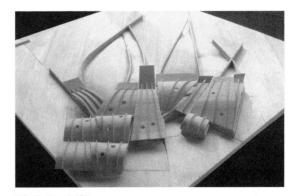

Finished library
The finished project becomes a series of eruptions that extend the landscape into spatial enclosures that in turn create their own topography.

Arcelor Pavilion, Esch-sur-Alzette, Luxembourg

This project was formed by establishing an elaboration of invisible lines on the surrounding site. The lines came from the wind, movement of trees, rain, historical context, and the relationship between the landscape and the city.

The models clearly show the progression from early studies of the landscape forces through development of the final design.

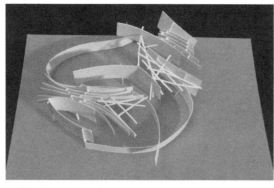

Initial concept

The lines of movement on the site and intersection between various axes come together in the project location.

Spatial volume

The project space is "discovered" in the body of the various looping conditions, and an ambiguity between what is enclosed and what is open is set up at this early stage.

Completed building

The building is lifted up off the ground plane, and exterior ramp space with patios is seen as additional opportunity to blur the lines of interior and exterior spatial understanding.

Development model

The interior space of the project is explored and focuses on developing the intersections between the various flows of the overall project.

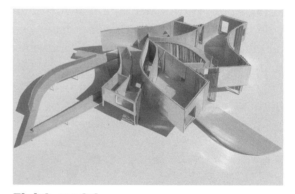

Finish model

At this stage, the model is built out to develop and delineate openings and architectural conventions such as wall thickness and occupiable space.

Gas Natural Building, Barcelona, Spain

The Gas Natural Building is sited in Barceloneta on a direct axis with the Triumphal Arch in Parc de la Ciutadella. This connection played a large role in the development of the project in terms of monument and gateway, but all forces that acted on the space of the site were taken into consideration. The fragmented volumes, which make up the larger one, respond to the smaller scale of Barceloneta. The dynamic confluence of these forces was studied through numerous models to produce reactions that cumulatively shaped the space in a deterministic response.

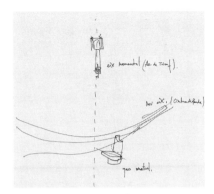

Triumphal Arch and axis
The initial drawing for the project studies the relationship between the arch and connecting axis to the site. At this stage, the marking of the site and the gate of the cantilever are already present as ideas.

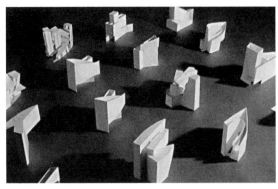

Envelope studies
The array of models demonstrates the extensive study invested to explore how the various site forces might act on the building mass to give it form. Each move has come about as a specific response to some condition.

Completed building
The completed building with its dramatic cantilever is ultimately clad in a uniform glass skin.

Site model
The site model highlights the relationship of the building as a strong corner entry into the low-scale, densely packed blocks of Barceloneta and the scale shift this represents.

Development model
Each section of the project under consideration is studied as a dialogue between components with different material readings. This direction is ultimately abandoned in the final schemes.

Santa Caterina Market Renovation, Barcelona, Spain

The market project was both a renovation of an existing market and the planning of the adjacent neighborhood. Various plans to preserve and use only a section of the original market were studied. The initial design studies looked at an extension of the forces from the existing neighborhood as they extended across the original walls. Ultimately, a large part of the perimeter wall was covered with the undulating tile roof as shown on the following page. The roof was studied through a number of models to determine its form and structure.

Initial roof study
The implications of the initial drawing to the left are built out as they intersect the existing walls as a wire frame study. The projection into the neighborhood blurs the line between rehabilitation and new impositions.

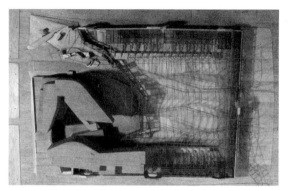

Roof study and adjacent area
The project focus is shifted to engage a large part of the existing perimeter with new buildings at the rear. The roof is modeled in wire at regular sections to explore its curving nature.

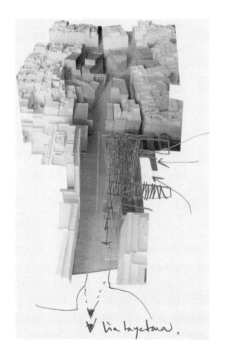

Detailed roof study
The entire roof system is developed in detail, including the large, bent laminated wood beams and the three large arch trusses that span the interior space. The long projection over the street shown in this model is not realized in the final construction.

Rear elevation study

A layer of wood infill framing and panels is modeled to study the closure of the roof and market space at the rear of the project.

Rear elevation

The built work above can be compared with the highly detailed model to the left. The laminated wood beams and purlins can be compared to the detail model of the roof system on the previous page.

Street approach

From the street, the entrance to the market is called out by the roof as it slides across the old walls and is supported by the branching columns.

Completed building

The roof structure draws in part on an early project by Gaudi for the school at the base of the Sagrada Familia. In this project, the roof arches alternated from front to back. However, the studies for this roof also took strong direction from the nature of gathered cloth and seeks to replicate the specific type of folding that occurs in the material.

The technicolor surface (better appreciated in color images), with its honeycomb tile pattern, is a major presence in the city. While only suggestions of its full impact are seen at street level, the surrounding neighborhood is given a new landscape at an upper-story datum.

Spanish Pavilion for Expo Shanghai 2010, Shanghai, China

The pavilion was developed as a sustainable solution that exploits the history of wicker baskets to define the space along the lines of basket volumes. While the wicker itself serves as a filter and as skin for the building, the mesh frame structure also uses the idea of weaving.

A number of model studies can be seen here, including small and full-scale panel mock-ups to test manufacturing techniques for them.

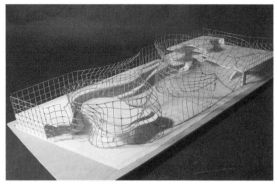

Wire frame

The space of the corrugated cardboard models to the left is translated to a wire frame construction to begin defining the actual structural conditions of the building. Digital modeling has been used to control the process.

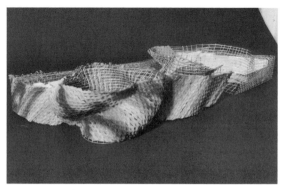

Woven skin

The frame is covered by woven paper to simulate the reedlike skin of the project. Digital models have been made of this phase as well.

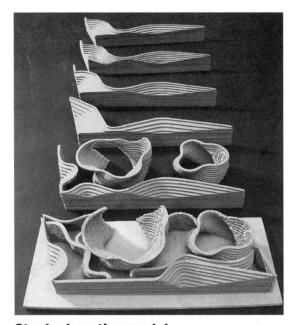

Stacked section model

The volumes of the baskets are explored using corrugated cardboard cut into individual sections.

Small-scale panels

A lexicon of model panels has been developed to cover all cases in providing a continuous skin over the irregular surfaces. Soldered wire and cloth are employed in the models.

Full-size panel mock-ups

Full-scale panels have been made in the office using bent wood and reed to study the details of the actual panels.

3XN

3XN is an innovative, groundbreaking Danish design firm. Their work has become well known through competition projects such as the Architects House in Copenhagen, the Glass Museum in Ebeltoft, and more recently the Liverpool Museum. The idea of continuous flow, perpetual surface, and overlapping spaces is central to a lot of their work and is pursued in the design stage through a parallel track of physical and digital three-dimensional modeling information. In this sense, the firm has carried forward all of the strengths of traditional paper models while incorporating all the advantages of digital modeling.

Renault Truckland, Lyon, France

This project was a competition for a new showroom and training facility for the Renault truck division. It was intended to be replicated in multiple locations and, as such, had no actual context. The designers used the idea of the highway and road maps to generate the space and made the initial scissor-section to connect floor and roof into a continuous space.

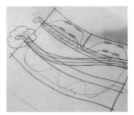

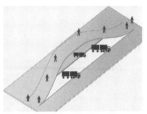

Scissor-section
The ground plane has been cut and raised in the manner of a bridge condition. The drawing diagrams how the track of this cut may be displaced horizontally to overlap other sections.

Woven strips
Combined sections in alternate schemes are explored digitally to create a topography for truck display and program space.

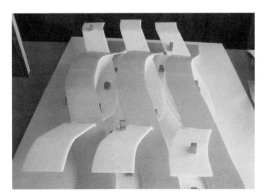
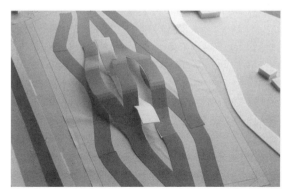

Truck display
One of the early foam core models sets out the patterns for truck display and green space as an interwoven condition.

Network
A larger network is modeled in foam core to explore connections to the landscape as the project meets the ground.

Layers in network

The basic interwoven body of the showroom and the larger network are integrated into a single structure.

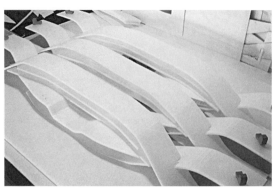

Model with interior sections

A model of the scissors pattern is made to include the interior space.

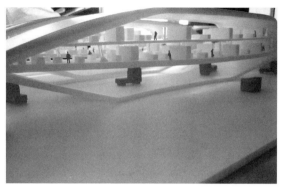

Interior space

The model is built at a larger scale, with interior components added to develop the section.

Development series

The pattern of contiguous showroom and office space is studied together at the larger scale with the truck display in evidence.

Digital model

The project is modeled digitally to include details and the pattern of the green spaces.

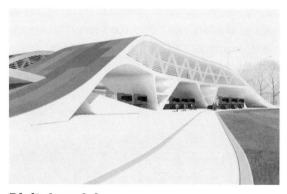

Digital model

The digital model is capable of simulating the actual character of the space and provides interior views from the ground plane.

Liverpool Museum, Liverpool, England

The site of the Liverpool museum was thoroughly interrogated to understand the flows of pedestrian movement, views, history, and other forces in the former car park. The scheme became a nexus of juxtaposing flow lines that link parts of the dock and open up views. Rather than a static container, the museum was conceived as a porous connector and can be passed through on the way to other locations and events.

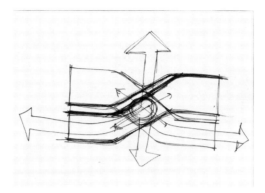

Initial sketch

This sketch for the scheme shows the basic organization of the overlapping paths created by the two crossing wings of the museum.

Schematic model

Early models of the project explore the implied ideas of the diagram to the left. In working with three dimensions, the idea of crossing space is played out on the vertical axis as well.

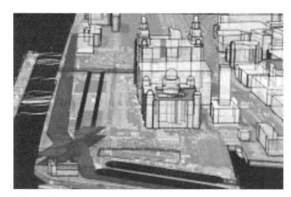

Site diagram

Analysis suggested a project that would take its cues from the nexus formed by the intersection of paths and views as they pass through the site.

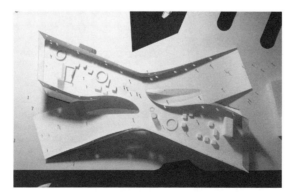

Development model

The scheme is increased in scale, and the path of the flow is refined as an interior condition. At this stage, plan suggestions of interior spatial components have been introduced.

Interior space

Study of the interior in three dimensions is key to understanding the overlapping nature of space between the two directions of flow.

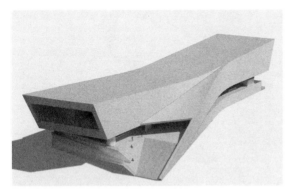

Development/finish model

The form of the building has been refined to convey its essential qualities. The large viewport focuses interior experience on key parts of the city.

Detailed finish model

With interior components added, the final model carries the details of the faceted stone cladding.

Longitudinal section model

The interior section was constructed in the longitudinal direction to develop the central core of the internal experience.

Transverse section model

The project model is cut in the short direction to study internal relationships not fully understood in the long direction. This is helpful in getting a physical reading of internal experience that digital models cannot provide.

Interior model

The interior space of the central nexus has been modeled at a large scale to fully control the sectional conditions at this location.

Cladding mock-up

Large-scale mock-up models have been made to develop ideas for stone cladding. At this scale, the pattern and texture of the scheme can be understood. Eventually a full-scale mock-up will be made to confirm the scheme.

BIG Bjarke Ingels Group

BIG is part of the new movement of innovative practices in Copenhagen that is transforming the European and world landscape with competition-winning projects. As the founding partner, Bjarke Ingels thinks of himself as a midwife that assembles existing ideas in new ways to create surprising mixtures. Many of the firm's projects have some aspect of the artist Escher's fascination with Möbius strips and serve to invest an element of improbability in the work.

Mountain House, Orestead, Denmark

Mountain House came about as the reinterpretation of an earlier project that excavated a sports hall from a mass of apartments to create a sloping set of units. In the current project, a sloping parking deck has been capped with apartment units and the mass pushed in to react to the footprint of its neighbor. See the diagrams below.

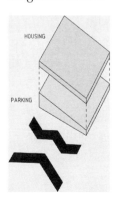
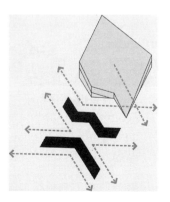

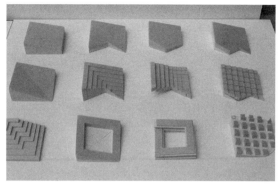

Massing composite models
The models above show various iterations that explored the basic marriage of the parking deck and housing on top.

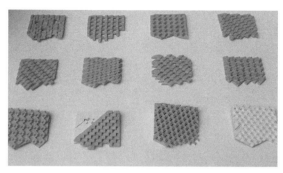

Housing unit models
The units cascade down the parking deck with private yard space in front. Multiple studies for the unit organization are shown.

Unit massing model
The basic scheme for the housing was in part an adaptation of Jorn Utzon's L-shaped courtyard typology.

Development study model
A larger model has been made in order to work out the relationship between parking and the units.

101

Parking interior
The space of the sloped zigzag interior parking deck is fully developed in this large model. Included in the deck is the first sloping elevator in Copenhagen.

Final model
The model of units and parking deck is completed and indicates garden areas with alternating plans to ensure daylight for the units below.

Final model
The model shows the screen wall wrapping around the parking deck. The wall must be open to the air to ventilate the deck but provide protection from ice and rain.

Mountain image
The accidental metaphor of mountain is used to provide an image for the metal screen that wraps the parking deck. The image is rasterized to black-and-white dot patterns and cut into the screen.

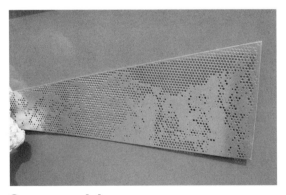

Screen model
A test model of the screen is made for the scale finish model. The image is cut with computer-assisted design (CAD)-controlled equipment.

Completed building
The completed building with its metal wrapping and reflective façades confirm the predictive powers of the model studies.

Scala, Copenhagen, Denmark

For this competition submission, BIG envisioned the project as a high-rise that served as a link between the traditional spiral tower emerging from a well-integrated city block and a pure functionalist modern skyscraper.

The twisting spiral of the form speaks to the transformation between the two conditions.

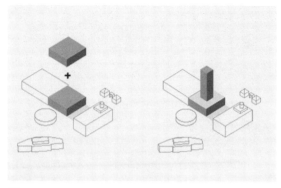

Diagram
The diagram shows the composite of two program blocks on the left, translated into a base and tower scheme.

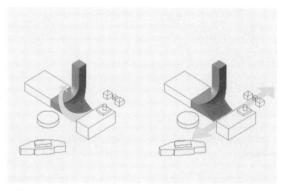

Diagram
The tower is transformed into the base as a spiral set of stairs that provides exterior program space. This type of torsional action on a mass is a formal opportunity afforded by the digital model.

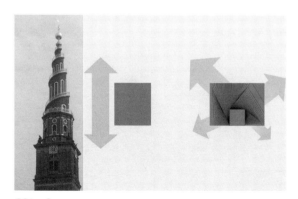

Site forces
The site is analyzed to identify forces on the building. The orientation of the base responds to the city grid. The diagonal corner ties in with key landmarks in the city and reflects the spiral of important towers to the city.

Study models
This collection of study models testifies to the intense investigation that has taken place to explore all aspects of the simple diagram for the project.

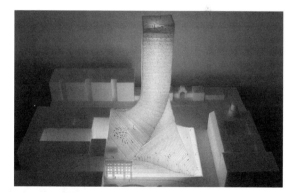

Final model
The final rendering of the project in model form is used to study the light given off by the project. As a result of the torsional spiral of the column, the tight mock brick pattern produces a moiré effect.

The Danish Pavilion, Shanghai Expo 2010

The Danish exposition hall was conceived as a sustainable project that would be filled with 1,500 bicycles, water from the Copenhagen Harbor, and the Little Mermaid statue. While several project alternates are shown from the initial stages of exploration, all have in common the idea of a continuous bicycle path.

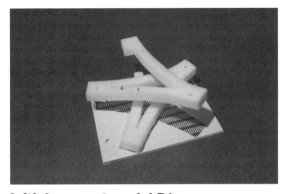

Initial concept model B1

A second alternate design scheme is sketched with this model using the idea of a continuous route with hard turns.

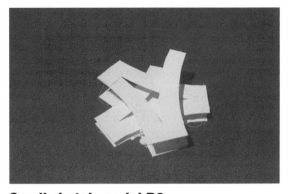

Small sketch model B2

The space of the concept model has been rationalized and expanded to provide the program space for the project.

Initial concept model A1

This project concept uses the diagram of an interwoven star pattern to provide the continuous path.

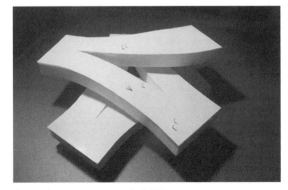

Development model B3

The project scheme is increased in scale to study and refine the path of the project as a massing model.

Final model B4

The scheme is rendered as a solid/void model to articulate the structure, openings, and interior wall disposition.

Concept model C1

To generate another direction, a small strip of foam is used and explores several methods of wrapping the space on itself. This proposal looks at a form of knotted space.

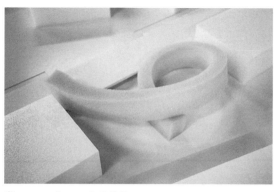

Concept model C2

The spiral of the project space takes a simple looping form that tracks across the site and provides the suggestion of a long entry ramp.

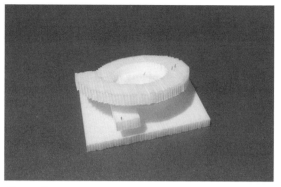

Sketch model

The small spiral is increased in scale and tested as an open loop scheme.

Concept model C3

The foam is wound in a tight spiral that, along with the knot, helps to set the direction for the project.

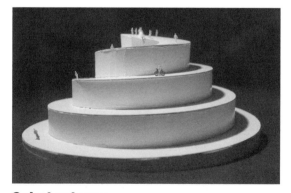

Spiral scheme

The idea of a spiraling tower is rendered as a larger massing model to study the idea.

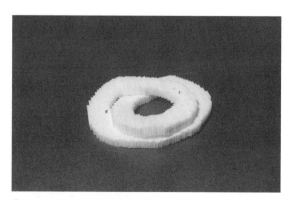

Concept model C4

The idea of the spiral is rendered as a much flatter loop that winds back on itself. Conceptually, this would be a combination between the idea of the knot and spiral.

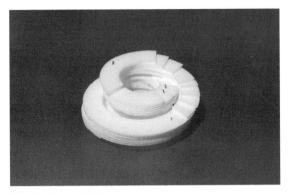

Sketch model
The space of the continuous spiral has been expanded into a deeper reading of space.

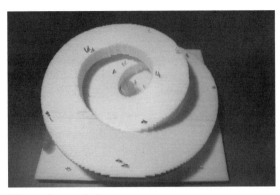

Sketch model
The continuous spiral is modeled at a larger scale to refine its mass and path.

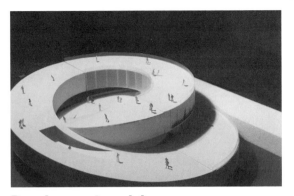

Development model
Detailing and entry paths are tightly rendered in this development model.

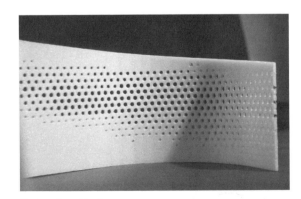

Façade study
The image for the façade is tested as a set of holes to provide light and send light out into the city.

Façade treatment
The image of the development model reveals the strategy for openings to be a mapping of an urban image on its surface.

Night image of model
The internal lighting of the model tests the reading of the building as a large glowing object in the city.

Henning Larsen Architects

This Danish firm has been established for over 50 years and participates in projects throughout the world. However, it's firmly rooted in the present time. Perhaps its best internationally known project in current years, the Copenhagen Opera House, forms a bridge between the firm's modernist history and contemporary practice. Currently, the firm is involved in many competitions, which situate its work in the nexus of innovative work by younger Danish and Dutch firms.

The Copenhagen Opera House, Copenhagen, Denmark

The Copenhagen Opera House is situated on Holmen Island and aligned with the Marble Church across the harbor. Its large roof frames outdoor patio space and connects the axis between the opera house and the church. The curved façade of the foyer space contains many balconies to enliven the experience of movement and reflects the large wooden shell that houses the performance space. A number of early schemes for the opera house are shown as it evolved from a glass box to a formable block of space with a semitransparent façade. The design work was initiated with a series of physical models that were seen as the best way to understand the space.

Initial glass design 1
The early designs for the opera house were conceived as glass enclosures containing the solid program spaces as floating objects. The outdoor space is present but is not covered in this scheme.

Initial glass design 2
Another glass design breaks the box down into a series of elements and begins to move out over the exterior space at the harbor front.

Mass design

This scheme changes direction and examines the building as a solid mass of space. The roof begins to overhang the exterior space, setting up the entry sequence.

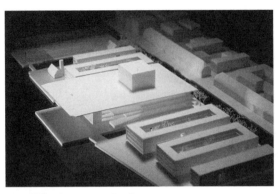

Modified mass design

Moving away from a totally closed experience, the foyer space begins to open up to the city with a glass enclosure under a large framing roof. This scheme ultimately is used to develop the final design.

Section model

The section model shows the key relationships between the backstage, fly space, performance seating, and foyer space of the opera house.

Site model

The direct connection across the harbor to the Marble Church in the distance becomes apparent in this model. While the scale of the opera house is much larger than the surrounding buildings, it maintains a horizontal reading.

Finish model

The final design for the opera house is modeled in great detail and includes the decreasing thickness of the roof plane. The façade for the foyer space was modeled at 1:1 scale in a large warehouse in order to fully detail it.

Samba Bank Headquarters, Riyadh, Saudi Arabia

The Samba Bank was approached as a large carved mass. Various proposals for the type of faceted volume can be seen below. The context model shows the kind of dense urban environment the bank would reside in.

In the final design, a large hole that relates to the center atrium of the structure has been implied by the clear glass opening in the otherwise patterned façade.

Massing models
The massing models for the bank use stacked sections of foam core to model the sculptural surface of the building. Digital models provided the information needed to create the various sections.

Light study
The large completed design model explores the possibilities of light in the building and is used to develop the overlapping glass panels in the atrium. The various layers of the glass are simulated with paper of varying thickness.

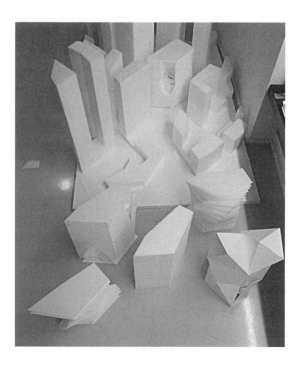

Opening design
The patterns of openings for the completed design rendered on the left are studied at a very large scale so that the details of the shifted oculi can be fully worked out.

The Scala Competition, Copenhagen, Denmark

The project was conceived as an urban development in three dimensions and sited next to Tivoli in Copenhagen. The building program has been placed in two slim towers that were doubled up to create a folded structure. The building scheme relocates Grabrodre Square to the 6th and 11th floors.

Models were used to explore the process of folding in order to establish the faceted form for the two towers.

Study models

The exhaustive process of exploration is clearly evidenced by the number of different models used to investigate alternate solutions. Although all of these models are related to the project diagram, they explore different solutions.

Model folding

The process of folding is used to arrive at the two interlocking forms of the tower. In this case, a mapping of the square helped determine the sides of the folded elements.

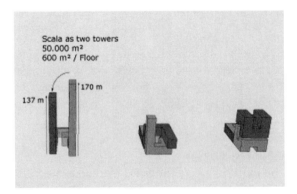

Project diagram

The idea of the two towers that have been folded together is illustrated in this early project diagram. The diagram clearly sets out the strategy for the subsequent model exploration.

Folded towers

The two towers produce a dialogue between each other and set up the raised courtyard spaces in the gaps formed by the introverted mass.

Final model

The final model in the square conveys the public nature of the building and addresses the problem of accommodating the large program without becoming a high-rise in the midst of the low-scaled urban block.

Massar Children's Discovery Center, Damascus, Syria

For the Massar project, the designers began with the idea of a rose with light filtering between the petals. The program spaces were located in the perimeter labyrinth and surrounded by a central space for people to meet. The models used to develop the design show the progression of ideas rooted in this centralized theme. The work was developed as a set of shells that interweave in a way that speaks about unfolding rather than the rational projection of a center.

Digital parametric modeling was also of great importance in controlling the project.

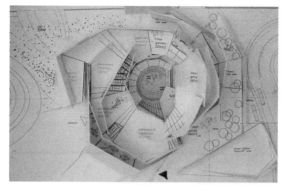

Program model

Working from plans, the program spaces and circulation suggest the varying types of experiences possible as they move around the center.

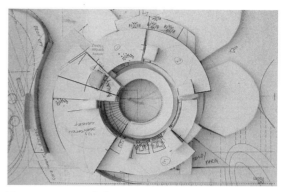

Program model 2

The elevation of floor plates provides further insight in understanding the spatial needs of the project and its possible relationships.

Finish model

The model of the completed project shows the refined detail of the opening patterns on the skin.

Sketch model

The programming exercise is now pushed forward as a three-dimensional interpretation of the spatial enclosure. The simple extruded walls of the earlier diagrams begin to contain the space as a volume.

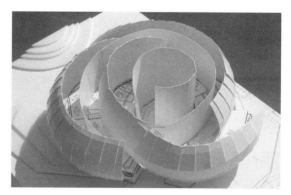

Development model

The method of achieving the curved walls is studied in this model and is refined to form a series of faceted elements.

Structural frame

The ability of the structural frame to carry the faceted wall system is explored at the level of a three-dimensional diagram.

Frame and wall

The frame is attached to the wall structure to understand how the two will act together. Individual vertical strips are used to deal with the nature of the curvature.

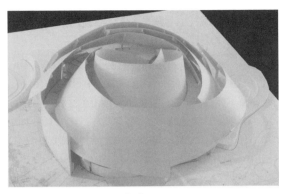

Development model

The set of wall relations is roughed out, and a larger scale and refinement on each wall is initiated.

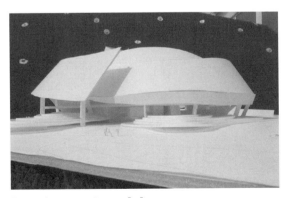

Development model

The walls begin to take on a specific relationship with the ground as the building is opened up to the site.

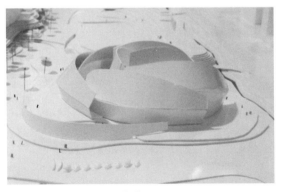

Development model

The wall shapes go through further refinement and become closer to their final resolution.

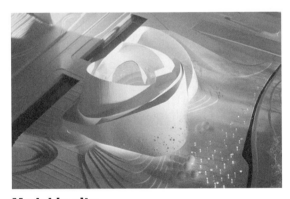

Model in site

The building and site are developed together. With the design now close to completion, the project begins looking at issues of light and skin.

Large-scale study model

A larger model is made to work out in detail the elements of interior components, structural frame, and skin.

Interior model

A large model without the frame and complete skin is made to study the interior space of the project.

Interior space

A digital model is made simultaneously at this point to obtain a clear reading of the interior experience and begin the process of parametric modeling.

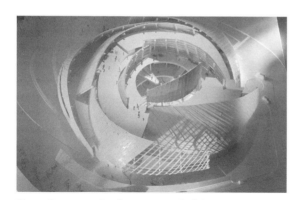

Development—large model

The large model provides the ground on which to work out the frame for the skin. By placing supporting members on the bias lines, the curvature is able to follow the frame without the need to radically bend the structural backup.

Skin model

Large panels of the skin are modeled with the opening pattern detailed. This three-dimensional rendering of the surface allows for a visceral understanding of the surface texture.

Skin mock-up

A full-scale mock-up of the exterior skin was assembled in the firm's office to understand the details for connecting cladding plates to their underlying frame.

RAPID PROTOTYPING

Using Digital Information to Produce Physical Models

In the past, the use of digital modeling programs and physical models traveled along largely divided paths. Now rapid prototyping (RP modeling) readily converts three-dimensional information to analog models. The presentation that follows explores modeling programs and RP processes with examples drawn from academic programs.

Computer Modeling

Modeling Programs

The ultimate aim of any design tool is to provide information in an efficient manner. Although a case has been made for the advantages of building physical models, computer modeling with rapid prototyping techniques can also provide valuable information and generate unique design directions and should be investigated for its advantages.

The speed and sophistication of computer modeling has increased rapidly over the past 15 years, but some debate persists over its ability to match the intuitive nature of physical modeling. Moreover, because of the extrusional logic used by many programs, XYZ coordinate points must be used to create diagonals and warped planes. Inputting these coordinates can be cumbersome compared to the directness of angling cardboard planes. This limitation is compensated for by the ease with which forms can be iterated. In addi-

tion, inherently common operations for the computer such as duplication, distortion, and overlay can be powerful tools for discovery.

The clear advantage of digital modeling lies in its ability to produce rapid prototyping model information, render the model, and produce construction documents after the model has been developed.

To implement construction documents and rendering effects, a different set of software is required in addition to the modeling program. To make RP models from the digital model, a graphics program is required. To render the model, rendering software or a "rendering engine" is needed.

Many of the widely used programs traditionally come with two-dimensional graphics software, three-dimensional modeling software, and scripting functions bundled together. Today, however, a real shift has been seen in how these prepackaged programs are seen and used. It is increasingly common now to use a base program in combination with a collection of plug-in applications from other companies. In the past, compatibility problems discouraged this type of customized interface, but these problems have been addressed to the point where movement between programs is not a barrier.

Any modeling program under consideration should employ what is referred to as *solid modeling*. This means that the forms it generates will appear as solids instead of only "wire frames," and when cut or manipulated will present solid surfaces. By simulating the way physical models behave, solid modeling

allows computer-generated models to be manipulated with greater intuitive ease.

Modeling programs can form surfaces by creating polygons or by using Nonuniform rational B-splines (NURBS). The polygon method works by defining planes with three points and combining them to define forms. The results are angular and not very pliable, as stretching, bending, and folding changes the smoothness of objects. The only way this can be overcome is by increasing the number of planes, which in turn increases the data load and slows processing significantly. The polygon method is the easiest way to define surfaces, and since buildings are traditionally made up of planes, most architecture software uses this method.

NURBS, on the other hand, use curve (spline) equations to define surfaces so that objects can be zoomed in on without any loss in geometrical detail. The nurbs are very pliable, like virtual dough, and are excellent for stretching and folding operations. Programs like Rhino and animation programs like Maya support NURBS.

Compatibility

An important aspect to consider in shopping for software is the ability to translate modeling information between different software packages. Although many companies claim compatibility with other software, in the past there were many problems in this area. For this reason, some designers preferred to use software with all three drawing components from a single source (modeling, two-dimensional graphics, and rendering applications). However, there are programs that are stronger in certain areas of application than others, and with today's improved compatibility they can be successfully integrated into your other software. Although the operation of these programs is beyond the scope of this book, information regarding some of the most popular software is offered in the following section. Most, if not all of these programs, are available for PCs (Windows) and Macintosh platforms, and all employ solid modeling.

See Chapter 6 for a discussion of the use of programs in select design offices.

Software Guide

Over the past 15 years, digital modeling programs have gained such widespread use as to be commonplace in every office and design program. While 3D Studio Max is widespread as a modeling program, as well as TriForma due to early entry into the field, programs such as Rhinoceros and Maya have seen increasing adoption. While Form Z still enjoys some use, its popularity seems to have waned. In addition, there are a number of lesser-known programs used, but most are similar in operation and contribute little that is new to the field of digital modeling. However, one niche program known as SketchUp is noted for its unique approach to modeling.

3D Studio Max

Company: Autodesk
(associated with AutoCAD)
This is considered to be a sophisticated program with good rendering capabilities. It is a little more complicated but once learned can be as easy to run. Professional practices stress the use of the program as completely compatible with AutoCAD and find this to be the most trouble-free method of working between modeling and orthographic drawings.

TriForma

Company: Bentley
(associated with Microstation)
The same things that can be said about 3D Studio Max apply to TriForma. TriForma is a powerful, sophisticated program, and for those who use Microstation, it provides a seamless program application.

Rhinoceros

Company: RSI 3D Systems and Software
Rhino, as it is known, is a true curved base program and supports NURBS. It was developed as an engineering program and is very sophisticated as well as intuitive in its operation of commands. Rhino has proved to be very compatible with other programs as any file can be opened in it. This is a great advancement and, combined with the intuitive capability with command tools, helps explains Rhino's ever-increasing popularity.

Maya

Company: Autodesk
Maya, like Rhino, is another true curved-based program that supports NURBS. Developed to model human forms for animation, it can incorporate the parametric properties of wind and gravity to make objects behave as they would in real space. Also, many find new perspective in a program that was not made by and for architects and engineers. One of the limitations to this program is that is can be hard to read alien files.

SketchUp

Company: Google SketchUp

This program is limited in application but is an interesting attempt to reconnect designers with the intuitive operation of the sketching pencil. The main program feature is that of inferring design moves. That is, when the mouse is moved in a particular direction, volumes begin to gain height or width accordingly. This is similar to the way Microstation and AutoCAD work and eliminates the need to enter coordinates. The process comes close to actual hand sketching but is limited by the program's assumption that all forms are intended to be orthogonal volumes. To deviate from this is cumbersome and can defeat the ready utility of the program.

Form Z

Company: AutoDysSys

This program is easy to learn, relatively intuitive, and inexpensive to purchase. The program primarily uses polygons to model forms, but later versions support some NURBS capability. Its rendering capabilities are not very sophisticated, so it is not highly thought of by those wishing to exploit this mode to the fullest.

Autodesk Revit

(Associative Building Information Modeling)
Company: Autodesk

Revit is a program produced by Autodesk that has found widespread acceptance in both architecture/engineering fields as well as the construction industry. It is essentially a three-dimensional (3D) modeling program that uses parametrics to integrate components and systems. The standard systems can be selected and modified, and then as the building dimensions change, the components such as wall systems change as well. This is very convenient and makes for instant construction sections and quantity take-offs by contractors and better information for owners. There are some limitations, though. Actual detailing usually has to be done in another program such as AutoCAD, and special systems are not supplied in the stock catalog supplied by Revit. However, this is a minor problem compared to its inherent design limitations, as the program assumes all projects are built in discrete floors and does not treat the building volume as one continuous space. Like SketchUp, it is also built around orthogonal assumptions, and to overcome this, it is necessary to go against the natural grain of the program.

Vectorworks

Company: Nemetschek North America

Vectorworks is used as the Apple/Macintosh counterpart to AutoCAD. However, it goes further, as it includes 3D modeling and rendering capability employing a similar rendering engine to Form Z.

Algorithmic Approach

An algorithm is essentially a program, a set of step-by-step procedures to establish a programming code for generating a type of behavior. When applied to architectural drawing and modeling information, this idea of interrelated behaviors can take two different but related paths, that of generative process and parametrics.

Generative Process

Generative processes are an extension of traditional approaches to form making in which a scripting function, essentially a programming code, is used to establish a set of rules that, once set in motion, are capable of generating complex forms. The code uses tools embedded in the modeling program such as move, scale, rotate, and so on, to define a set of sequences that then act on a given form or plane. These resultant forms come into being or are generated as a result of the internal logic that is followed by the scripting code. This process tends to divorce the design considerations from subjective aesthetic evaluation.

Parametrics

Parametric modeling, or associative modeling, refers to a process by which all the information related to materials and component systems in a building or design are combined and associated with each other in a single model. Therefore, changing one component or aspect will automatically adjust all other affected components. A good example of this would be how changes to the model such as reducing wall height or taking one foot out of the building dimension are dealt with. In this case, the parametric properties of the model automatically modify every aspect of the building that would be affected by the change. Another example of the capability of parametric responses would be presented in the varying sizes and shapes of stone cladding panels on a building façade with complex curves. Each stone is relatively similar but not of equal dimensions or shape. As the panels change, the digital model automatically adjusts the dimensions of the receiving frame and connections as well as the panel.

Plug-ins

Plug-ins are essentially mini-applications, used in many cases for rendering and scripting. As mentioned earlier, with the recent shift in the way modeling programs are combined, plug-ins are increasingly used to extend the capability of the programs.

An abbreviated list of plug-ins includes the following (see appendix for company & web site information):

Rhino Rendering

Rhino rendering is a rendering engine sold by Rhino that can be used with other programs.

Brazil

This is a rendering engine used with Rhino and other programs.

V-Ray

V-Ray is a rendering program used with all programs.

MEL

MEL (Maya Embedded Language) is the scripting program add-on for Maya.

Generative Components GC

This is a scripting program from Bentley.

Grasshopper

Grasshopper is a shorthand graphic interface that has been developed to allow designers to construct scripting code visually without knowledge of any of the actual underlying program code required for scripting.

Flamingo

This is a ray-tracing program for Rhino.

Penguin

This is a very useful nonphotorealistic rendering program.

Outputting Complex Geometry

One convenient advantage of modeling programs is being able to generate and control complex curvilinear solids. While it can take considerable time to make physical patterns for these forms using traditional methods, various techniques can be used to translate the 3D digital model into patterns for assembling complex forms.

Lofting

Lofting is a term derived from boat building and refers to the definition of form by means of a series of sections, laid out at regular intervals, and then connected with lines (or planks in the instance of boat hulls). Usually, the forms are complex curves, also known as compound curves. For this reason, drawing programs attempting to draw complex curves have employed logic similar to lofting hulls in describing the forms. Lofting can be used to create a physical model by cutting sections of the model at regular intervals and then cutting sections at 90 degrees to the initial cut. The resulting parts can be cut by hand or laser and assembled to build any form.

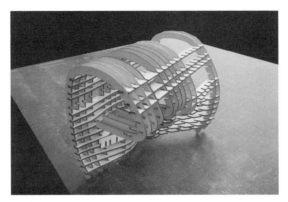

Lofted model

Stacked Sections

One of the most direct output methods related to lofting is to employ stacked sections. The primary difference between lofting and stacking is that in stacking, sections are connected to each other directly with no space left between them. This makes a solid surface and, while it may take more time, produces a better approximation of the shape. To create the components for a stacked model, the digital model must be cut into a series of sections that match the thickness of materials to be used for assembly. The layers or sections are printed out to scale and then typically cut with a laser to produce a set of sections that can be stacked to replicate the form.

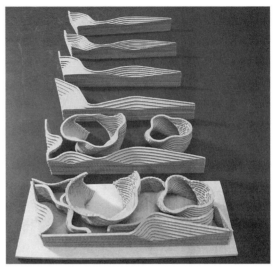

Stacked section models

Unfold/Unroll

Unfold, also known as unroll operation in some programs, resolves any form into planar components. These patterns can be printed out and joined at the seams to recreate the form.

Forms are drawn in the program with true, smooth, three-degree curved surfaces. The forms have two directions known as U and V (basically vertical and horizontal). To unfold them, the curves in one direction or the other are reduced to one degree, producing a hard facet or pronounced seam between each section. The choice of directions is usually based on which direction will most approximate the true nature of the original form.

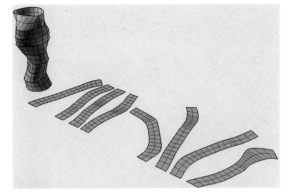

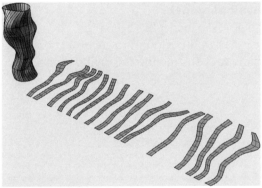

Unfold/unroll

The unfold operation in the U and V directions is pictured above. In the U direction (top), the complex form of the digital model is resolved into a series of strips that go around the form. The hard bends can be seen in the assembled shape at the intersection of each strip.

In the V direction (bottom), the strips have been taken as a set of vertical bands around the form. The smooth vertical curves have been broken into seams so that the form is no longer smooth as you move around it.

Squish/Smash

Squish/Smash is an idea related to the unfold operation, but instead it flattens the form to create a two-dimensional pattern. In doing this, it assumes that the material to be used has some level of elasticity and will reinstall the surface area lost in this process. Part of the parameters for carrying out the operation is to define the degree of elasticity for the material to be used. The ratio is then set automatically in the program to compensate for this.

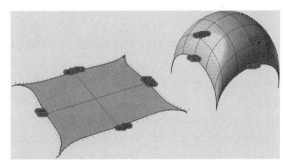

Squish/Smash

In the images above, the domelike form of the digital model, representing some type of stressed skin, has been flattened to form a two-dimensional surface. The surface must be cut from material with the elastic properties assumed by the program to regain its proper physical shape.

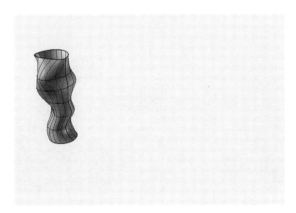

Modeled form

The modeled form is smooth in both directions as can be seen by the path of the wire frame lines.

Digitizing
Inputting Modeling Information

In a converse operation to outputting modeling information, there are cases whereby models created through analog process need to be converted into digital models. At its most basic level, this can be accomplished by measuring the XYZ coordinates of a series of points, inputting these points, and then connecting them in the drawing program. This process is similar to translating models to drawings as described in the appendix. However, the hand process is cumbersome, so it is more common now to use a digitizing machine. This consists of a pointer on an arm that records the XYZ coordinate in space. The key to creating an accurate translation is to divide the model at all inflection points, spacing the points equally and close enough together to allow for smooth connections between them. Lacking inflection points, as on smooth curves, the curves need to be divided at regular intervals as in the lofting process. Digitizers can come in large sizes, which are then wheeled around the model (see Frank Gehry RP2), or affordable tabletop models that are fully capable of measuring many model sizes.

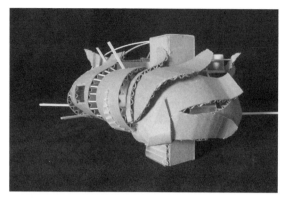

Physical model
The physical model has been built, then measured point by point to create a coordinate system for constructing the digital model.

Digital model
The digital model has been constructed using the XYZ point measurements from the model on the left.

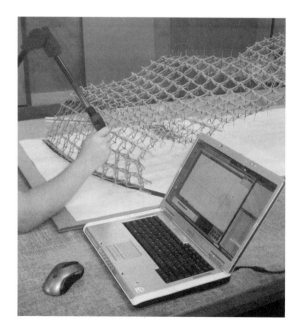

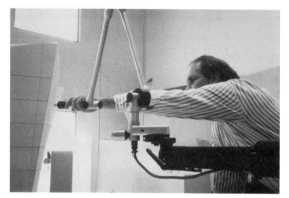

Digitizer arms
A small digitizer arm for small model inputs is shown on the left. Above, the digitizer arm used by Frank Gehry is at work. The arm base can be moved around the model and has a zero reference point built in.

Rapid Prototyping

Over the past 15 years, a bridge has been created between physical model building and digital modeling. This bridge is referred to as *rapid prototyping* or RP. With RP technology, physical models can be made directly from three-dimensional computer models. Although the use of digital modeling programs has become widespread, the direct comprehension offered by the physical model is important to many designers. To fill this gap, RP models, initially developed for industrial prototypes, were adopted by architectural design firms. In the past five years, physical models produced directly from digital information have become widespread. Many design programs have some form of RP equipment, and a number of design offices own their own equipment or have models made regularly.

Considerations of RP Modeling

Interface

One of the main reasons to use RP is when design work is already being developed with digital media (i.e., modeling program). If this database, developed by the digital modeling, did not exist, the process would be considerably slower than building paper working models.

Speed

Given that digital information is available, RP models can be made automatically without involving much of the designer's time. Small models take around 12 hours, and they are usually made at a stopping point in the design process.

Complexity

One of the most common RP modeling tasks is that of making complex curvilinear shapes. This type of form could be made from plastic material such as clay, but conversion into dimensioning systems presents barriers.

Staging

RP models can be made at any stage, but a typical way of working may be to create a computer-generated massing model, then output a physical model. Next, return to the computer and develop an architectural language, then output a model again. As the project is developed, there may be a switch to paper models to look at larger-scale issues. Due to cost and time, there may be a tendency to produce a limited amount of study models. However, because of the potential for efficiency, models of completed designs are easily justified.

Cost

In the past cost has been an issue with RP models. Typically, information is sent to a company who owns the RP equipment, and for $200 (plus shipping), a small model can be made. Compared to employee costs of a day or two of work, this is a relatively small sum. Compared to an hour of work producing a paper sketch model, it can seem expensive. If multiple RP study models are needed, costs can mount up quickly. The answer to this seems to be in owning RP equipment. One of the popular in-house solutions is a powder-based printer made by Z Corporation. Compared to other processes and larger equipment, the $19,000 price tag has been coming down over the years, but other competitors are entering the market, such as V-Flash with a $10,000 machine. This trend is expected to continue until the equipment becomes truly affordable for every office. At this point, laser cutters are a bit more affordable and are commonly seen in offices.

Modification

While it may be possible to modify or edit RP models in some way, they do not lend themselves to this type of direct exploration. Each model stands on its own, and adjustments must be made to the computer model. This is a significant difference from working with paper models.

Hybrid Models

Since RP machinery can make forms that may be difficult to render by hand, many models are made up of a combination of hand-cut parts and RP components.

Finish

Computer-controlled model building is an accurate process; however, due to the way in which the processes work, tooling marks tend to produce a rough appearance. This does not present a problem for study models but requires a finishing treatment if clean, tight surfaces are desired. Sanding, cutting off stems, filling, and painting are common finishing tasks.

Types of Modeling Processes

Many processes and variations on the basic equipment are used to make 3D RP models. A full explanation of each tends to make the field a bit confusing; however, there are really only two basic methods: additive and subtractive.

Additive

Additive processes build up models by laying down very thin layers or sections of the model. They can do this by spraying melted wax (fused deposition modeling), spraying glue on powder (powder printers), dripping plastic (3D plastic printer), or producing a chemical reaction that hardens liquid (stereo lithography). Additive equipment can be very expensive as the model size becomes larger. To work around this limitation, models can be made in several parts.

There are special advantages and cost bases for each type of process; however, the 3D printers used most often by architects and other visual designers are stereo lithography (STL), powder printers, and more recently plastic printers.

Subtractive

Subtractive equipment takes away material by cutting or milling it in sections. Few processes use this method except for computer numerically controlled (CNC) milling.

Translation of Files

Before modeling programs can be converted into RP models, the files must be converted to STL files. Drawing programs such as 3D Studio Max can convert drawing files to STL as part of its built-in commands. Other programs may need to use a stand-alone program to make the conversion. These files resolve all forms into small triangular facets and then slice them into sections to direct the buildup or cutting of layers.

3D Printers

3D Powder Printers

Powder printers use a vat of powder and an ink-jet printer head to spray glue or binder on the powder in thin layers. After a section is sprayed, it hardens and the bed lowers so another section can be added. The models do not need stems to support suspended parts, as the loose powder supports the hardened parts. On completion, models are blown off, and the unused powder is put back in the vat. The type of powder has been evolving over the years, and more recent formulations have improved the smoothness of the models. Models can benefit from a sealer to further smooth and strengthen them.

3D Plastic Printer

A recent addition to the market, the V-Flash FI 230 desktop modeler is probably the most affordable solution currently available. The printer works in a similar fashion to powder printers and laser sintering machines but uses a plastic material as its medium. Its accuracy is reasonable, but there is a need to clean the support material off the model afterward.

The 310 powder printer from Z Corporation
This machine has a bed capacity of an 8″ cube. If larger models are desired, they must be made in several parts and pieced together. Models take 4 to 12 hours to print, depending on size.

The V-Flash 230 printer
This machine has an 8-in. bed capacity. Printing time is similar to the 310 powder printer. The machine to the right of the printer is used to clean and cure the model after it is complete.

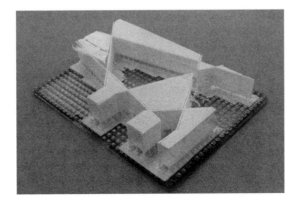

V-Flash printed model
Without powder to support the parts, the components are suspended by stems of plastic. These parts must be cut off after the model is finished.

Stereo Lithography

In a similar process to powder printers, stereo lithography uses a laser to trace a section of the model in liquid. The area traced hardens when hit by light, then the model bed lowers into the vat of liquid to the depth of the next section. See Chapter 6 for a discussion of the use of RP in select design offices.

3D Printer Examples

The following pages represent some of the model types and exploration methods well adapted to RP modeling.

Conversion to STL Files

The models on this page show the original computer model ready for conversion to an STL file along with the resultant printed models.

Digital model
The digital model is ready for translation into STL files and then to be printed out.

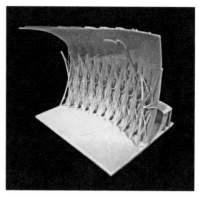

Printed model
The RP model has been printed using the computer model and shows the design of the frame as it originally appears.

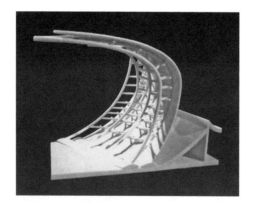

Printed model
The digital model has been printed again. The physical model carries the level of detail present in the digital model and has a modified structural support system. Making variations is one of the advantages of RP models.

3D Printer

Multiples

With RP models, a number of variations can be explored with relative ease. This is a great help when developing design directions, as the chance to look at alternate designs consumes very little actual fabrication time. This advantage means that simple changes in the digital computer model can be output with comparative ease. The only real drawback is that each model takes a number of hours to print out.

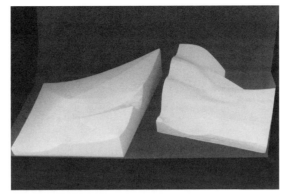

Multiple Variations

Multiples can easily be explore on complex organic forms that ordinarily would be difficult to model and discourage exploration.

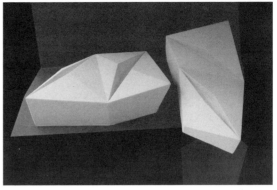

Multiple Variations

Multiples can look at small differences in what is basically the same design organization.

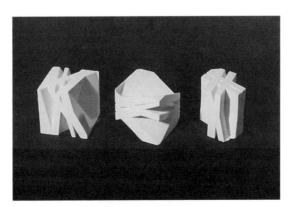

Multiple variations

Variations on a basic design idea are explored in three different organizations.

Multiple Variations

Multiple studies can be achieved readily for any conceivable form.

Massing

The most basic set of forms is that of the mass model. However, mass models of complex curves are not easy to construct by hand. This type of modeling is well suited for RP 3D printers.

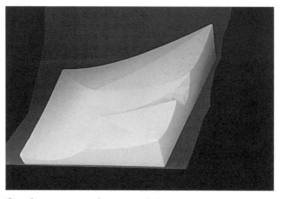

Surface massing model
Massing the surface form of an undulating contour is well suited to the RP printer.

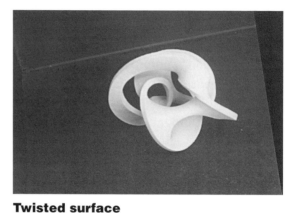

Twisted surface
While not a massing model in the strict sense, this abstract interwoven form showcases the capabilities of the powder printer.

Compound curve massing
The most fluid shapes with three dimensions are easily translated by the powder printer.

Delicate Forms

Hollow curved forms and envelopes described with delicate lines are a natural extension of the kind of massing models suited for RP printers.

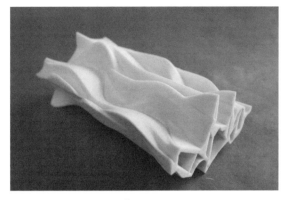

Hollow construction
The flowing form of this RP powder-printed model shows up the machine's ability to create shell-like hollow forms that can address the internal experience of space.

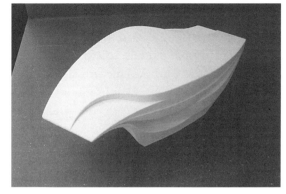

Massing with detail
While this form is essentially a massing model, revealing no internal space, it carries the surface delicacy of the project expression in all its details.

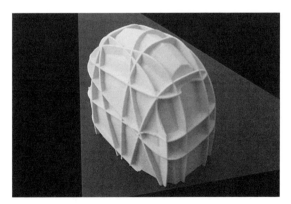

Massing model with detail
Another massing model with surface detail, this model from the powder printer incorporates a layer of fins along the surface that would be much more difficult to build by hand.

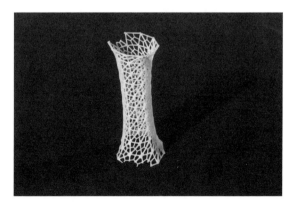

Fine detail
This model reads as an open column due to the filigree of its surface. However, it can be seen as a single mass described by the fine web of structure that only a 3D printer could impart at this scale.

129

Project Development

Printed models can be used in the same manner as traditional models to explore design development. The models pictured here show general relationships and subsequent refinements as they have been developed in the digital model.

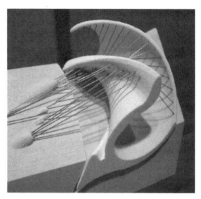

First-stage massing

In this model and in the image shown to the right, the development progression of moving from the general to the particular can be seen. This model expresses the gestural sweep of the project only as a translation of massing.

Second-stage developed model

In this model, the previous iterations have been articulated in a way that explores the skin and structure of the project gesture.

Development chain

In the three models above, the progression from first iteration to exploration of openings and structure can be seen.

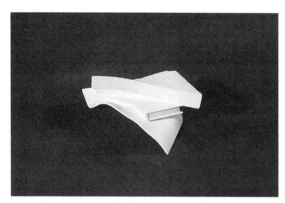

First-stage massing

In this model and in the image shown to the right, the development progression of moving from the general to the particular can be seen. This model explores the relationship between the two layers of the building.

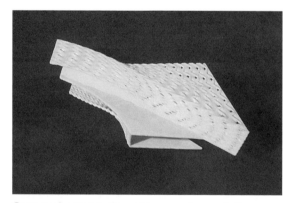

Second-stage development model

In this stage, the model develops a reading for the skin. Its fine surface pattern is easily articulated with the powder printer.

Skin/Cladding

Many studies can be made that look at developing alternate ideas for the surface treatment of buildings. These explore the lines and patterns inherent to various strategies such as disruption, overlay, and torsion.

Surface model

A model of surface exploration with computer drawing below the model. Folded space is used to manipulate the flow of surface form.

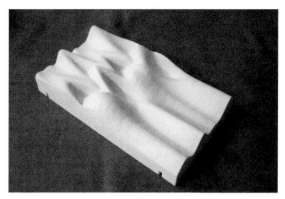

Undulating pattern

A regular pattern of surface patterns is modeled in the 3D printed model.

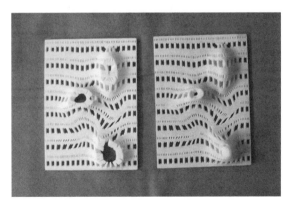

Pattern disruption

A model with a regular pattern has been disturbed by intersecting other volumes and using them to distort the surface.

Sculptural twisting

A surface has been cut and twisted in the computer program and output as the 3D model.

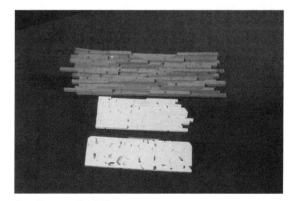

Surface cladding pattern

Elements have been overlaid and perforated to explore options for building cladding.

Building Complete Architectural Models

From an architectural standpoint, models of the entire building or sections of a building are some of the most useful applications of the 3D printer. This takes advantage of the printer's full capability. Both complex form making and intricate detail carried by fenestration patterns can readily be achieved.

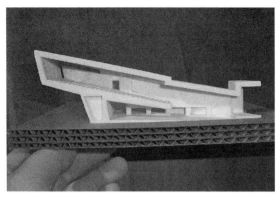

Section model
Small but accurate models of building sections can be made quickly with 3D printers simply by cutting sections in the digital model.

Building model
The building model surface can reflect all the detail of the project design to a degree that would be very difficult to cut by hand.

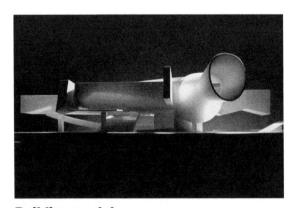

Building model
The combination of curved and planar forms is modeled seamlessly with the powder printer.

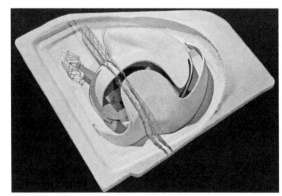

Thin shell
A thin sculptural shell can be achieved by conventional plaster methods but is far easier using the powder printer.

Building model
The complex curves of this building are automatically translated with accuracy from the digital model. The finished surface has been sealed and painted.

Laser Cutting

While RP modeling has evolved as a complete modeling system, computer-guided laser cutters have their place in producing components. Laser cutters work by tracing lines of flat material with a laser beam, which produces enough heat to cut through the material. The laser beam is guided by two-dimensional CAD drawings. Laser cutters are typically used to cut flat sheet goods such as styrene or cardstock in order to make a kit of parts for hand assembly. However, the beam does not have to be set to burn all the way through material. Laser cutters can also be used to etch mullion patterns on plastic, creating highly detailed glazing systems. This type of process lends itself to finish model building.

Most of the model parts covered under outputting digital information with processes like lofting and unrolling depend on parts that are cut by a laser cutter. However, parts can be cut by hand as well.

The ability to cut parts cannot be carried out without some thoughtful direction. That is, components should be manufactured in such a way as to reflect the correct reading of a building or component.

Laser cutter
Model parts can be fed to the laser cutter from modeling programs and divided into discrete sections to cut sheets of cardboard, Plexiglas, or wood.

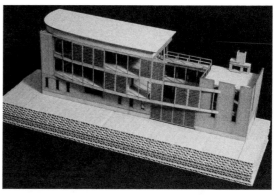

Laser cut façade
Building façades and plans can be cut from the laser and assembled by hand. The CAD floor plans must be reduced by the thickness of the modeling material used before cutting, or plan lines will cut through the façade at every level.

Stacked laser-cut model parts
Parts can be cut matched to the material thickness and stacked to create a solid, continuous surface.

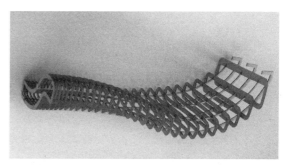

Lofted laser-cut model parts
Parts can be cut as regularly divided sections separated by space and connected by parts cut from transverse sections. Assembly can be facilitated by notches created in the parts in the digital model. Assembly can be challenging.

Chipboard mock-up for a lamp
Parts can be laser cut and assembled by hand.

Boolean operation built out
Laser-cut model parts have been assembled to illustrate the subtractive and additive forms created by digital Boolean operations.

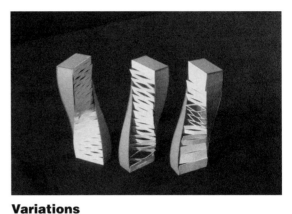

Variations
Three alternate treatments of façade design for this torqued volume have been cut using the laser and assembled in the twisted frames.

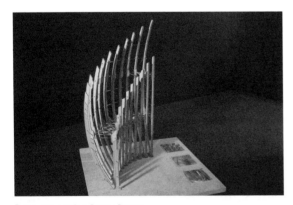

Laser cut structure
Finely detailed structural components have been laser cut and assembled to build a mock-up of structural system.

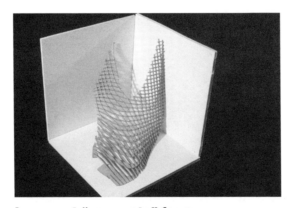

Laser cut "egg crate" form
Sections have been cut in both directions at equal intervals and assembled to test the results from modeling the form as assembled parts versus a 3D printed modeling (as shown to the right).

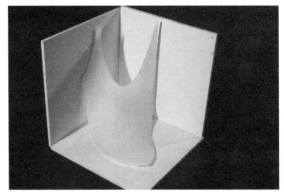

Stereo lithography printed model
The smooth surface of the printed model can be compared to the surface described by the "egg crate" laser cut version to the left.

CNC Milling— Computer Numerically Controlled Cutting

CNC milling equipment is essentially a form of advanced router controlled by a computer. CNC process is used both for accurately cutting heavier material such as plywood and carving out forms using subtractive methods. Like other forms of RP equipment, the CNC cutter is controlled by CAD drawings and uses 2D and 3D drawings, depending on the type of parts to be cut. CNC milling is often employed when larger models are needed. In some cases, full-scale details and building components are made.

While the process of cutting out flat planner objects is fairly easy to understand (the drill bit follows the computer lines and cuts on the side of the bit), cutting material away for 3D shapes is a bit more difficult to conceptualize.

To understand the process, picture a spinning drill bit. If the bit is moved sideways after contacting material (commonly foam in architectural models), it can cut a line in the surface. By moving the bit slightly up and down and making many passes, any contour can be cut.

Water jet cutters are a variation on CNC processes and can be used to cut a variety of relatively thick metal parts.

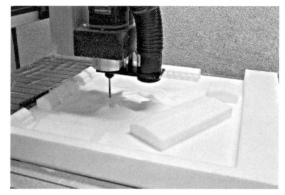

CNC milling head
The CNC routing bit cuts the material away one pass at a time, slowly raising and lowering the head at each pass as needed.

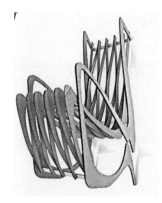

CNC cut furniture
The component parts for this chair have been cut as flat plywood parts by the CNC cutting bit.

CNC milling bed
The CNC cutter for medium-sized projects cuts using a routing head mounted on a moving arm over the large cutting bed. Movement of the arm and head is computer controlled.

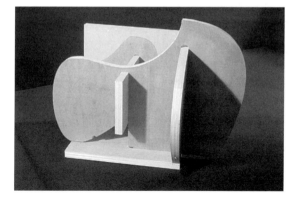

CNC model
The model parts are cut from 3/4" plywood. It is possible to cut the parts in one pass, but at times multiple passes may be needed to get through the material. This usually depends on the equipment capability.

Five-Axis CNC Milling

To cut away material for shapes that are more than just surface forms, the bit needs to be able to approach the material, from all sides (five different axes). To accomplish this, the drill head is mounted on a rotating arm, and the work bed is turned automatically to access the underside. For an example of five-axis milling, see Chapter 6.

CNC Milling Finish

The choice of cutting tools will determine the appearance of the model. Small-diameter bits using many passes will produce a smooth surface. Large bits, taking out a quantity of material, will produce rough patterns. Many times, large bits are used at first to speed the job up, then small bits are used to finish it. The finish is also affected by the path of the bit. All of these finish considerations are design choices and should be planned whenever working with CNC models.

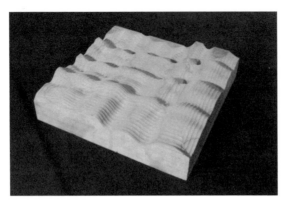

CNC site model
The model has been cut with a bit size in wood that leaves a definite pattern in the material. The cutting pattern has also been set to traverse around the model.

CNC site model
The tooling pattern of this model has been controlled to produce two readings: a smooth surface and a definite pattern groove. For the groove, a large bit has been used.

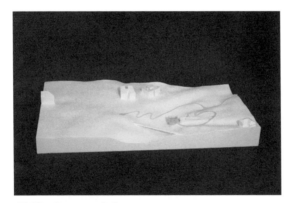

CNC site model
This site model has been cut in foam using a fine bit to produce a smooth finish with very few tool marks.

Fabrication

Full-scale translations of complex-curved or faceted components can be made to fabricate projects. The forms are typically broken down into triangulated units that are small enough to conform with the change in plane of the overall shape. The following projects represent examples of those using various computer-controlled manufacturing equipment to translate computer-generated design work into full-scale implementation. They are typical of many of the projects being carried out in academic programs in an effort to understand and exploit the capabilities of RP design models.

Pavilion Project

A bridge is designed with a digital model using a highly triangulated structural system. The component parts have been output and cut with CNC equipment out of dimensional lumber.

Initial computer model
The pavilion is designed in the computer and employs structure that is triangulated to provide support as well as conform to the shape of the pavilion.

Computer drawing of pavilion
The scale of the initial digital model can be compared to the actual construction.

Pavilion transported to site
The entire pavilion has been prefabricated in a shop and transported to the site to be placed on its foundations.

Completed pavilion
The completed structure is mounted on foundation points and offers a space for contemplation.

Wave Installation

A simple wave design is created with the digital model, and its parts are fabricated with the laser cutter from corrugated cardboard. The components are assembled to create one self-supporting form.

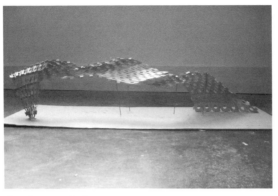

Scale model
The computer model is output as component parts, fabricated with the laser cutter, and then connected to form the entire shape.

Component mock-up
Full-scale components have been cut to test the assembly.

Digital model of the wave
A simple wave form is made, then divided into component parts to allow the curve of the form to be modeled with incremental small parts.

Wave form and connection detail
The wave mock-up is extended to test for structural support. At the same time, small connection details are developed and tested.

Completed wave installation
The completed wave is run through the hallway for which it was designed.

DIGITAL PRACTICE

Combining Digital and Physical Model Information in Professional Practice

This chapter explores the digital/analog modeling relationships found in current design firms. The discussion extends to the role of digital information in the design process and the use of rapid prototyping (RP). Examples of RP such as computer numerically controlled (CNC) milling and three-dimensional (3D) printing are shown as they occur in the course of the work.

Morphosis

From a conversation with architect Ben Damon:

Morphosis has traditionally designed with drawings and physical models. With the shift to computer modeling, there was a desire to see virtual space rendered in physical space at regular intervals. RP provided this capability and led the firm to become one of the first architectural practices to purchase RP equipment.

The way that Morphosis works between the computer and RP models is probably exemplary of the way this relationship has developed for many firms. For Morphosis, the computer is perceived as the best way to speed up exploration, so concept and massing models are initiated with the computer. From this stage, the designers engage in a period of back-and-forth dialogue between a number of small RP models and the computer models. Each generation of RP models is changed and explored in the computer. Then large paper models are built to study interior spatial relationships. The computer also is felt to be important during the design development stage as all changes to the computer model keep the drawings automatically updated and provide a high degree of accuracy. Typically, firms that do not own RP printers send files out and have models made at an interim design point and on completion. Having the model printer in-house has changed all this and facilitates an ongoing dialogue between physical and virtual models. Also, difficult forms and complex curves can now be explored with confidence and control. The printer can also be used to make full-scale details.

RP models at Morphosis are used in the form they are printed with limited attempts made to improve their slightly rough appearance. Their primary concern is to learn something from the model, and they accordingly regard all of their models as study models.

When asked about the eventual shift to all digital information that many consider inevitable, Mr. Damon responded emphatically, "Physical models will never go away...we will never be able to completely shift over." His feelings were based on the removal imposed by the computer, whereby the depiction of space is divorced from the tactile process. For Morphosis, physical models offer a way to understand space that cannot be seen or felt in the computer. Also, physical models are viewed as the most powerful and accurate vehicle for communicating with clients.

Morphosis relied on Form Z for computer modeling in the past but has shifted their model work into TriForma to take advantage of the seamless interface with Microstation.

Rensselaer Polytechnic Institute's Electronic Media and Performing Arts Competition

The RPI project serves as a good example of RP capabilities. Due to the ability to transfer modeling information directly to the powder printer, the designers were free to explore form beyond what was previously possible (without using clay or other plastic mediums). The project proceeded by fitting the program to a fixed configuration, then draping the enclosure around it. Earlier interest in the egg form was used as a starting point, then pushed and pulled in a Boolean approach to arrive at the refined shell. Due to the relatively small size of the 8" cubic printer bed, the model was tiled and made up of six or seven separate pieces.

Rensselaer Polytechnic Institute's Electronic Media and Performing Arts competition

This model is one of a series made to design the performing arts building. It was developed using Form Z and a 310 powder printer from Z Corporation. It is made of several pieces in order to overcome the size limitations of the printing bed.

Rensselaer Polytechnic Institute's Electronic Media and Performing Arts competition

This section model of the building illustrates the advantages of being able to output different cross section and scale studies. Once the computer model is in place, this can be done with very little additional time or expense.

Mack Scogin Merrill Elam Architects

Mack Scogin and Merrill Elam have a long tradition of designing and developing projects through physical study models. Some of these can be seen in this chapter. Like many firms, the way they work has evolved to include computer modeling. It is probably accurate to say that most of their projects are currently developed on parallel tracks. One track uses physical models to develop the project and the other track uses computer modeling images to communicate and study aspects of the project. This has not led to the kind of reliance many have come to place on the computer model as the primary generator of form. Rather, the computer is used to control and generate those things that it is best suited for, such as complex organic forms, while physical models are used extensively for all other studies. Large-scale physical interior models are felt to be particularly valuable in understanding space.

The firm uses Form Z Rhino and AutoCAD as their primary digital programs. RP has played a role in their model making as well, but like computer modeling, it is generally limited to organic forms. This typically results in a hybrid construction with the majority of the model made in-house and special parts being sent out to be made with stereo lithography (STL).

Illustration

The projects shown in the following examples are from two projects that illustrate both ends of the spectrum. The Children's Museum is almost entirely modeled with RP; however, it is instructive to see that the generative and explorative studies are made with traditional sketches and physical models.

Conversely, the Fine Arts Center has been made mostly by hand with special sections made as RP components.

The Children's Museum

This project uses a combination of methods to explore and develop the design. The initial move is started with a hand drawing, then a foam model is made to capture the dimensional suggestions of the drawing. Computer models are drawn to give precise definition to the space. Finally, an RP STL model is output to produce physical confirmation of the space.

The Pittsburgh Children's Museum
The hand sketch of the project is ambiguous and suggestive in the way clearly defined computer drawings typically are not.

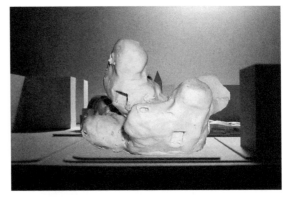

The Pittsburgh Children's Museum
A foam sketch model attempts to interpret the space implied by the drawing.

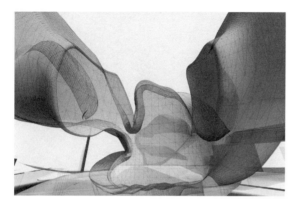

The Pittsburgh Children's Museum
A computer model of the space is made to refine the space and program fit.

Fine Arts Center, University of Connecticut at Storrs

This project uses a hybrid approach. STL models are made only of parts that are felt to be too complex for hand modeling techniques. These parts are first assembled with each other (to overcome size limitations of the modeling equipment) and then assembled with the hand-cut components of the entire building model.

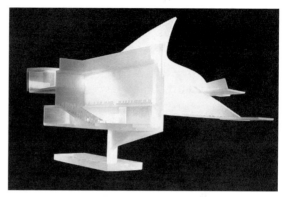

Fine Arts Center, University of Connecticut at Storrs
The flowing curvilinear parts on the rear section of the building have been RP modeled as a collection of several parts and attached to the hand-cut parts.

The Pittsburgh Children's Museum
A stereo lithography model output from computer modeling information.

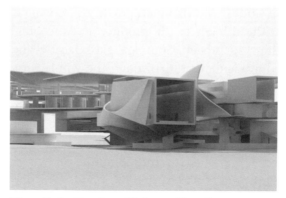

Fine Arts Center, University of Connecticut at Storrs
A computer rendering of the building shows the section of the building where RP has been employed.

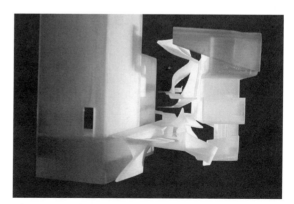

Fine Arts Center, University of Connecticut at Storrs
The stair components are made from several RP pieces and incorporated into the hand-built model.

Eisenman Architects

From conversations with Larissa Babij and Peter Eisenman:

Peter Eisenman's office has a long history of exploring space with the extensive use of physical models. Over the past 20 years, the computer has come to play a large role in the design process, but it has not replaced physical models. The primary advantages of the computer are the ways in which it can handle complex space and extend conceptual possibilities. At the same time, the physical model plays an important role in understanding what has been created and developing large-scale studies. In response to these methods, Mr. Eisenman made these comments, "I develop in the computer because you can do things in the computer you cannot do in the 3D model, but you model them to understand what they are really like. There is always a conscious dialogue between the computer model and the three-dimensional model.... We work back and forth between computer models.... I make all my spatial corrections on three-dimensional models.... With the computer you can just jerk anything around ...with three-dimensional models, I can see what is really happening...what the space is going to be like because you know it is an analog of the space."

Mr. Eisenman's office uses Rhinoceros for many projects as well as 3D Studio Max. (AutoCAD is used for 2D drawing). The choice varies depending on the project, but Rhinoceros appears to be the most applicable.

Physical models are built for the most part in the office. The computer models provide a great degree of control over the work, both in the design process and for the actual building drawings. Sections are cut through the Rhino computer model to get a precise reading of how the building needs to be built. The physical models are also important in checking what has been done in the computer in order to correct things such as spatial conflicts.

The City of Culture, Santiago, Spain

The example shown is from the City of Culture in Santiago, Spain. Over the years, Peter Eisenman has developed a working method as a form of spatial excavation in which he overlays a drawing of the historical map of the city, the city grid and the topography. This composite is then manipulated to begin making spatial interpretations. For the City of Culture, the first manipulations were made with Rhinoceros to produce a conceptual drawing model. Complex glass façade and soffit elements run through the whole project. Conceptual computer drawings were translated into large-scale detail models to explore these elements. Changes made to the models were measured by hand and conversely applied to the computer drawings. This process was carried back and forth during the entire development phase of the project.

The City of Culture, Santiago, Spain, Biblioteca soffit wireframe drawing
A computer drawing of the soffit is made to begin informing the space.

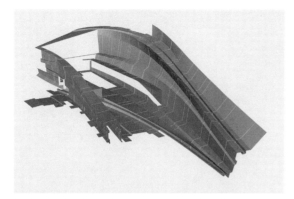

The City of Culture, Santiago, Spain, computer rendering of soffit
The drawing is refined and rendered in the computer.

The City of Culture, Santiago, Spain, Bienale model
The computer drawings are translated into hand-built physical models to refine and understand the quality of the space.

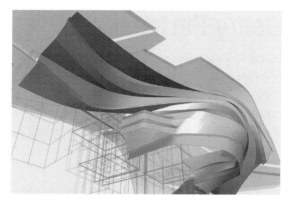

The City of Culture, Santiago, Spain, Music Theatre—computer rendering
A computer drawing initiates the interior space of the theatre.

The City of Culture, Santiago, Spain, Biblioteca soffit model
The computer drawings are translated into hand-built physical models to refine and understand the quality of the space.

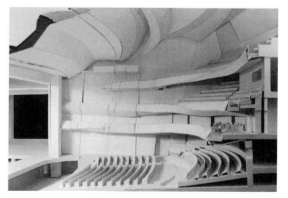

The City of Culture, Santiago, Spain, Music Theatre—physical model
The computer drawing is translated into a hand-built physical model to refine and understand the space.

Gehry Partners, LLP

Frank Gehry's office represents a unique case in which two poles of design methodology coexist. The office probably has developed one of the most sophisticated digital systems for project delivery in the industry, while at the same time adhering to traditional physical modeling methods.

In a recent lecture by James Glymph, head of Gehry Technologies, he stated that, although they had tried many approaches to design development using computer modeling, in the end the computer proved to be too slow. The computer is viewed as an additional tool, good at some things, such as refining design, and not particularly good at others. As Mr. Glymph was quick to point out, "It would be a serious mistake to think it could replace models and drawing entirely." The key program for generating 3D computer models from physical models is Computer-Aided Three-Dimensional Interactive Application (CATIA), an aerospace program developed by Boeing aircraft. The models are marked at intersections and grid points. The points are digitized to define XYZ spatial coordinates, then fed into Rhinoceros and rationalized into curves. This information is transferred to CATIA, where it is hyperrationalized, and the final computer model is completed. Details such as the many varying stone panels and support points are mapped as "accurate plugs of program" with parametric modeling programs. These drawings can be pushed and pulled in the computer model to produce automatically adjusted components.

Once the computer models are finished, 3D drawing models can be transmitted directly to fabricators and contractors. This process has allowed Gehry to gain precise control over production and costing.

Keeping in mind that many of the things computers can draw have little connection with actual material properties, the office is developing a program to model the behavior of planes that can bend and fold using defined rules. The planes will exhibit the properties of gravity and indicate when stress limits have been exceeded.

As shown in the Walt Disney Concert Center project on the following pages, design development makes intensive use of physical models. Physical modeling exploration is typically intensive, with around 30 to 40 physical models produced for each project. Computer modeling rarely comes into play. At some later development stage, the physical model may be digitized and output as a rapid prototype for further study.

The Walt Disney Concert Center

The models shown here represent a classic model progression in Gehry's office. Very little of what is explored and developed at this stage involved digital modeling. To fully appreciate the process, it should be noted that the stages shown here represent only five out of at least 20 different models.

The Walt Disney Concert Center stage 1
The first phase of the project came as a result of a competition entry and defined the space as a ziggurat and pavilion.

The Walt Disney Concert Center stage 4
After further refinement of the program, a collection of blocks were used to correlate the spaces with building form. At this point, a tower was included in the project.

The Walt Disney Concert Center stage 10
The space of the main hall is defined at this point and surrounding components are experimented with. Shown here are the vestiges of the competition pavilion, dome, and ziggurat.

The Walt Disney Concert Center stage 15
At some point, the idea of working with flowing theatre curtains begins to inform the exterior reading of the building planes.

The Walt Disney Concert Center stage 20
The final model shows a rethinking of material and final rendition of the flowing planes.
Note: The tower has been deleted from the project.

WDC acoustic model
A large-scale model (very large) was made of the concert hall to enable consultants to test and adjust acoustic qualities.

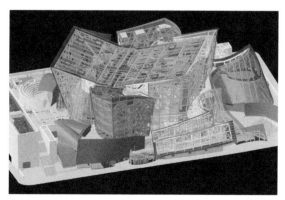

WDC CATIA model
After inputting and refining the information, a computer model of the entire building, structure and mechanical systems is generated with CATIA.

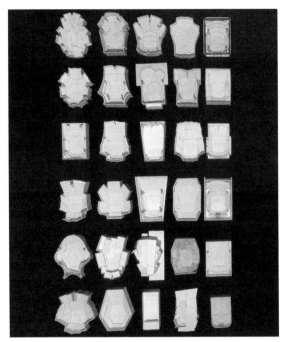

WDC theatre space study models
This image shows the exhaustive array of study models made to develop the concert hall. These are all hand-made models and are typical of the kind of 3D rigor the office brings to every project.

WDC digitizing
The large final model is being marked in preparation for the digitizer.

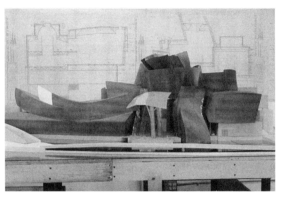

Bilbao Guggenheim CNC milling model
In many cases, the flowing forms of the project are output to make a large CNC milling model such as this one. The CNC process is better suited for large models (see Chapter 5).

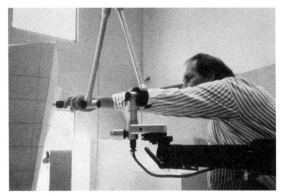

WDC digitizing
Each of the many intersecting points is recorded by the digitizer to be translated into a CATIA computer model.

The Barcelona Fish

The Barcelona Fish (produced in conjunction with the 1992 Olympics) provided an information base for design methods used in future projects.

In this case, the project was fully developed with hand-built physical models, then translated into digital information.

Distortions can be made by the computer drawing, so it was important to confirm its accuracy with a rapid prototype model.

The Barcelona Fish physical model
The physical model of the fish has been completely worked out at this stage.

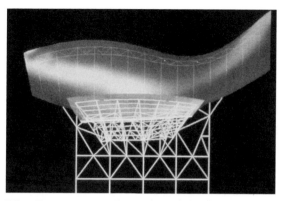

The Barcelona Fish computer model
The model is digitized, a computer model drawn and output to make an RP model.

The Barcelona Fish built
The built fish carries the intent of the original model and provides an information base for future projects.

Garofalo Architects

From conversation with Doug Garofalo:

Doug Garofalo represents the end of the spectrum pursuing form making beyond Euclidean concepts with sophisticated modeling interfaces. The evolution of computer modeling programs and their integration has had a radical effect on the way he approaches architecture. Unlike many practices discussed in these pages, Mr. Garofalo's firm does not employ any physical models during design development. For the flowing, continuous space he is exploring, traditional modeling is felt to offer either too many limits or too little control.

To facilitate the exploration, he uses Maya, a modeling software developed for the animation industry. The program is sophisticated in modeling complex curves and uses spline curves to define space rather than faceted and triangulated surfaces. Mr. Garofalo finds it to be intuitive to operate and allows objects to be pushed and pulled similar to the way actual plastic objects might react. Form Z and other mainstream modeling programs are felt to be limiting in two ways. Not only do they approximate curved space with triangles, but a traditional architectural attitude concerning the generation of form (through extrusion and Euclidean block building) guides much of the operative commands. In contrast, working with Maya opens doors on worlds that have yet to be discovered.

Mr. Garofalo's work has been translated using various RP processes, but he finds CNC milling is best suited to the larger constructions.

The Cloud Project

The production of the cloud piece is an excellent illustration of how future construction delivery will be handled. In this case, all information is taken from the computer model and seamlessly fabricated by computer-controlled machinery. A large CNC five-axis milling machine can be seen at work at CTEK in Los Angeles. This same company makes many of Gehry Partners' projects, using technology developed for the automotive industry. Even with the large-scale capabilities of the CNC equipment, the parts are so large that they must be made in several sections and spliced together.

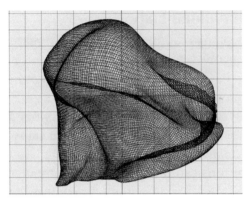

The Cloud
Meteorological information is used to make a 3D digital map of a particular cloud. This computer model is then sent directly to a CNC milling machine to begin cutting the parts.

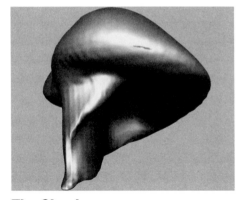

The Cloud
The cloud is refined and rendered in the computer.

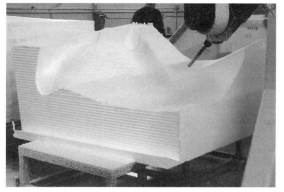

The Cloud

Guided by the computer model, the drill bit of the miller makes many passes over the surface of a foam block to cut away material.

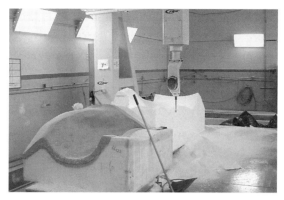

The Cloud

The rough-cut foam mold is then coated with a material like automotive filler, recut, and sanded to refine the surface. The miller arm and frame can be seen in the background.

The Cloud

Each component part is reinforced with steel rods, and attachment edges are embedded.

The Cloud

The parts are taken out of the mold, fitted together, and sanded to transition smoothly into each other.

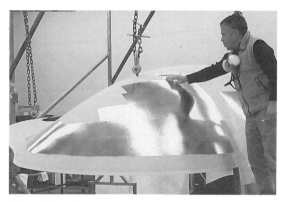

The Cloud

The surfaces of the parts are laminated with thin sheets of titanium metal.

The Cloud

The completed cloud is hung from the gallery ceiling.

Antoine Predock

From conversation with architect Peter Arathoon:

Antoine Predock's practice represents another office with a strong tradition of studying projects through models. Projects are typically initiated with sketches and clay models. Far from simple concept models, these models include a direct relationship to program and can be used as a guide through the life of the project. In regards to these models, Mr. Predock explains, "When a project is formative or embryonic, the drawings are often terse and immediate, a kind of encoding or DNA that will inform the making of the building. These preliminary or anticipatory drawings lead to three-dimensional clay models, which can be very tiny; three-by-five inches like Cal Poly, or very large, like the one for Agadir, which is five feet long and three feet wide. I am still exploring as I work with the clay, but I am working toward a finality. Compared to a drawing on paper, the models are very real; they are the building. They are not massing models; they rationally address section and plan."

The office augments their 3D approach to design with a Z Corp. powder printer. With this and Form Z, projects are refined with RP methods.

Currently, all projects are initiated with drawings and clay models, and RP is employed to refine and update the model. However, other roles are envisioned wherein a project might be initiated with Form Z and RP, then moved to the clay models or, eventually, be completely executed in Form Z.

Like many offices based in traditional models and expanding into RP, Antoine Predock's office views the RP models as a great help in communicating with large groups but sees them as an added tool rather than a complete replacement for the clay models.

As the model bed of the Z Corp., the RP printer is a relatively small 8-in. cube, most of the RP models the office makes are small-scale studies of building and site relationships. However, larger sectional studies are made of single rooms by assembling several RP components. Likewise, RP components are used in conjunction with traditional wood and paper model parts. All model parts are made in-house by the designers and are the focus for Mr. Predock when working with the design staff. The office has also recently purchased a laser cutter that they use to make orthogonal parts.

The office uses Vector Works, a Macintosh–based computer-assisted design (CAD) program popular on the West Coast, for 2D drawing. This program and Form Z make up their primary digital drawing software.

Clay Models

Clay models are unique to Antoine Predock's office and represent the kind of direct connection that carving and forming spaces by hand offers.

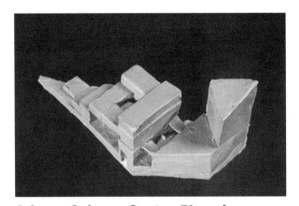

Arizona Science Center, Phoenix, Arizona

This study is removed from the site and context to reflect a singular building study.

Classroom/Laboratory/Administration Building at California State Polytechnic University, Pomona, California
One of the small 3-by-5-in. studies placed in context with the campus buildings.

Clarke County Government Center
This model appears to be much larger and operates at the scale of a small urban inhabitation.

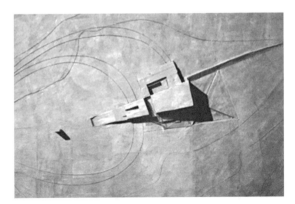

Spencer Theatre for the Performing Arts
The clay provides a strong relationship with the site, becoming an extension of what usually are conceived as separate systems.

Coop Himmelb(l)au

Coop Himmelb(l)au has traditionally relied on the generation of sketch models and drawings to initiate projects. Their energetic spaces have always questioned barriers. As a result, the integration of computer modeling into their practice has not engendered a radical shift in their design direction. Rather, its primary impact has been to provide another means of extending the radicalized rigor for which they are known.

An illustration of the continuity of working methods can be seen in the Wolfsburg Science Center model. It is unclear if this direction was suggested by the possibilities of RP or merely exploited the process as an expedient way to control the work. In any case, it is instructive to see that the initial studies are made with paper models in which intentions are already clear. Only after some period of development is the apparatus for conversion injected into the process.

Because the exacting nature of the digitized model brings about a perceived loss of possibilities, digitizing is avoided until late in the design process. They address the predilection toward an open-ended process with this explanation: "In this predigitized state, the models exhibit a certain fuzziness that allows a layer of interpretation to come into play." This chance to read the model for inference and ambiguity is similar to the richness offered by the layered sketches and drawings.

Aside from the computer's role as an aid in realizing modeled forms, Coop Himmelb(l)au also uses it to generate topological studies such as those shown for the BMW showroom on the following pages.

The Open House, Malibu, California

Their description of the design process for this project is at the core of all the office's work and extends to its attitude toward digital media. "Created from an explosive-like sketch drawn with eyes closed with intense concentration, the hand acts as a seismograph, recording those feelings created by space. It was not the details that were important at that moment, but the rays of light and the shadows, brightness and darkness, height and width, whiteness and vaulting, the view of the air."

The Open House, Malibu, California, initial drawing

The multivalent reading provided by layers, indeterminate lines, and smudges offers a number of readings that are unique to this kind of marking.

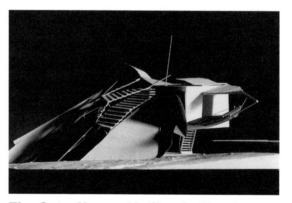

The Open House, Malibu, California, interpretive study model

The spirit of the drawing finds space in a model made from the drawing above.

The Open House, Malibu, California, final model

The final model translates all the energy of the drawing into a crisp, finely edited set of delineations.

The Open House, Malibu, California, computer rendering

The digital rendering attempts to make a reality of the space, but in some ways domesticates the raw energy of the model.

Musée des Confluences, Lyon, France

This museum is a public place providing access to the overlapping and hybridized knowledge of our age. The architecture is characterized by interactions, fusion, and mutation of different entities and combines the typology of a museum with the typology of an urban space.

To do this, the design process is hybridized as well. Along with a genetic section sketch, the topological space of the digital model is pulled and distorted to discover an urban landscape, while surfaces and nodes merge inside and outside into a dynamic sequence of spatial events.

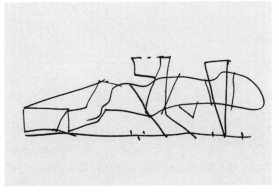

Musée des Confluences, Lyon, France
Initial sketch section.

Musée des Confluences, Lyon, France
Initial computer topology.

Musée des Confluences, Lyon, France
Building space emerging from computer topology.

Musée des Confluences, Lyon, France
Digital rendering.

Science Center Museum, Wolfsburg, Germany

This project responds architecturally to changes in the scientific worldview such as the logic of "either/or." In this case, a mutating fluid form acts as a metaphor for the infinite scientific process of gaining knowledge. A large featureless exhibition space provides a neutral body that is transformed by plugging and adding additional bodies. The sculptural, open proposition is typical of the way Coop Himmelb(l)au's office approaches a project. In this case, RP modeling is introduced at the end of the process to gain full control of the space.

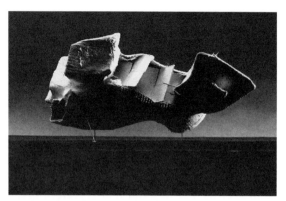

Science Center, Wolfsburg, Germany, initial sketch/concept model

This model captures the feel of the working strategy, but even at this stage is connected with the program.

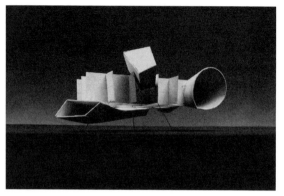

Science Center, Wolfsburg, Germany, development paper model

A refined manipulation of the rough study achieves flowing, continuous space with only paper as material.

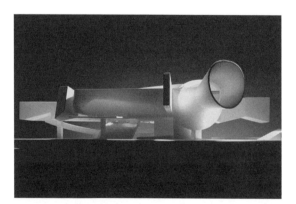

Science Center, Wolfsburg, Germany, RP final model

The model space has been fully refined and yet retains the enigmatic nature of the studies.

BMW Welt, Munich, Germany

This project consists of a center for brand experience and vehicle delivery, a marketplace for differentiated and changing uses, and a sign for the BMW Group. It consists of a large, permeable hall with a sculptural roof. The small section drawing for the project is typical of the genetic sections that have informed Coop Himmelb(l)au's projects from the beginning. Even with the integration and expansion of ideas enabled by digital possibilities, these small drawings remain relevant to the process. The physical models almost negate the need to rely on digital aids as they carry all the spatial complexity that one associates with digital production.

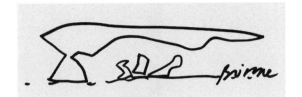

BMW Welt, Munich, Germany
Formative section sketch.

BMW Welt, Munich, Germany
Interior view of model.

BMW Welt, Munich, Germany
Physical model.

BASIC ASSEMBLAGE

Basic Techniques for Assembling Model Components

This chapter presents a catalog of basic modeling techniques. Many of the same examples are presented throughout the course of the book in the context of step-by-step models (see Chapter 9).

Cutting Materials
Cutting Sheets

Cutting sheet material such as chipboard and foam core is accomplished by applying light pressure on a knife and making multiple passes as required for material thickness. A sharp blade is needed, as well as a steel edge with nonslip backing or steel-edged parallel bar. *Note:* Sheets should be cut on a cutting mat or other protective surface such as heavy cardboard.

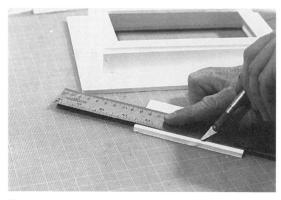

Foam core

Foam core is cut using multiple passes, similar to chipboard. Foam core will dull blades very quickly, and they must be changed often to avoid rough edges. The blade can be angled for mitered joints.

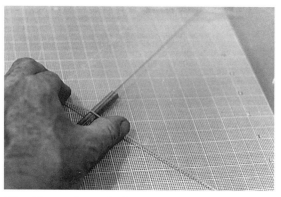

Plastic and acetate

Plastic sheets are not cut through but must be scored with a sharp blade. This requires a little more pressure, and the score should be made in one accurate pass. After scoring, the score line should be placed over a hard edge such as the knife handle and broken by pushing down on both sides. To help cuts break cleanly, the raised edge may have to run continuously under the cut.

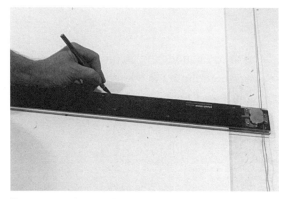

Paper and cardboard

These materials are cut by pulling the knife in several passes, depending on thickness. A steel-edged parallel bar can be useful for making multiple components such as a series of parallel strips.

Balsa wood sheets

Balsa sheets can be treated similarly to heavy cardboard and foam core. Like foam core, balsa sheets are prone to rough edges if knife blades are not changed regularly.

Cutting Sticks and Wire

Sticks employed in model making are primarily made from wood, plastic, or wire. Most of these can be cut with a modeling knife, but as they grow large or harder (as in the case of wire and metal rods), saws and snips will be needed.

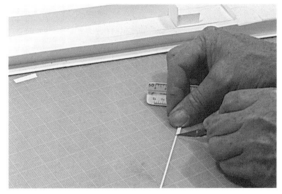

Plastic sticks
Small rectangular sticks are cut in a similar manner to wood sticks. The ends can be squared with sandpaper.

Large wood and plastic sticks
For larger shapes, the modeling saw and miter box is needed. For difficult cuts, place the raised edge on the bottom of the box over a table edge and saw forward. Chipboard in the box bottom will protect the saw edge.

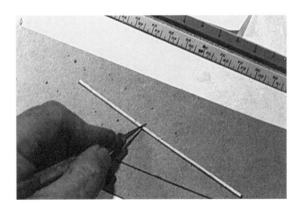

Wood sticks
Small sticks can be cut by pressing down with the knife. Basswood sticks require more pressure and a slight sawing action. Rough edges can be squared with sandpaper.
Note: Dull knife blades will crush the wood.

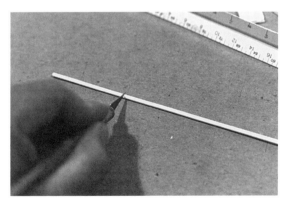

Round wood and plastic sticks
Round sticks should be cut by rolling the knife. Small sticks can be cut completely through, but large ones should be scored and broken on the cut line. Rough ends can be dressed with sandpaper.

Wire and metal rods
Small wire snips can be used to cut rolls of copper and steel wire. Heavy electrical dykes are needed for harder rods. A small hacksaw and miter box will be needed to saw bronze and copper tubes.

Cutting and Drilling Holes

There are a number of uses for cutting holes in modeling sheets. Holes can serve as simple notches or sockets to receive other parts; they can provide a positive connection in the modeling base for a series of columns, or they can penetrate a number of common parts to create multiple floor plates.

Holes can be made by cutting or punching with the knife or using a small electric drill. If the knife is used, the No. 11 blade with its thin, tapered point provides the best results.

Creating sockets

Holes cut into the partial depth of foam core create a positive seat to insert columns. To excavate, insert the knife to the desired depth and rotate the blade. Make a tight fit, trying not to overcut the hole diameter.

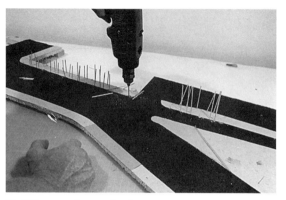

Drilling column holes

For speed and greater accuracy, an electric drill is useful. An added advantage is that holes can be excavated to greater depths without widening the entry point as a tapered knife blade tends to do.

Punching column lines

For quick studies, holes can be punched with the knife. The material will need some thickness such as that provided by corrugated cardboard. Holes can almost be simple slits that sticks are pushed into.

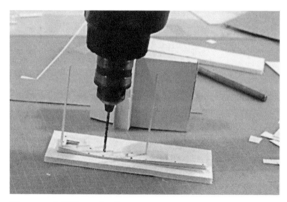

Gang drilling holes

For multiple layers such as floor plates with column penetrations, the plates can be stacked using pins to keep them aligned and drilled through their entire depth. *Note:* A base sheet is used to protect the cutting board.

Trimming and Clipping

In the course of model building, it is often useful and necessary to make cuts directly on the model.

These cuts can be used to make modifications to a study model, refine a model, fit parts, or clean up connections.

Most trimming and clipping can be accomplished with a knife, scissors, and a small triangle.

Cutting new openings
Openings can be cut with relative accuracy directly on the model using the triangle as a guide and a very sharp knife. Rather than making several passes, push through the material and cut or saw in one pass.

Trimming and modifying
Scissors can be effectively used on study models for quick cuts. They are less disruptive to lightly glued joints and are capable of making clean, straight cuts over small distances.

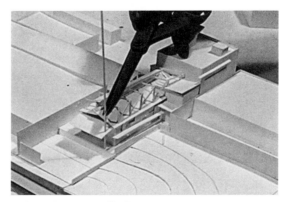

Trimming and fitting
Small sticks can be trimmed in place with scissors, as their pincer action is less disruptive to delicate joints. This method also provides accuracy for fitting new parts to existing ones.

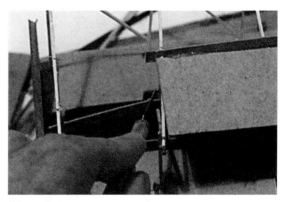

Cleaning up connections
Edges and other protrusions can be modified with the knife by cutting or carefully shaving overlapping connections.

163

Attaching Parts

Attaching Planes

Model building for study purposes should be an ongoing process with little time spent waiting for parts to dry. To this end, most materials are assembled with white glue.

When applied properly, white glue will dry quickly; however, cuts must be straight for this to work. In instances where drying time is not fast enough, aids such as pins or tape can be employed. It is important not to over-glue model components, as this tends to make them tear and deform when disassembled for experimentation.

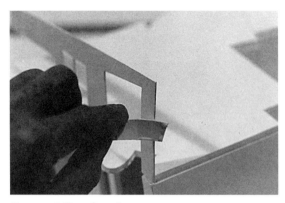

Assembling in place
Glue can be applied to the material edge of assembled pieces directly on the model.

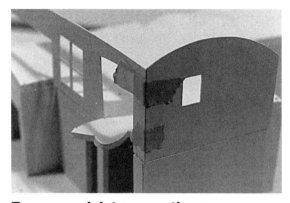

Temporary joint connections
For edges that do not dry immediately, use drafting tape for temporary connections. After 10 or 15 minutes, the tape can be removed. *Note:* Avoid masking tape or Scotch tape, as they will tear paper surfaces.

Placing glue
When working with glue, keep it in a pool. This helps it to become thicker and reduces drying time. Using a small cardboard stick, very lightly coat the edge of material. Too much glue will cause joints to dry much more slowly.

Joining parts
Press edges together and ensure that they are flush. After several seconds, the connection should be dry enough to hold on its own. Further drying will take place, but the part can be worked with right away.

Pin connections
Joints can be temporarily held together with straight pins and removed when glue is dry. In cases where joints will be hidden, pins can be pushed in all the way. The end of the knife handle is useful for setting and sinking pins.

Alternative Attachment Methods

Several adhesives, other than white glue, are also appropriate to paper constructions, each with advantages and limitations. In applications where face gluing is encountered, such as in site models or paper coverings, the water content in white glue tends to buckle the paper. In these instances, adhesives such as Spray Mount, hot glue, or double-faced tape are better choices.

Face-gluing contour models
White glue is effective for thick materials such as corrugated cardboard. For site models that are to be experimented on, glue should be distributed in lines to allow alterations to the layers.

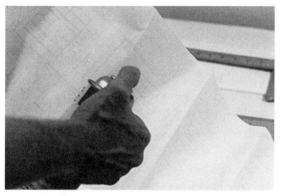

Nonbuckling spray adhesives
Apply a light, even coat of adhesive to attach cover materials and paper site contours. Site model contours can be modified as desired; however, holding power is limited.

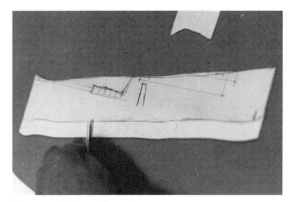

Face-gluing sheets
White glue can be used on thick materials such as foam core and corrugated cardboard. For permanent, well-jointed connections, the glue should be spread evenly over the entire surface interface.

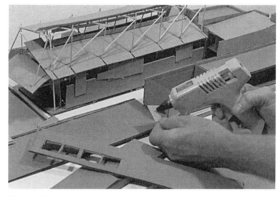

Hot glue
Due to quick setting time, hot glue is useful for quick sketch and study models where finished appearance is not demanding. Hot glue is also strong and can be used for reinforcing, but it tends to vibrate apart when moved.

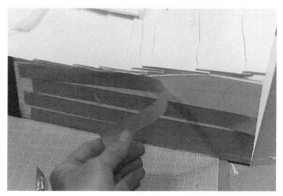

Covering with transfer tape
Fill in area with strips, pull away paper backing, and attach cover sheet. Although this is an effective nonbuckling method, the cover sheet must be correctly aligned, as there is no chance for further adjustment.

Integrating Forms

One of the key exercises in exploring readings between elements is to engage the parts in various relationships.

The rough study model makes this exercise quick and effective. Rather than avoiding difficult connections where model parts must share the same space, parts can be held in relative attitudes and quickly cut away, allowing the designer to visualize adjustments.

After final arrangements have been selected, the rough cuts can be recut or refaced. See "Converting" in Chapter 2.

1. After building separate forms, the two parts are placed in approximate plan relationship and traced at the point of intersection. *Note:* For angled relationships, the plan location of entry and exit can be different sizes to reflect the diminishing penetration.

2. The point of penetration is cut out on the box top. *Note:* Material could have been removed from the cylinder instead of the box to achieve the intersection, but the cylinder would have been prone to come apart when removing this much material.

3. Lines from the point of intersection are cut down the face of the box with the aid of the small triangle. *Note:* Blades must be sharp to do this without damaging the box. Scissors are sometimes better employed and create less disruption.

4. Material is removed from the box, and the parts are engaged by sliding the cylinder into the cut.

Attaching Sticks

Attachment methods appropriate to wood, plastic, and metal differ, depending on the material and the level of finish desired.

Wood sticks typically use white glue. Hot glue can be used in applications where more speed is desired.

Plastic sticks are attached with specially designed acetate adhesive, although model airplane glue can be used with some success. It is possible to glue plastic sticks with hot glue for quick studies, but the plastic surface can reject the glue. When attaching plastic sticks to paper, white glue or hot glue must be used in place of the acetate.

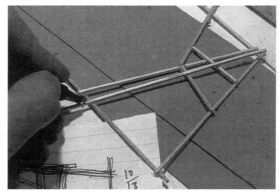

Wood sticks
Apply a touch of white or hot glue to the end of connections and joints. To keep glue from sticking to working surfaces, place construction on top of plastic food wrap or another nonstick surface.

Attaching in place
Apply a drop of acetate to end of stick and place it in contact with existing framework. Light sticks can be released within a few seconds and remain in place to dry.

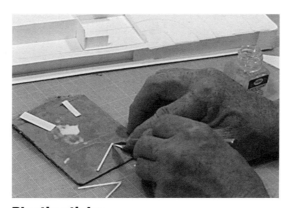

Plastic sticks
Place a drop of acetate on end of knife blade and transfer it to the joint. The material should be ready to use in less than a minute.

Attaching dissimilar materials
Plastic components must be interfaced with paper using white glue, as acetate adhesive will not work with paper or cardboard.

Attaching Plastic Sheets and Wire

Relatively standard methods using acetate adhesive are employed for plastic sheet connections and offer predictable results.

Wire and metal connections in model applications present several problems, and no one solution is ideal. Since white glue does not adhere well to metal, the most practical and effective alternatives are hot glue, super glue, Zap-A-Gap, and solder. Of these, only hot glue and Zap-A-Gap will interface with paper with relative success. Even then, results are mixed, and a combination of drilled sockets and white glue may be necessary to achieve the desired connection.

Attaching plastic sheets 1
Spread a thin line of acetate adhesive along the edge of the material. *Note:* A third hand is provided by the needle nose pliers.

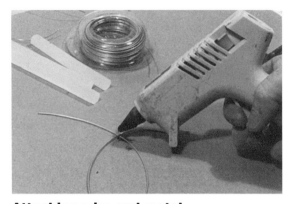

Attaching wire and metal
Hot glue can be used; however, joints will not hold if rotated. Super glue and delicate handling is another alternative. White glue can hold to a degree but must be dried for several hours.

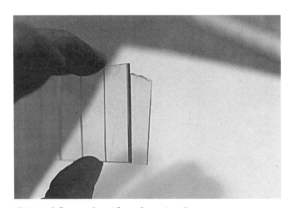

Attaching plastic sheets 2
After applying the acetate adhesive, hold the edges together and wait a minute or more before testing. Joints will be fragile, and attaching them can be time consuming. *Note:* Cuts must be straight, or it will be difficult for the glue to adhere.

Acid core-solder connections
Heat wire with soldering gun near connection point. Test wire temperature with the end of solder. When the solder melts, apply it to connection point and allow to cool. Do not melt solder directly with soldering gun.

Fitting Components

Aligning Edges

Once a model is partially constructed, irregularities such as minor misalignments, offsets because of material thickness, and stretched blueline drawings are inevitable despite attention to accuracy.

To help ensure tight connections, model components cut from plan and elevation drawings should be checked with the emerging model dimensions before assuming blueline templates will produce parts that fit. To keep component edges plumb and square, a small triangle can be used. The triangle is particularly important for vertical alignment since there are not any drawing lines to follow.

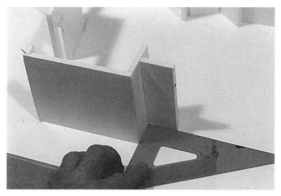

Aligning plan components
Place a small triangle at wall intersections and align the parts with triangle edges. For angled intersections, use an adjustable triangle. If walls are short, template the angle off the triangle, cut out shape, and use to align the model.

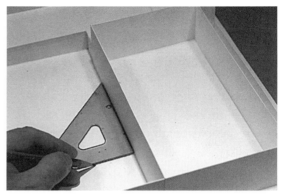

Drafting on the model
Small triangles can be used to draft guidelines on the model. This is useful when a model is being made without drawings or when new components are added.

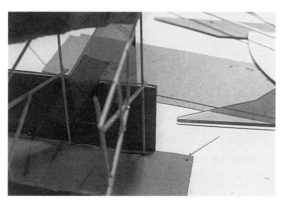

Vertical alignment
For vertical alignment, hold part directly against the triangle or mark guidelines on the adjoining wall face.

Detailing Connections

As models become larger and more refined, joints reflect greater levels of detail. Edges should read clearly and be accurately scaled. Thicker materials should be dovetailed to conceal interior layers, particularly with the use of colored boards with nonintegral interior layers.

Several conventions are used to code building parts. One of the most commonly employed is the use of standing edges to simulate parapet walls at the perimeter of low-slope roofs.

90-Degree foam core intersections
Cut a line into the foam filler equal to the thickness of the intersecting wall, and scrape away all the foam down to the paper backing. The remaining paper face can then fit neatly over the edges of intersecting walls.

Corner detailing
Another method of achieving tight-fitting corners is to cut the material on an angle as shown. The cuts must be accurate for a good fit, but the angle can vary on the tight side if only one side is exposed.

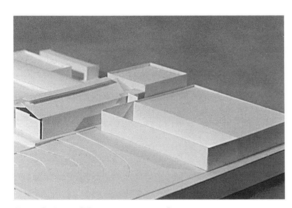

Roof detailing conventions
The plane of the low-slope roofs on this context model have been set slightly below the perimeter walls to create a parapet wall. This convention helps code the roof plane as being visually different from the ground plane.

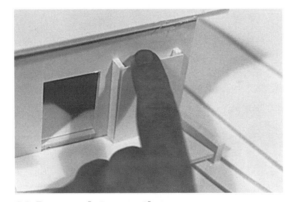

90-Degree intersection
The wall is placed in relation to its adjoining parts. As the wall is fit together, the edges will meet without any of the core material being revealed.

Compound joint detailing
Joints that angle in more than one direction, or *compound joints* such as shown in the upper right corner of the illustration, can be made by cutting and adjusting test fits, then templating the two ends onto a single piece the full width of the opening.

Handling Small Parts

As model parts become more delicate and refined, it may not be possible to place them by hand. A few simple tools can be employed to help make clean connections.

In the illustrations to the right, tweezers, needle-nose pliers, and a modeling knife are used in various applications. Although their uses can overlap, certain tools are better suited to particular situations than others.

Knife edge placement
By inserting the tip of the modeling knife into the paper edge, components can be guided into place. Care must be taken to lightly engage the knife, or parts can be pulled free when extracting the blade.

Tweezers for delicate members
The automatic-release spring action of tweezers allows placement without disturbance, and they can handle parts, such as plastic, that a knife cannot easily penetrate.

Knife face placement
Parts can be placed with the knife by gently inserting the knife in the face of the material. Too much blade engagement may leave visible marks in the surface.

Plier grips
Although it is not as easy to release objects from pliers as from tweezers, needle-nose pliers offer a steady grip for positive placement. By keeping one finger inside the handle, they can be gently opened to release components.

Shaping and Reinforcing

Making curvilinear shapes from various material can be accomplished in a number of ways. Many specialized techniques are covered in Chapter 8; however, two very common techniques for curving and warping planes are useful at even the basic levels of model building. Planes can be rolled or applied to a series of curved frames.

After pieces have been curved, they can be cut along bias lines to form a number of derivative shapes. Planes also can be made to fit curved armatures and warped in an infinite variety of ways.

For larger components, holding an accurate radius on curved pieces requires some type of reinforcing elements. These can usually be hidden inside wall lines or disguised in some way, as they are not really part of the building. This is not to say that they may not become part of the building, because these components may generate ideas for holding the actual building radii and be incorporated into the design.

Reinforcements are also useful under long spans of thin board and at wall edges to support planes and roofs inserted into perimeter walls.

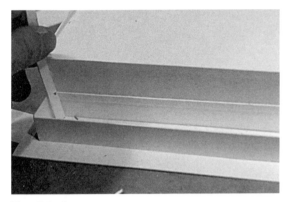

Roof ledger

A ledger strip has been attached to the wall slightly below the top so that the roof can be dropped in and carried on an even line. The cardboard stick is being used to press the strip against the wall until it sets.

Curving cardboard

Board can be curved by rolling it over cylindrical objects. It can be pulled across small cylinders for a tight radius or molded on larger objects for gentler curves. Forms should be slightly over rolled then relaxed to fit.

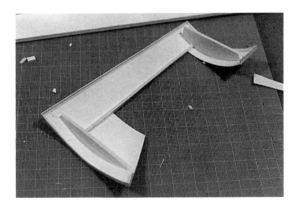

Reinforcing curves

To maintain large radii, curved reinforcing sections of foam core have been glued into place. *Note:* Edge fascia detailing using scaled curved pieces.

Warped surfaces

Thin plastic Mylar sheets and tracing paper can be glued to wire or cardboard frames and made to conform to various compound curves. *Note:* Mylar tends to simulate the qualities of glass but is less pliable than paper.

Templating
Transferring Drawings

One of the quickest methods for transferring drawn information to modeling components is to template them. This is done by cutting through the drawings to score the material below. The drawing is then removed and parts are attached using the score lines as a layout guide.

Alternately, the plans can remain mounted to the model surface and built directly on top. Aside from the visual distraction, this sometimes causes problems as the walls are glued to the drawing, and the drawing is attached only with spray adhesive.

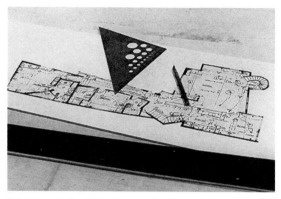

Plan readied for transfer

In a typical operation, the plan is secured to the modeling sheet with spray adhesive, then traced lightly with a knife using drafting edges. The plan is then removed, and the lightly cut lines are followed when placing components.

Cutting in elevations

The drawing is cut through to create the fenestration pattern. To avoid over cutting the corners, finish cuts from the opposite side. *Note:* Only the larger window mullions have been reproduced. See "Scale" in Chapter 2.

Spray adhesive

Apply a light, even coat of adhesive in a well-ventilated area, then spread out the plan smoothly on the material surface by attaching corners and smoothing it down from one end. For large plans, a third hand may be needed.

Drafting with the knife

Even without plans, a layout can be drafted onto the modeling material with a knife just as one might draft on paper with a pencil.

A cut elevation

A finished elevation is attached to a model. This can be done a number of times to study different opening schemes in the context of the building.

Templating Parts

Parts can be templated, that is, traced directly from the outline of another component or measured directly from drawings without the use of a ruler.

For complex connections, the process may have to be repeated several times while adjusting the new part each time to fit into the desired form.

Typical templating application

A form can be cut to the model shape by tracing around the form and cutting out the desired piece. In the illustration, a top for an irregularly curved conical tower is made quickly using this method.

Templating contours

In a manner similar to projecting contour lines in a section drawing, a side cover is made by placing the modeling material next to the existing model contours and tracing the profile.

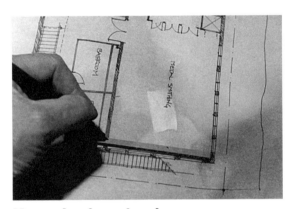

Measuring from drawings

As the model proceeds, parts such as ledgers and other components can be marked directly from the drawings.

Templating complex forms

For complex forms, a rough version can be cut or approximated from several spliced pieces, then transferred to another sheet with adjustments. This can be done several times until the final piece fits accurately.

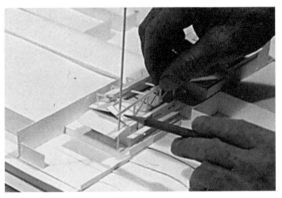

Projecting lines

Accurate cuts on the model may be located by extending a line with a straightedge to find the intersection point with another component.

Templating Multiples

A template can also be a device that is used repeatedly to reproduce a single item. Templates can be made and used for model building. A very practical application is using a template to make a series of repetitive roof trusses.

This technique can employ a range of approaches from drawing a simple template to building a model jig for mass assembly.

Drawn template
A simple template can be made by tracing the design on paper and laying each new component over the drawing.

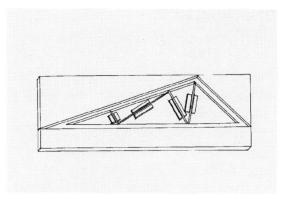

Block-type jig template
Pin-type jigs can be improved by cutting blocks and gluing them to a base to form the boundary edges for truss members. Block-type jigs are stronger and may be needed when making curved trusses.

Cast multiples
Multiple elements also can be cast from a single mold using plaster or anchoring cement. See Chapter 8.

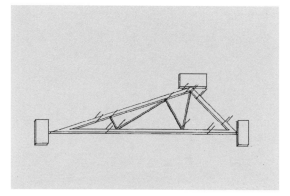

Pin-type jig templating
Pin templates can be made by inserting straight wire pins in a base and laying members inside the defining points.

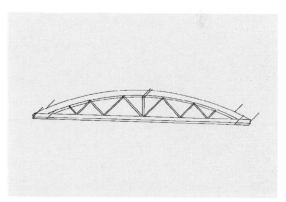

Braced curve template
Curved members can be made by pinning the two ends and using restraining pins in the middle. Once web members are installed and end connections made sound, the truss should hold its shape without the pins.

Finishes

Fenestration

Fenestration, or the act of creating windows and glazed openings, can be accomplished in a variety of ways.

Guidelines for denoting openings should be to keep them simple and to detail only what can be accurately depicted at scale. *Note:* It is usually better to avoid drawing openings on surfaces.

For alternate glazing simulations, overlays can be used as well as plastic sheets with applied mullion patterns.

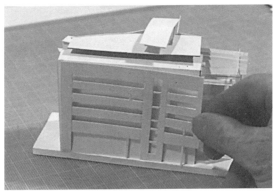

Fenestration overlay
A simple overlay can be cut and placed on top of a base sheet to provide a subtle reading of openings.

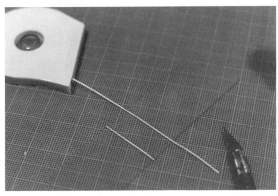

Art tape on plastic sheet
Art tape can be stretched across plastic to create mullions, using score lines as guides. Trim the tape ends after they have been pressed down.

Curtain wall glazing
Even small models can use plastic glazing sheets to create glass walls. For small areas and curved pieces, thick acetate can be used. As size increases, sheets of thin plastic will be needed to maintain rigidity.

Scoring mullion lines
Lines can be scored in plastic with the knife to serve as the actual mullion pattern or as guidelines for applying art tape.

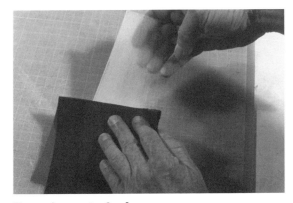

Translucent glazing
Translucent glass can be made from plastic or thin Plexiglas sheets by sanding one side with very fine paper.

Surfacing

For simple presentation models, final detailing and finishing can be accomplished through clean construction and a few simple techniques.

Surfaces can be covered with additional layers of paperboard to clean up exposed joints and create opening patterns. Edges can be detailed to convey correctly scaled depths.

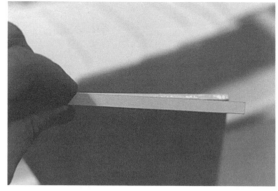

Edging detailing

Museum board strips, cut to the scale of fascia details, are adhered to the edge of 1/8" foam core roof panels. The factory edges of foam core and cardboard sheets are too thin to convey the correct reading for 1/4" scale.

Painting

Models can be cleaned up and finished by light spray painting. Flat automotive primer is recommended as an undercoat for heavy spray painting to prevent paper buckling.

Covering

The model is in the process of being covered with colored construction paper. This is applied by coating paper with spray adhesive, or for more permanent applications, transfer tape can be used.

Sanding

Rods and sticks can be sanded by rubbing them back and forth across a sheet of sandpaper placed on a flat surface; 100-grit paper will serve for most purposes.

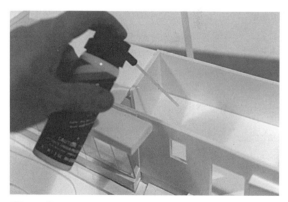

Cleaning

Models littered with postconstruction debris can benefit from cleaning with blasts of compressed air.

Site Work

Solid Contour Model

Select a material thickness that will scale to the desired grade steps. In the example, the scale is 1/8″ = 1′0″ and the corrugated card board is 1/8″ thick, representing 1-ft. grade steps.

Adhesive Guide

Spray Mount (Spray-Type Adhesives)

Paper and chipboard models work best with spray adhesives, because the water in white glue tends to buckle the material. Foam core can work with either spray adhesive or white glue. For study models, spray-mounted model layers are much easier to modify.

White Glue

For heavy materials such as corrugated cardboard, white glue may be needed for strength. It can be spread evenly for permanent construction or applied in lines to allow for removal of the layers. White glue can take up to 12 hours to dry when applied to the face of the material.

Hot Glue

Hot glue can be used but can be difficult to disassemble for modifications. Moreover, as the model is moved around, hot glue tends to lose its grip.

1. Use a copy of the contour map to template cuts (apply with spray adhesive to keep it from shifting). The copy can be cut to score the surface of the cardboard, or a pizza cutter can be rolled over the lines to transfer marks to the material.

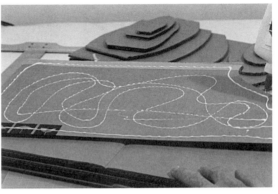

2. Starting with a full sheet the size of the site, cut away the first contour line. Glue this sheet to a base sheet the size of the entire site.

3. Cut away the next contour from another full sheet, and place this one on top of the first contour. All layers can be stacked first without gluing. When prestacking layers, splice lines should be marked and grades labeled to help guide reassembly.

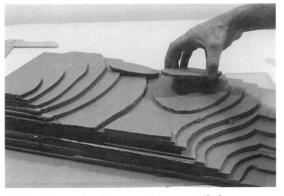

4. Continue stacking contours until they are small enough to use partial sheets, as for hilltops and other small sections. Grades can be lightly labeled on each contour to aid in counting elevations and controlling site work.

Drying

After gluing, the model is weighed down with books or magazines to press layers tight until dry.

Hollow Contour Model

Hollow models are built in a similar manner to solid ones, but only partial sheets are needed.

Contours can be either cut away to insert building volumes or built up around buildings. *Note:* Be careful not to cut along each contour without providing extra material for overlap between the sheets.

See Chapter 9, "Case Study A," for an example built directly on the model.

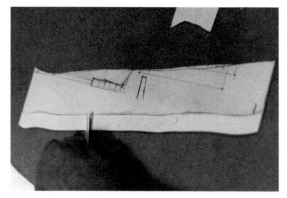

1. Cut sheets with enough area behind the contour line to supply adequate gluing surface (about 1/2" to 11/2", depending on the size of the exposed piece and the weight of the material). Mark edges to keep glue out of areas that will be exposed.

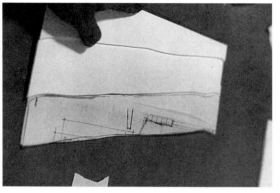

2. Splice the successive contour layers to each other and provide support from below to hold the construction at the proper slope. This can be done by building a series of columns or templating a section with graded steps that follow the rise of each contour.

3. With the majority of contours in place, the cavity below is clearly evident, as well as the overlapping splices between partial pieces.

4. Small grade sections can be completed off to the side and installed as a unit.

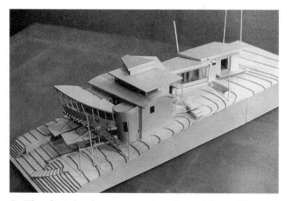

5. The finished construction has side walls added to support the edges at the proper rate of rise. To cut support walls, lay the model on its side and template the pieces. Side pieces can also be drafted as a section projection of the contour map.

Site Foliage

For design studies and simple finish models, it is best to treat foliage and entourage simply and abstractly. Elaborate simulations can easily overshadow the building, both in terms of its psychological importance and in the way they visually obscure the project.

Illustration

The examples offer simple but effective methods commonly used to provide unobtrusive site foliage.

Foliage

Trees have been created using lichen placed on small sticks. The lichen does not interfere with the ability to see the project and works well at small scales.

Foliage

Simple trees have been made by stacking layers of cut paper on wooden sticks. This method works better for larger-scale foliage.

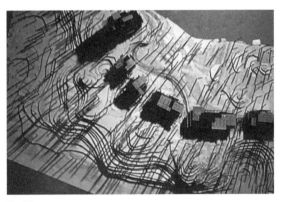

Foliage

The trees have been treated very abstractly by using bare plastic rods to give a sense of wooded density without interfering with the perception of the building.

Foliage

Dense foam can be sanded and shaped to create massing trees and plantings.

Model Base Construction

A number of bases are shown throughout the chapters of this book, and the discussion on contour models in Chapter 2 provides the basic information for base construction. However, some general guidelines are given here.

The main objective of a base is to support the model without warping or sagging. This is easily accomplished on small models but requires reinforcement and heavier material as models gain weight and size. Deep reinforced bases, Gatorboard, and plywood offer solutions in such cases.

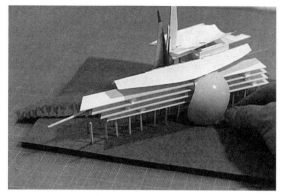

Sketch model base

Small sketch models can be built on pieces of corrugated cardboard or foam core. Layers can be stacked in rough simulation of sloped sites.

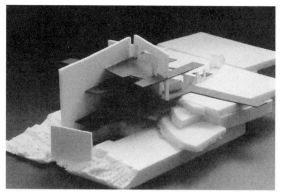

Study model base

Foam can be used to create quick grade simulations and provide instant rigidity.

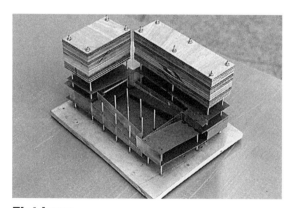

Flat base

For heavy models such as this solid wood construction, plywood or Gatorboard can be used to make a flat base.

Reinforced bases

For large models with flat bases, boxes with top and bottom surfaces can be built and reinforced with internal strips running at 90 degrees inside the box. Increased box depth will add strength.

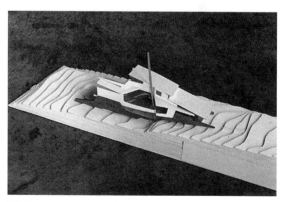

Hollow contour bases

Although solid contour models tend to become rigid of their own accord, it is necessary to reinforce the internal spaces of hollow bases with cardboard uprights and horizontal strips.

ADVANCED ASSEMBLAGE
Advanced Techniques for Form Making

With the proliferation of design work that explores curved/warped spatial concepts, this chapter provides a range of ideas for realizing these forms as hand-built models. A variety of simple chipboard to cast resin shapes is presented.

Because sculptural elements are sometimes needed only as components of a model, many of the examples present ideas for creating individual shapes that can be expanded to entire models if desired.

Found Objects
Modifying Objects

Many shapes, such as cones, spheres, and other complex forms, can be found in a variety of everyday objects and provide quick, accurate solutions. To match the qualities of other materials, such as paper, they may be painted or plastered. The problem in employing these materials is finding a match at the scale of the model.

Generally, found objects are not exactly the right size or shape, but by altering shapes such as cones and spheres, a large variety of secondary shapes can be generated.

Found objects can also be manipulated to integrate conventional modeling components. This may involve cutting, breaking, melting, unraveling, distorting, penetrating, and so forth to achieve the desired integration.

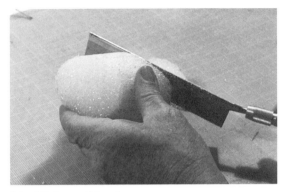

Modifying objects
Styrofoam cones can be sawed at an angle to alter their shape.

Modifying objects
Plastic packaging can be cut with a knife to produce secondary forms.

Modifying objects
This pasteboard cone has been truncated to change its form.

Modifying objects
A small fragment from a light bulb is used to create a curved wall surface.

Assemblages

This model type is made with found objects and other fragments to generate ideas.

By reading ordinary objects at another scale, the objects may be used as architectural elements. The resultant combinations can suggest forms not readily achieved with conventional materials.

Objects are most effective when used in combination with conventional model components and manipulated to yield secondary forms.

Found cardboard assemblage

A model using found chipboard elements. The body of the model has been cut from a cardboard dome. Sectional frames create the spherical crowning element; see "Transparent Forms" in this chapter.

Found object assemblage

Found objects and common modeling materials such as plastic rods have been combined to produce this quick assembly. *Note:* Forms such as the spray paint cap have been cut to integrate elements.

Stone assemblage

By assembling several configurations from fragments, interesting relationships can be uncovered that other materials may not suggest.

Stone assemblage

Not only can the fragments provide a ready collection of forms, but the material qualities convey a sense of weight not found in paperboard constructions.

Metal and plaster assemblage

A variety of objects, including metal balls, rods, and a cast-plaster site, have been used to create this assemblage.

Planar Forms
Curved Planes

Many curved shapes can be made using common paperboard materials as well as wood and metal (see "Alternative Media" in the Appendix). These can be assembled as complex planar forms or used to cut patterns for curvilinear solids.

The projects on the right employ simple curved planes. Cardboard planes can be curved by rolling them over curved objects. Techniques for curving metal sheets are shown on the following page.

Curving chipboard
The sweeping component of this sculptural model has been made from chipboard sheets. The sheets are precurved and attached to a series of "ribs" at the edge of and inside the form.

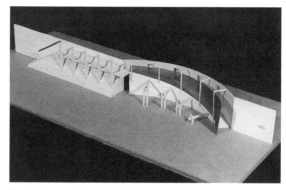

Curving thin wood
Balsa sheets can be used for curved sections on small models. Gluing the sheet to a base or intersecting edge can help hold the curve. *Note:* For thick wood, cutting a series of lines on the back side will allow it to curve.

Section template
To create a curved wall with a specific form, a template has been made by cutting a series of sections. Skin can be wrapped about this in panels to produce an accurately modeled wall.

Curving corrugated board and foam core
To achieve a smooth curve, board should be cut at about 1/8" intervals through the top layer. *Note:* The lines on the cone shape radiate from a center.

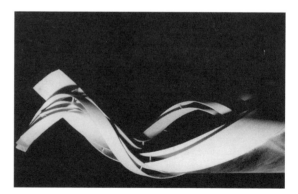

Bending thin wood sheets
Thin basswood sheets can be soaked in hot water and curved, then held in place to dry.

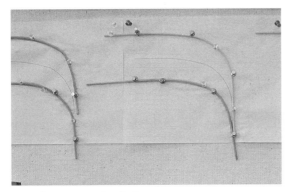

Curving wood sticks
Wood sticks can be curved to hold their shape by soaking them in hot water and pinning them in place until dry. A printout of the desired curve is used to guide the sticks into the exact curve.

Working with thin metal sheets
Thin metal sheets can be cut and bent easily. Bolt patterns can be embossed on the surface by hammering lightly with a pointed metal object such as a nail or punch.

Cutting metal
Sheet metal can be cut with tin snips or metal stud shears. It can be cut from a variety of materials, including metal ducts (shown), aluminum flashing, and copper and bronze sheets.

Bending metal sheets
Small pieces of thin, flat metal can be curved by holding the edges and pressing with the thumbs. The sheet will need to be overbent slightly to hold the desired curve when released.

Bending metal sheets
Sheets can be rolled over large objects such as this gallon paint can to introduce curves in the same way cardboard is curved.

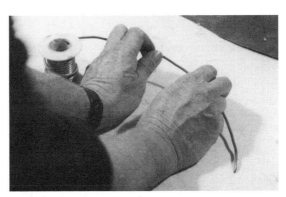

Bending soft metal rods
Small copper rods and lead solder can be bent to smooth radiuses by using the thumbs and pushing outward. For longer pieces, sections can be bent incrementally by moving down the wire down one section at a time.

Planar Solids

Platonic Planar Solids

Rectangles/Pyramids

Simple platonic volumes can be cut from solid blocks of wood (shown below) or made by joining flat planes. One of the most common shaped volumes in architectural modeling is found in the hip roof.

The following steps detail some of the points to be noted in constructing a simple hip roof form.

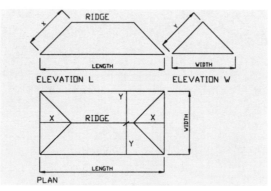

1. Elevation and plan drawings need to be made to obtain true plan dimensions for the four face components. To determine plan dimension X, use X dimension on elevation L. To determine plan dimension Y, use Y dimension on elevation W.

2. Cuts should be angled inward to achieve a mitered edge. If this is not done, the material thickness of all but the thinnest sheets will collide at the joints.

Wood massing model
The volumes for this model have been cut on a table saw. This method can be much faster than forming the volumes with cardboard planes. The blocks can be sanded to upgrade the finish when desired.

3. The small triangular face on the right (being put in place) has not been undercut with an angle. In comparison to the tight fit of the same element on the opposite side, this joint illustrates the potential for rough, unresolved edges.

4. Pins are used to hold the balsa sheets for assembly.

Complex Planar Solids

A large variety of planar forms can be made by attaching flat planes to define space. Several examples are shown using planes in a variety of ways.

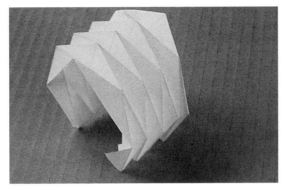

Folded planes

A triangulated arch structural system can produce space through simple folds in paper stock.

Planar solids

Chipboard planes have been used to model these forms. *Note:* The planes have been made to warp as they follow curved surfaces.

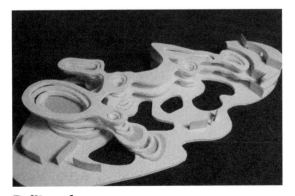

Built-up forms

Complex curves can be created by stacking sections to describe the form.

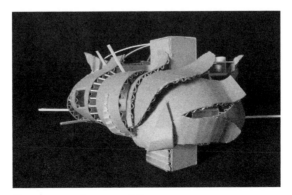

Compound curved forms

Compound curves can be achieved by using a shell-like assemblage of curved planes. In this case, the material is of corrugated cardboard and has been molded to its limits.

Basswood mass model

Shapes have been cut on the table and band saws to produce multifaceted volumes.

Transparent Forms
Exterior Skeletal Frames

These models are similar to wire frame drawings; however, whereas the "wire frame" employs a minimum amount of members to describe the edge conditions, the "skeletal frame" incorporates a sufficient quantity of members to describe the surface of the form. These models have the advantage of allowing the viewer to see through to interior space.

Two approaches to frames:
1. Create a series of frames or lines using individual members.
2. Bend and warp hardware cloth, screen wire, or other malleable sheet material.

Chipboard frames

By cutting successive frame segments from chipboard, any form can be described through the visual connection of their repetitive outlines. The inflection lines can be connected to further help describe the form.

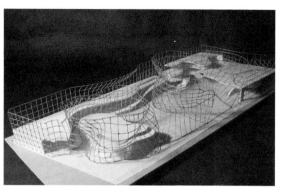

Warped hardware cloth

The model has been constructed using hardware cloth bent in various configurations to define spatial volumes.

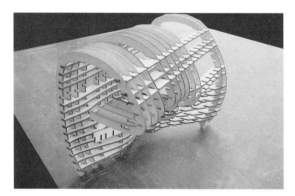

Shape using a series of sections

A complex volume can be described by cutting sections at regular intervals and attaching the frames with members cut in the opposite direction. Frames for this model were cut by a laser cutter (see Chapter 5).

Frames and planes

A solid/void model that uses repetitive frames to describe its surfaces in combination with solid planes.

Warped plane

An armature of sticks broken up into small sections that can follow the movement of a flowing plane has been constructed and can be filled in section by section to describe its surface.

Covering Frames

Skeletal frames can be covered with different materials to achieve the appearance of solid forms. This technique often offers the most controlled method for modeling complex curved shapes. Techniques related to this idea can be seen in the following section on working with plaster in regards to covering malleable screen wire.

Covering chipboard frames
A variety of shapes can be made from strips of chipboard and covered with lightweight tracing paper.

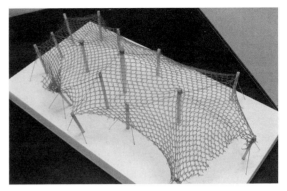

Screen wire volumes
The shapes inherent to tension structures can be replicated with a variety of mesh materials. The open web of synthetic cloth can simulate the properties of the skin.

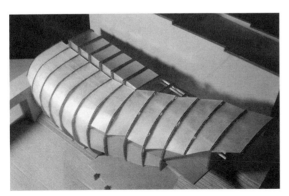

Covering corrugated frames
Repetitive frames can be infilled with flexible material like Mylar and acetate to describe the form. In this case, the acetate has been sanded to simulate translucent material. This also helps give it mass.

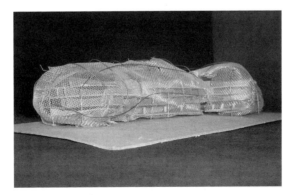

Making a screen form
Screen wire (both metal and fiberglass) can be used to follow the compound curves of surface planes. A series of floor plates with an internal wire frame provides the anchoring points needed to hold the screen in the proper form.

Covering frames
Elastic stocking material was stretched over a series of frames and varnished to produce this form.

Interior Skeletal Frames

Transparent wire frames, which outline the edges of space like three-dimensional (3D) drawings, may be built to understand interior relationships between intersecting geometries. The spaces at collision points would normally be obscured by exterior wall surfaces, but because only the edges can be built, overlapping spaces can be seen and developed.

To give definition to the space, it is helpful to build out all solid surfaces, such as the floor plates, that will not obscure the area of study.

Inexpensive and easily manipulated plastic drinking straws can be used for this study. The straws work well, as they can span large distances and be cut with scissors and connected with Scotch tape. Other inexpensive materials to be considered are cardboard strips for curved lines and balsa sticks or ribs cut from foam core for larger spans.

Interior study

An open frame has been built to define the limits of the space, but keep the interior open so that the internal space can be understood and developed.

Transparent mixed media

Screen wire, or something a little more open in its mesh, can be used to define the planes of the volume and reveal the internal space.

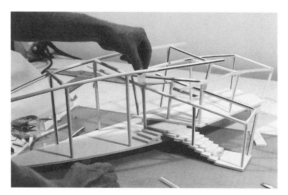

1/2″ House entry study

The limits of this house model are described by drinking straws. By looking through the model, it is possible to visualize the relationship between the intersecting planes of the interior projection at the entry stairs.

Transparent media

By providing only the structure of the skin for this project, the internal relationships are open to exploration and evaluation.

Transparent Plastic

It is sometimes desirable to incorporate plastic in models for transparent layers and bases. These materials offer similar advantages to skeletal frames in allowing the viewer the ability to see through to interior spaces. They can also be used to build visually interactive layers.

In all but the thinnest sheets, plastic usually means the use of Plexiglas. Plastic and acetate sheets for glazing (addressed in earlier chapters) are related to these thicker sheets but do not require special equipment to fabricate.

Material

Plexiglas is available in clear and colored 4 ft. × 8 ft. sheets. Thickness can start as small as 1/16" and progress to 1/8", 1/4", and 1/2". Many suppliers sell scrap sheets that can be used if smaller pieces are required.

Equipment

Plexiglas sheets of approximately 1/16" can be cut with scoring knives or tools and broken similarly to thin plastic sheets. Thicker sheets require power tools like those used in working with wood. For more information, see "Plastic and Foam" in this chapter.

Fluid Plexiglas

This model attempts to translate the material properties of water. The Plexiglas can be heated in an oven (on very low heat) and distorted to form the waves.

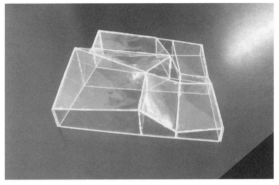

Transparent plastic model

Thin Plexiglas can be warped to a degree to form distorted volumes like this one. The key is to provide planar edges that the warped parts can attach to.

Translucent plastic models

The two models on the left achieve an ephemeral quality by using thin acrylic sheets and sanded Plexiglas. The material quality of these sheets yields a reading that is crystalline and flowing.

Curvilinear Solids
Pattern-Cut Geometric Solids

Geometric, or platonic, solids such as the sphere and cone can be made from assembled sheet patterns. The advantage to constructing them this way is that, unlike found objects, they can be made to fit exact scales.

The resulting spherical forms will be slightly flattened as true spherical segments are curved in two directions; however, the results will be acceptable for spheres with diameters up to about 4".

Sphere Pattern

The sphere is made by dividing the desired volume into a series of segments similar to those described by longitude and latitude lines on a globe. About 24 segments are needed to create an acceptably even pattern. More segments can be used, but at some point, they may become too small to handle. If fewer segments are used, the sphere will start to appear flattened at the sides. Techniques used to assemble the segments are shown on the following page. *Note:* Computer models use the unfold feature to resolve volumes into flat patterns similar to the example. After edges are joined together, almost any shape imaginable can be produced from them. See "Computer Modeling" in Chapter 5.

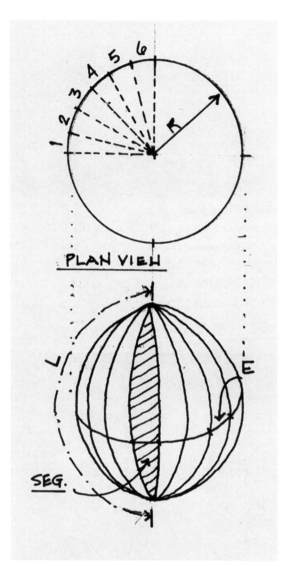

Conceptual view of segment (seg.)
Dimension E = circumference (2TT R) divided by the number of segments.
Dimension L = half the circumference.
The plan view at the top shows the layout of six segments in one quarter of the circle.

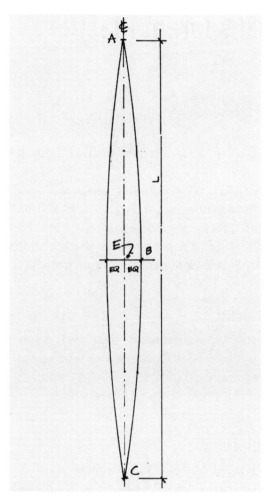

Layout for one segment
1. Draw a center line equal to dimension L.
2. Cross the center line with marks equal to dimension E.
3. Draw a three-point arc through points A, B, and C.

Note: The sides of the segments must be curved as shown to fill space at the edges. Simple triangular shapes will not work.

Cone Pattern

Cones can be constructed as a measured pattern or rolled from paper to quickly approximate the desired size and shape.

The construction of a measured cone is shown on the right. A rough cone assembly is demonstrated at the far right.

To produce a measured cone shape, the pattern shown below should be followed.

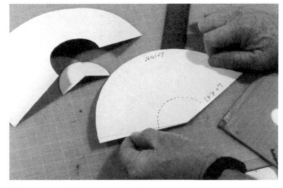

Measured cone pattern
A pattern cut from poster board to form a cone with a 2″ radius (dimension L) and 4″ height (dimension H). The angle between L radius legs is 158 degrees. *Note:* An extra tab has been glued to the edge to join the seams.

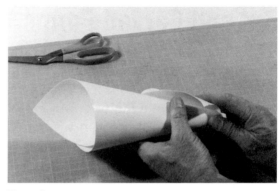

Rough cone
To make a rough cone, material can be rolled tightly at one end and glued together.

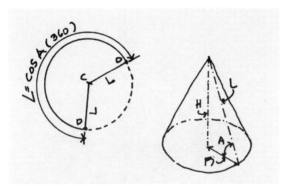

Measured cone pattern
L = square root of dimension H2 + R2.
To find angle A, use H/R = TanA.
The pattern will be the smaller part of the pie with the dashed line along the curve.

To build the cone:

1. Draw two lines (L and L) from a single point joining at the angle shown (cos A (360)).

2. Measure out on lines to find L and draw a circle from this radius.

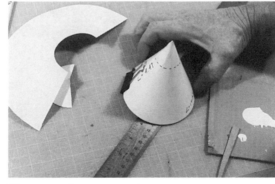

Measured cone pattern
The cone has been joined at the seam using a clamp until the glue dries. A second cone may be cut from the top to truncate the form, as shown by the dashed line around the top of the cone.

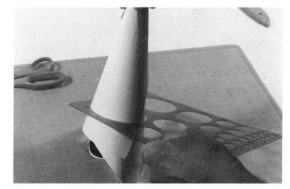

Rough cone
To trim, a circle template can be passed over the cone, traced, and cut as desired. For angle cuts, slant the template and trace around the cone.

Cut and Carved Forms

For quick assemblages, wood blocks and Styrofoam can be cut on a table or a band saw to provide a large range of shapes. Polystyrene foam can also be cut using a hot wire cutter. Scrap lumber from construction sites works well for this type of assemblage and is relatively inexpensive.

For more on equipment and wood types, see "Alternative Media" in the Appendix.

Shapes cut on the band saw
Shaped forms can be easily cut on a band saw from blocks of wood. The saw can be used to do rough carving, as done by a knife, but much more quickly.

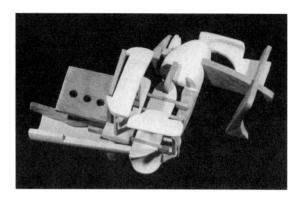

Carved and sanded wood
Given time, wood can be cut, sanded, and carved to make any shape imaginable.

High-rise assemblage
A model for a high-rise tower built from band-sawed wood, balsa sticks, and chipboard.

Styrofoam
Blocks can be carved with saws or Shurforms and sanded into shapes. They can also be covered with plaster. *Note:* Use fine, even-celled blocks such as those sold for modeling or used for flower arrangement bases.

Carved Styrofoam shapes
This Styrofoam massing model has been carved from polystyrene foam with a hot wire cutter, then sanded smooth for a high level of finish.

Cutting and Carving Wood

A variety of affordable hand and power tools can be used to cut and finish wood model parts. The following illustrations give some suggestions as to how each can be used to shape and cut wood blocks. *Note:* Although power drills are not shown, they are useful for a variety of tasks and can be used in a manner similar to the examples shown in Chapter 7, "Cutting Materials," and Chapter 9, "Case Study C," for cutting/drilling holes.

Carving wood
Shapes can be carved from blocks before or after shapes have been rough-cut with power tools. Small hobby chisels can be used, but professional wood carving chisels will make the job go much faster.

Cutting curves
Curves can be cut in plywood and boards with an inexpensive jigsaw. These saws are limited to wood about 3/4" thick. Thin metal can also be cut by using metal-cutting blades.

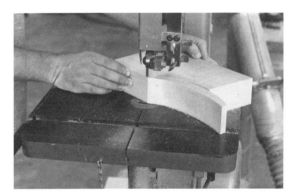

Cutting curves
Using a band saw is the quickest way to produce rough shapes before carving and sanding. The bed can be angled for compound curves.

Sanding blocks
Wood blocks may be smoothed with the belt sander using 100-grit belts. Shapes can be carved using coarse belts. In many applications, shaping wood on the sander may be more effective than using carving chisels.

Cutting blocks
Wood blocks can be quickly ripped from larger pieces of wood on the table saw. *Note:* Always use a push stick, as shown, instead of your hand when working close to the blade.

Building with Plaster and Anchoring Cement

Molding plaster is a versatile material that can be used to make a variety of shapes. It is inexpensive, sets rapidly, and can be sanded to a smooth finish.

Building with plaster can be extremely messy and should be done over a disposable surface.

Anchoring cement is similar to plaster in its behavior and mixing instructions. It is useful for simulating concrete and can be stronger than plaster. In many cases, it will require internal reinforcing.

Several methods are available:

- Making forms and covering them

- Covering existing shapes

- Pouring into molds

Conventional molding plaster
Molding plaster is flexible and readily available. To mix, add water, then pour plaster in (sifting it to avoid lumps) until an island appears on the surface of the water. The ratio will now be correct, and plaster can be mixed.

Precoated plaster cloth
Precoated plaster cloth is best suited for covering wire forms. Simply wet cloth by dipping it in water, then cut into strips as needed.

Anchoring cement
This is a much stronger alternative to plaster and conveys the qualities of concrete at model scale.

Building with Plaster

The following examples demonstrate the making of curvilinear forms by covering screen wire shapes with plaster and a pre-coated casting gauze.

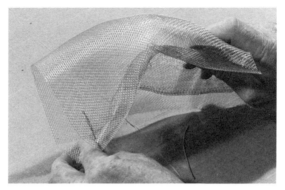

1. Screen wire is cut with scissors, molded into the desired form, and held in place with pieces of wire and string. *Note:* Materials such as hardware cloth can be used for armatures, but it is helpful to cover them in screen for plaster application.

2. The wire is then stuffed with newspaper to help prevent the plaster from falling directly through the screen. *Note:* This step may be omitted if falling plaster is not a problem.

3. A thin mix of plaster is made, and newspaper strips are dipped into the plaster and draped over the form. Usually, the plaster must be applied to one side at a time, allowing it to set before rolling the form over and coating the opposite side.

4. After the paper layer is finished and has set, a thicker batch is mixed and the paper is coated with a layer of pure plaster. When cured, this layer can be sanded smooth. Any remaining pockets or gaps can be filled with additional plaster and sanded smooth.

Building with Precoated Plaster Cloth (Rigid Wrap)

Typically, precoated plaster cloth is used to make casts for broken bones. This product, which can usually be found at craft or medical supply stores, is much easier to control than conventional plaster. A common brand of this cloth is sold in craft stores as Rigid Wrap.

The initial smoothness of this product and lack of waste, as compared to traditional plaster, should be evident from the example.

Papier-mâché mixes made from thinned white glue can be used to make similar strips.

1. Plaster-coated gauze is used to cover a screen form by cutting strips from the roll and dipping them in water.

2. The gauze backing eliminates the need to back up the screen with paper. By crossing directions with additional layers of material, the form can achieve much greater strength.

Screen covered plaster

These forms have been made using a process similar to covering wire forms. Screen is pushed through a shaped hole and formed, then covered with papier-mâché strips made from brown paper dipped in thinned white glue.

3. After the finished form is allowed to set, a final layer of pure plaster can be smoothed over the surface to fill rough areas. When fully cured, this coating can be sanded to an even finish.

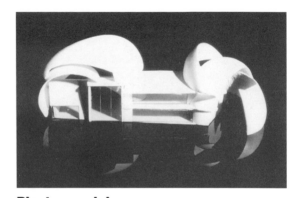

Plaster model

This model was made using similar techniques to that of covering. A series of warped and twisted shell components have been individually crafted, sanded, and assembled into one model.

Covering Styrofoam

Styrofoam is often coated with plaster to disguise its porous surface and match paper modeling materials such as museum board. Once plaster has set, it can be sanded smooth.

Plaster-covered ball

1. A layer of plaster is spread over the ball. Often, this must be done on one side first. After this side has set, the other side can be coated.

Plaster-covered bowl

This half-oval shape has been covered with a thin coat of plaster. *Note:* The shape was carved from a block of Styrofoam.

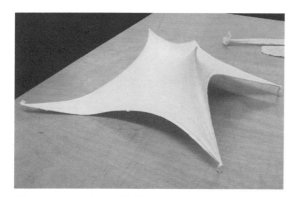

Plaster-coated cloth

A tensioned form is made using cotton cloth held in place with strings and props to form it. The cloth can then be covered with a thin plaster mix to impregnate the cloth. This will set and yield a rigid form.

Plaster-covered ball

2. The ball is sanded smooth. Plaster tends to clog up sandpaper and will require the use of several fresh sheets for final smoothing.

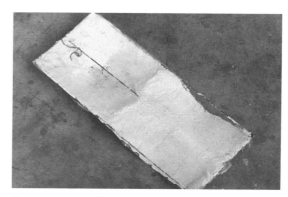

A plaster surface

This warped plane was made by stretching screen wire over a wire frame and covering it with plaster. *Note:* Gauze was used instead of newspaper to carry the plaster.

Coating Chipboard

Existing shapes can be covered with a layer of plaster for texture or to match white paper. Spackling or premixed sheet rock finishing compound can be used for this as well. Integral color can be achieved by mixing a small amount of powdered dye in with the plaster or spackling. Chipboard is used as a base because it allows the plaster to grip its relatively porous surface. Although it offers the simplest form of backing surface, this material is not ideal. The water content inherent in plaster can cause it to lose its form, and the surface grip is such that plaster may flake off after it has dried. These problems can be partially solved by using heavier material reinforcement and by gluing cloth to the surface to provide extra gripping power.

Spreading plaster on chipboard
Plaster can be spread directly onto chipboard and sanded smooth. Several layers may be required to achieve the desired consistency.

A plastered model façade
The surface of this building façade has been covered with spackling to produce a textured finish. *Note:* Integral color has been used on one of the layers to provide contrast.

Plaster contours
Although contours can be covered with plaster, a negative mold of the site can also be made and cast in plaster. See "Molding with Plaster and Resins" in this chapter.

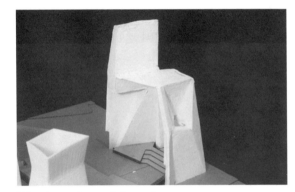

Plastered model surfaces
The model above is made from chipboard and has been covered with plaster to achieve the stucco-like finish.

Molding with Plaster and Resins

Plaster can be poured into molds to form a variety of shapes. Pouring plaster is particularly advantageous when making multiples of the same form and for pouring monolithic (solid) curved shapes.

The molds are constructed as the negative of the desired form. This method is similar to forming techniques for cast concrete, and concrete formwork manuals are full of ideas.

The processes that have been discussed to this point have been additive in nature; that is, the shapes and forms were built up by attaching pieces. The molding process is different from this, because before an object can be formed, its opposite or "negative" must be constructed.

Plaster must then be poured into the form or negative to yield a "positive" shape. Forms can be poured as solids or backed with cloth to create "thin shell" forms.

The following projects were made using casting techniques. Basic casting and mold-making techniques are illustrated in more detail on the following pages.

Multiple forms
The multiple forms for this multistory study were made using a wire frame mold. Successive pours were popped from the mold and strung together on the three columns.

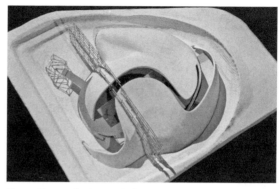

Powder print model
This model was actually made from a 3D powder printer, but similar shells can be made using plaster in a negative form by pouring in successive layers of plaster and draining the excess until the shell is thick enough.

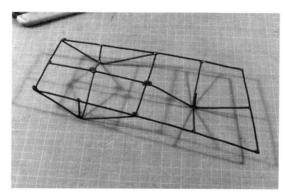

Molding frame
This frame was covered in tape and used to create the plaster mold for the example above. *Note:* The mold was greased with petroleum jelly to keep the plaster from sticking. Nonstick cooking spray such as Pam can also be used.

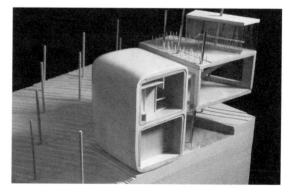

Fiberglass model
This model has been made from fiberglass sheeting and resin layered over a mold, similar to boat construction. Several sheets are needed as well as a final coat of urethane before sanding smooth and painting.

Basic Casting

Casting plaster and other materials involves the use of a mold or negative. This form will be the reverse or "negative" of the form you are trying to make. For example, if the desired form is a half of a sphere, the mold will be a bowl. To remove the casting, the mold must be flexible or slightly conical. If sides are "undercut" or have a lot of texture, the casting may be caught in the mold. A release agent is needed to help keep the material from sticking to the mold. A thin coat of petroleum jelly can be wiped on the form, or an aerosol cooking oil can be lightly sprayed on the form.

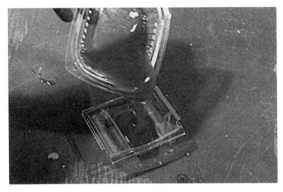

Project A—pouring resin
Following product mixing directions, polyester resin has been combined with a catalyst and poured into a plastic mold that can be peeled off. Common release agents cannot be used, as they will react with the resin.

Project A—cast resin and mold
The mold is peeled from the hard resin casting. Resin offers a very smooth surface finish. It can also be bought as a clear casting resin at craft stores. *Note:* Dyes of various colors can be added to clear resin, as desired.

Project—pouring the mold
Plaster has been poured into a muffin pan sprayed with a release agent. This mold is ideal, as the sides are slightly conical. If the sides sloped in the opposite direction, the casting could not be extracted.

Project B—reinforcing the casting
Wires or sticks can be pushed into the wet plaster to reinforce the casting. These act like reinforced concrete, supplying tensile strength to the material.

Project B—casting and negative mold
After about 30 minutes, the plaster can be pulled from the mold. *Note:* The "positive" form of the plaster is the opposite of the "negative" form of the mold.

Casting Molds

Casting molds or "negatives" can be made from a variety of materials. They do not need to be elaborate constructions. All that is required is that they hold the plaster until it is set in the desired shapes.

The examples on this page discuss some of the possibilities.

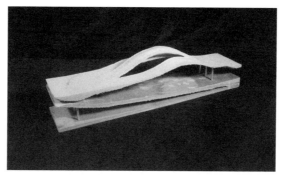

Sand casting

A box mold can be filled with sand. The sand can be shaped and a layer of anchoring cement poured on top. When finished, the sand is shaken out. Successive layers can be built up to create multilevel structures.

Plaster site model

This model was made using clay and other objects to create the negative for the casting.

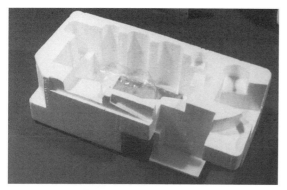

Found object mold

Interesting mold shapes or "negatives" can be found in packing spacers and other found objects. The shapes that would result from pouring this mold must be visualized by reversing the image of the negative volume.

Plastic mold

Clear plastic molding material can be bought or found as a variety of packing items. This molding material can be peeled away from the casting, allowing the use of limited "undercuts."

Casting in a wood box mold

A wood box may be built by nailing sides to a baseboard or holding the sides with weights as shown. All of the objects higher than the sides of the box will become holes through the casting. *Note:* A release agent was sprayed on.

Malleable Materials

Malleable materials such as Lizella clay and Plasticine can be easily formed to take on complex sculptural shapes. Of the two materials, Plasticine is generally used because it does not dry out and crack. In addition, because it is not water based, it can be used in combination with paper materials.

It can be difficult to achieve hard edges with malleable material, and they often require internal wire and wood supports to maintain their shape. However, there is no need to build a negative form (as required in casting plaster models), and subtracting parts is relatively easy.

Clay is worked using sculpting tools such as cutting loops, shaping sticks, kitchen knives, and smoothing boards.

For forms that will set hard after molding by hand, materials such as Sculpey, a ceramic hybrid available at craft stores, can be molded and fired in an ordinary kitchen oven.

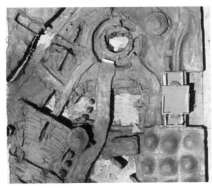

Malleable site model
A Plasticine site model can be molded in a similar manner to the actual site soil and used for quick studies. *Note:* It can be difficult to transfer final grade elevations from this type of site model.

Working with Plasticine
Cantilever projections can be supported by inserting wire or wood rods through these sections into the body of the model. The material is easier to work when it is warm. Hand molding will help transfer body heat.

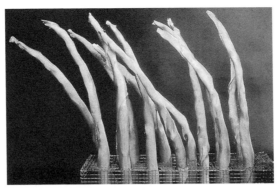

Plasticine concept model
This spatial interpretation of the book *Everglades: River of Grass*, by Marjory Stoneman Douglas, is facilitated by the plastic qualities of clay materials.

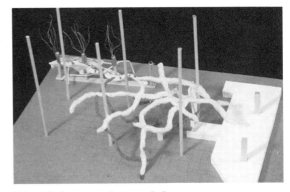

Plasticine scale model
Plasticine lends itself well to the exploration of a 3D network as in this small model for an inflatable project.

ASSEMBLAGE CASE STUDIES

Step-by-Step Case Studies of Assembly Techniques

The following projects trace the evolution of three designs from early conceptual stages to finish models. Many assembly techniques and strategies presented in Chapters 7 and 8 are shown to convey possible applications in the context of evolving designs.

Case Study A: Residence

Stage 1—Initial Sketch Studies

Strategy

With the project parameters in mind, the designer makes alternative sketch models from small schematic scaled drawings and pencil sketches. After exploring different approaches to generate ideas, an individual or hybrid model is selected for further development.

Assembly

Rapid construction techniques using knife, scissors, and hot glue.

Project

A 2,000-sq.-ft. house on a narrow infill lot.

Scale 1/16″ = 1′0″

Models measure approximately 2″ × 3″ (actual size) and are kept small for initial studies. *Note:* Even at this scale, the model is not built as a pure massing model but is treated as a solid/void model to understand the contribution of openings to the overall composition of forms.

Materials

- Poster board
- 1/16″ foam core

Illustration

Five alternative approaches are made to generate ideas and explore a range of directions. Work is begun using small measured schematic drawings, with each model employing a basic formal strategy to organize its moves.

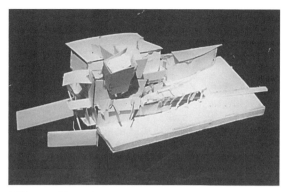

Alternative 1

This scheme is organized as a linear grouping. It becomes readily apparent that the program will need a second story to preserve any yard space.

Alternative 2

This scheme concentrates the program on the second level in another linear side-loaded organization (based on Alternative 1).

Alternative 3

This scheme uses a central drum as the focal point for its organization and covers the entire buildable area with a single-story solution.

Alternative 4

This scheme engages two volumes with all other spaces expanding from them. With modifications, this scheme is selected for further study with a development model. See "Case Study A, Stage 2" on the following page.

Alternative 5

This scheme employs a courtyard defined by a second-story bridge.

Stage 2—Manipulation and Focusing

Strategy

The general direction of the sketch is increased in scale for further study and development. Alternative solutions for different sections of the model are also considered.

Assembly

The model is assembled with relative speed but more accurately than the sketch model. Parts are lightly adhered using white glue with the intent of cutting and changing the components as the model progresses. A number of building and editing techniques are illustrated during the construction of this model.

Project

A 2,000-sq.-ft. house on a narrow infill lot.

Scale 1/8″ = 1′0″

The scale of the sketch model is doubled in size for this study. The increase allows for more detail and refinement but is still small enough to lend itself to quick alterations and visualization.

Materials

■ Two-ply museum board paper

Illustration

Alternative 4 is selected from the initial studies and rebuilt for further study. The raised section at the rear of the initial model is immediately lowered to the ground plane. This "tail" is then modified several times to explore different readings.

At this level of study, the development model must show all solid/void relationships to provide the next level of information.

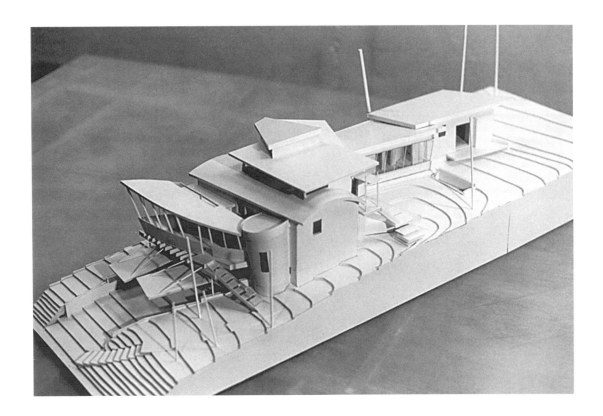

1. The plan is transferred with a knife to the base sheet. *Note:* Although scaled plans should yield accurate parts, adjustments must be made to compensate for the thickness of materials and to conform to small variations that occur in the actual model.

2. Walls are erected and small parts put in place with the aid of the knife point.

3. The shape of the conical stair tower roof is templated directly off of the model. Because this shape varies in its rate of curvature, direct templating is one of the most dependable ways to achieve an accurate fit.

4. The second story is held in place to make a rough template for the curving roof plane.

5. A finished roof is made by adjusting the rough template and recutting the part until an exact fit can be achieved. *Note:* For forms that change geometry in three dimensions, it is difficult to cut shapes that will fit perfectly the first time.

6. An initial "tail" wing is tacked together with the glue gun.

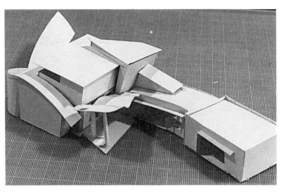

7. The "tail" is edited by cutting with scissors.

8. Openings are cut directly on the model. *Note:* If needed, these can be cut accurately by using a small triangle to guide the knife edge.

9. The resultant openings with small shading additions.

10. A wedge is cut out of the box to try out another angle on the tail.

11. The move is rejected, and the wedge is reattached to the box. *Note:* It helps to save all parts that are cut off for replacement if the modifications are not satisfactory.

12. The walls of the tail are broken open to study the potential for other arrangements.

13. Using scissors to cut out small pieces directly on the model, attention is directed to developing the front of the building. *Note:* Attention should move around the model so that one area does not become overdeveloped in relation to other sections.

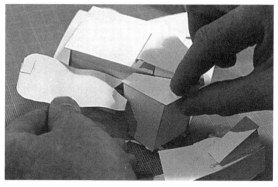

14. The knuckle formed by the stair tower between the main body and the tail is redesigned.

15. Returning to the rear of the model, a third alternate façade is considered, and the tail is rebuilt one more time. The final parts have been recut to match the level of finish on the other sections.

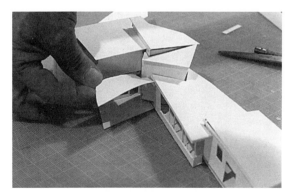

16. An alternate patio covering is considered as the investigation nears completion.

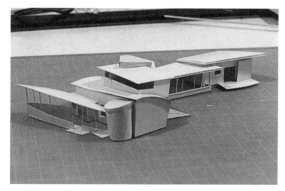

17. The completed development model is shown. *Note:* The site has not been addressed on this model, although it was included at the sketch model stage and has been explored in terms of the way the building will relate to it.

Stage 3—Finish Model and Site

Strategy

With the basic relationships established, the model is again increased in scale and built with greater accuracy.

The presentation/finish model can also be considered an advanced type of study model, as it affords the focus for designing details such as glazing patterns, site elements, interiors, and roof treatments.

Assembly

A number of new techniques and materials applicable to finish models are included in this example.

Project

A 2,000-sq.-ft. house on a narrow infill lot.

Scale 1/4″ = 1′0″

This is a typical scale for fully developed house models as it allows sufficient size for detailing.

Materials

- Three-ply museum board paper
- 3/16″ foam core

Illustration

The model is built as an example of the level of finish appropriate for formal presentations. The abstract detailing relies on implied material simulation. Items that cannot be reproduced accurately at 1/4″ = 1′0″ scale (less than 2″) are not included.

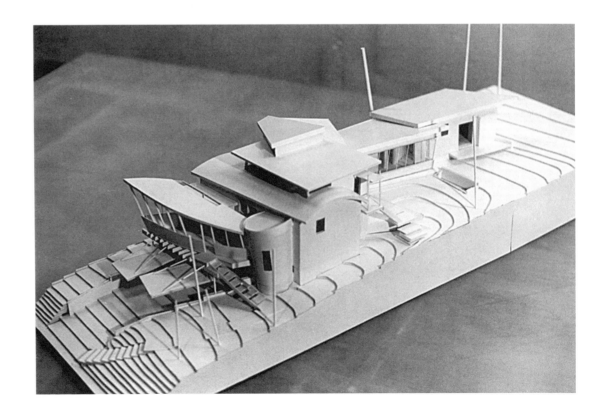

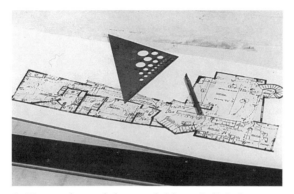

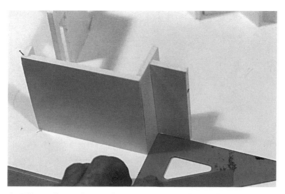

1. The surface of the model base is lightly scored by tracing a set of floor plans with a sharp knife. The plans have been spray mounted and are removed after the wall lines have been transferred. *Note:* Apply spray outdoors.

2. The plans have been removed, and the basement walls are laid out along the scored lines. A triangle is used to ensure accurate corner joints and vertical alignment of walls.

3. Wall connections are held together with straight pins. This speeds construction by allowing successive joints to be made without waiting for glue to dry. *Note:* Corner angles have been cut at 45 degrees to allow paper to meet without exposing the Styrofoam core.

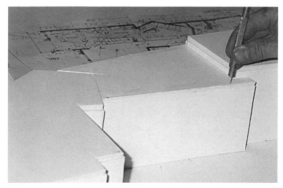

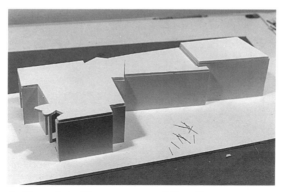

4. After glue is dry, pins can be removed or pushed in if the heads are hidden by other parts of the model.

5. Completed basement and first floor are shown. *Note:* Site contours will be built up around the basement level.

6. Using drawings to template the façade, museum board is cut to include only the dominant mullion details.

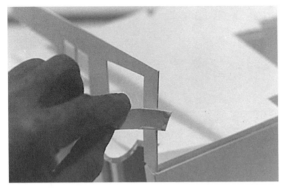

7. A thin line of white glue is applied directly to the wall edge.

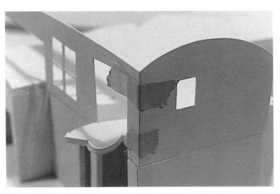

8. A wall joint is held in place with drafting tape until glue can set.

9. Walls continue to be constructed on the main floor of the house.

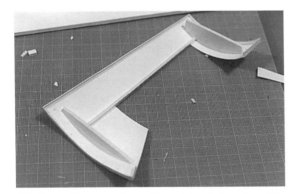

10. A rough curved roof is cut to determine fit, as demonstrated on the development model. The final cut for the roof is reinforced with hidden bracing to maintain radiuses at each end.

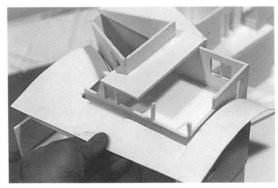

11. The roof is placed on the second floor. Supports allow the roof and the second floor to be taken off for interior model viewing.

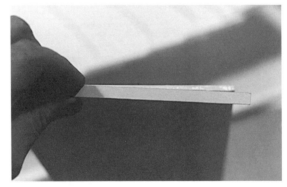

12. Exposed foam core roof edges are covered with museum board. *Note:* Edges should be scaled to their intended depth rather than letting the given thickness of material remain inaccurately sized. In the example, edges have been cut to read 8" and 10" at scale.

13. A conical entry tower is made from museum board by rolling with a round marker.

14. Street face components of the first floor are assembled.

15. A roof for the conical tower is templated directly off the model using discarded model material.

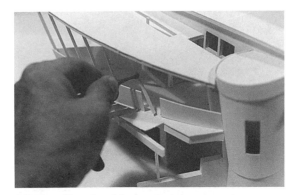

16. Detailing is added, using tweezers to handle the finer elements.

17. The basic body of the model is completed and ready for the site contours. See "Site Work" in Chapter 7.

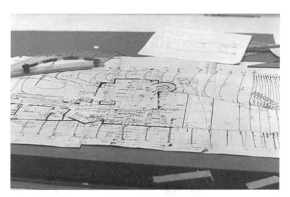

18. A hollow site contour model is constructed directly on the model by using a site drawing with 6-in. contours and 1/8" foam core. At 1/4" = 1'0" scale, each layer of foam core is equal to a 6" change in grade.

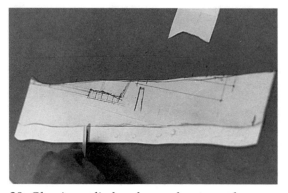

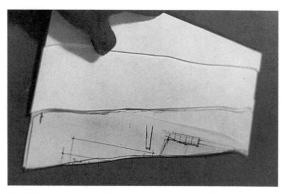

19. Contours are cut between the lines with a 1″ projection beyond the contour to allow a tab for gluing the successive layers together.

20. Glue is applied and spread out evenly. *Note:* The line of the contour above should be marked so that glue will not get on the material past this point and be exposed. The paper template can also be left on to protect this area until it is in place.

21. The overlapping contours are glued to the 1″ projection on successive contours. *Note:* This type of site model can be built from the top down instead of from the base up as in the solid contour model.

22. After several contours have been connected together, the section is supported from below and attached to the body of the building.

23. Individual contours are continued down the side of the house.

24. A completed side is shown.

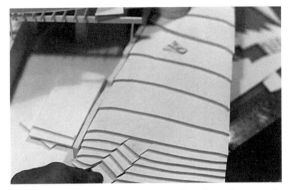

25. The opposite side is completed and a notch is cut for the location of site stairs.

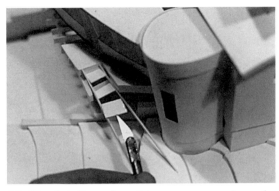

26. Site details and ancillary components such as the entry stairs can now be assembled.

27. A pilot hole is drilled in the foam core using the knife tip.

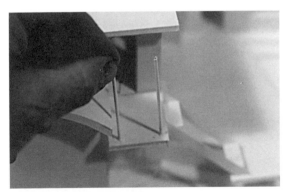

28. White plastic rods are cut and glued in the resulting sockets for canopy columns.

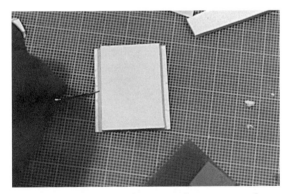

29. Foam core is cut down to the paper and scraped clean to hide the foam at the corner joints. *Note:* This can also be done by cutting joints at 45 degrees, but this technique becomes difficult to control when joints do not meet at 45 degrees.

30. The completed piece is installed over foam core wing walls and effectively covers the exposed foam edges with a clean corner connection.

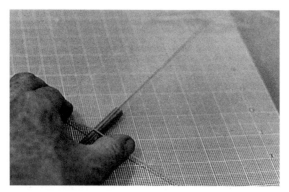

31. Plastic sheeting is cut for the window wall area by scoring with the knife and breaking over the handle.

32. Glazing mullion lines can be made by scoring with a knife or marked for the application of adhesive design tape.

33. 1/32″ wide white adhesive design tape is pulled across lines and trimmed to simulate 11/2″ mullions at 1/4″ = 1′0″ scale.

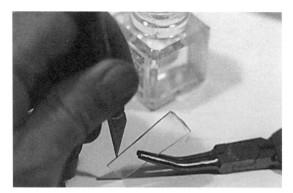

34. A very thin line of liquid acetate Plexiglas adhesive is applied with the knife edge.

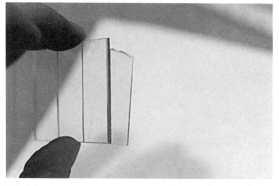

35. The two pieces are pressed together and will set, for handling purposes, in about a minute.

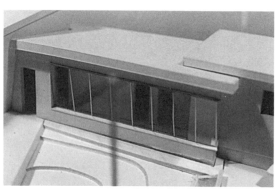

36. The completed window wall is installed in the building face.

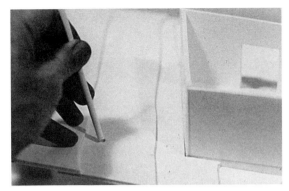

37. Large plastic rods are inserted in the site to serve as abstract trees.

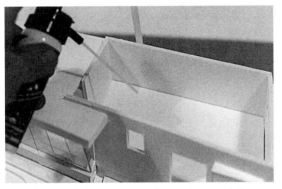

38. The model interior is cleaned out with compressed air.

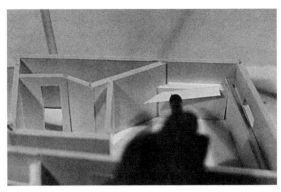

39. Interior components are then built out.

40. A set of scaled stairs is inserted into the circulation tower. *Note:* 1/8″ stacked foam core serves well as a scaled representation of 1/4″ scale tread risers at 6″ each.

41. Finally, rough interior side supports for the contours are installed. *Note:* Drafting tape is used to draw the materials tightly together until the glue can set.

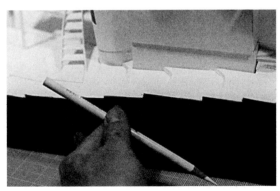

42. Finished museum board side covers are templated directly from the contours.

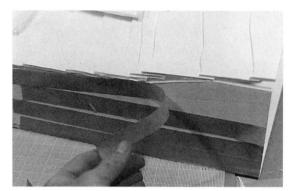

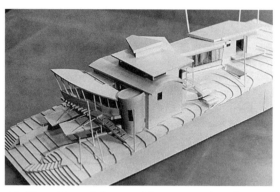

43. The sides are attached with a special adhesive transferred from a paper backing onto the material face. *Note:* Large, flat expanses of water-based glue will warp paper, spoiling the clean surfaces.

44. The sides of the model are completed. *Note:* Facing over rough cuts can convert studies to finished versions without rebuilding. See "Converting" in Chapter 2.

45. The second floor has been built so that it can be removed for a clear view of the kitchen millwork and living space. Keeping the other roofs on helps define the interior spatial qualities.

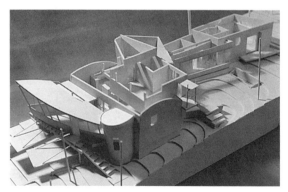

46. The rest of the model can be opened up to display various interior sections as well.

47. Construction proceeds on the project, and a 1/2" = 1'0" scale framing model is built in two sections (front section shown in the illustration) to work out all of the loading and member detailing. The model is consulted daily during the framing process.

48. The house is completed, and modeling projections can be compared.

Case Study B: Sculpture Foundry
Small-Scale Finish Model

Assembly

The model demonstrates assembly techniques for small plastic rods as well as the building of context and site.

Project

A sculpture foundry and classrooms (addition to existing facility)

Scale 1/16″ = 1′0″

A small scale is selected to accommodate the site context and minimal detailing.

Materials

- White two-ply museum board
- White plastic sticks

Illustration

The finish model is constructed both to confirm design decisions and to present to clients without the distractions of the rough assemblage.

1. Drawing information is transferred with the knife to the model base, and additional lines are drafted directly on it as required.

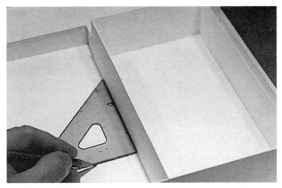

2. Lines are checked for squareness as the model proceeds and adjusted to fit the emerging construction. *Note:* Bluelines become slightly stretched when printed, and, if not checked, transferred construction lines may result in poorly fitting details.

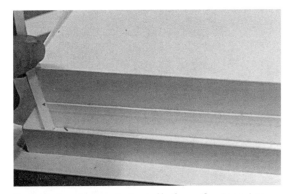

3. A gluing ledger is installed on the interior wall of the building. *Note:* The roof beyond is already showing signs of sagging due to the thin, overspanned material. The installation of reinforcing strips under the roof could have avoided this problem.

4. The knife is used to handle delicate parts.

5. The flat rooftops are placed below the wall edges. *Note:* Tweezers can help when handling small pieces.

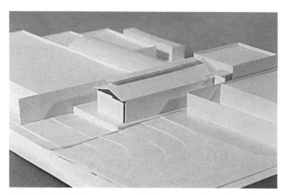

6. The initial mass model is completed, and the truss frame is detailed using thin, white plastic modeling sticks. *Note:* The accepted convention is to locate flat roofs below wall edges so the resulting parapets can be read on the model.

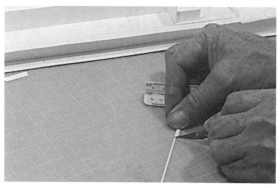

7. Small plastic sticks can be cut by pressing down on the knife. Larger sticks and rods must be scored and broken or sawed. Ends can be sanded to a clean, square finish.

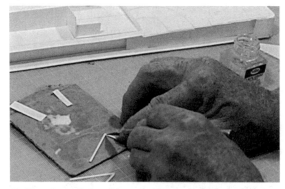

8. Plastic is joined by placing a small drop of solvent on the joint with the knife tip. *Note:* It is helpful to apply glue over a surface, such as plastic food wrap, that will not adhere to the material.

9. Truss components are glued to the paper with white glue.

10. Subsequent components are installed.

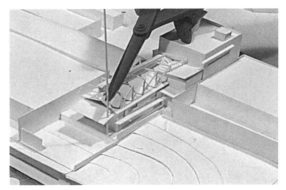

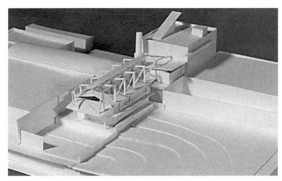

11. The exact length of additional components is measured directly from the model.

12. Scissors are useful for trimming pieces, as their pincer motion can be less disruptive to delicate constructions.

13. The small finished model, when side lit for contrasting shadows, can convey a surprisingly rich level of information.

Case Study C: Office Building

Stages 1 and 2—Sketch and Development Model

Strategy

The sketch model can be used in concert with basic scaled drawings to visualize a general design direction. Once the building begins to emerge, the model can be used as a focal point to help visualize additional moves.

Assembly

The example demonstrates techniques for constructing multiple floors and glass walls.

Project

A five-story office building.

Materials

- Poster board
- Plastic sheet for glass.

Note: For small models, thick acetate can be used, but it is not rigid enough to be convincing at larger scales.

Scale 1/32″ = 1′0″

A small scale is selected to reduce the building size for initial sketch studies.

Illustration

The model was generated using scaled schematic plans and sketches. The basic construction was then used to visualize refinements to the design.

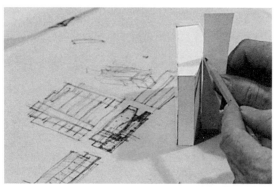

1. Scaled plan and section sketches are measured to produce initial model information. Curved pieces and other components are measured directly from the model to fit the construction. *Note:* Hot glue has been used in places for speed.

3. Additional plates are traced from the original plate to keep cuts uniform.

2. A drafted floor plate is attached to cardboard using a light coating of Spray Mount, and lines are transferred with a knife. The paper plans are then removed. *Note:* Spray Mount should be applied in a ventilated area.

4. Column centers are marked on stacked floor plates and gang drilled. *Note:* Two columns have been pierced through all four floors to hold them in place. Straight pins can be used for the same purpose.

5. Columns are passed through the floor plates. *Note:* Notches in the circulation shaft have been cut to receive the floor lines.

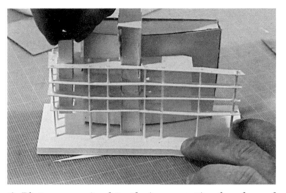

6. Plates are raised to their respective levels and inserted into the shaft slots. *Note:* Connection points are premarked on the columns. The completed unit is attached to the building; body and additional shaft elements are inserted through the floors.

7. Thin Plexiglas sheets are cut for atrium glass and covered with white art tape for mullion designs. A small steel triangle is used for scoring acetate with the knife. Plastic sheeting can be broken along scored lines. *Note:* Avoid thin acetate.

8. Plexiglas is assembled using an applicator brush.

9. The partial Plexiglas construction is fitted to the body of the building.

10. The model is used to visualize terminating roof elements.

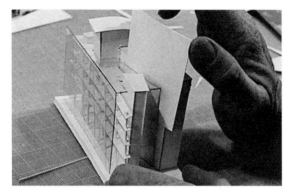

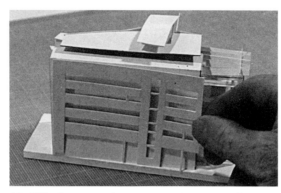

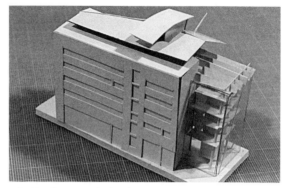

11. The Plexiglas construction is completed, and areas about to be enclosed are refaced with museum board to give the model a finished appearance. Selective parts can be recut as needed; however, refacing is generally less disruptive.

12. Window openings are cut in an overlay sheet and applied to the building face. This method is more practical than attempting to cut holes through the existing model.

13. Understated shadow lines generally read better on small models. *Note:* Additional facings can be cut and applied over all the original cuts to continue elevating the model's finish. See "Converting" in Chapter 2.

TOOLS
Equipment and Materials

This chapter presents the equipment and materials needed for making simple study and finish models.

Equipment

The following equipment includes both simple basic tools suitable for most study model construction as well as some of the more specialized tools for working with wire and other materials.

Basic Equipment

The equipment used for the majority of modeling needs is made up of a collection of basic equipment.

Expanded Equipment

Most of the equipment used for making sculptural shapes is similar to that used for other types of model making; however, several specialized tools can be helpful when working with alternative materials like wood, wire, metal sheets, and clay.

Aside from the power tools needed for woodworking, most of these tools are relatively inexpensive. For more information on woodworking and metal equipment, including hot wire, drill press, band saw, and other equipment, see "Alternative Media" in the Appendix.

Drafting tools
A set of common drawing tools used to lay out the model parts.

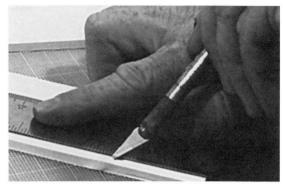

X-ACTO knife and No. 11 blades
The primary knife. Keep knife sharp with frequent blade changes. Blades are most economically purchased in packs of 100.

Steel ruler
The primary cutting edge. The ruler should have a nonslip cork backing. For economy, a wooden ruler with a metal edge can be used. Avoid aluminum rulers, as they will dull knife blades very quickly.

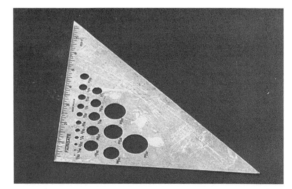

Metal triangle
Used for right-angle cuts and drafting with the knife. Unfortunately, most metal triangles are made of aluminum, but plastic triangles with steel edges can be found at some suppliers.

Scissors
For quick study models and editing cuts.

Small plastic triangle
Used to square and level model parts for accurate assembly.

Hot glue gun
For quick assembly and hard-to-glue materials like metal. Can be very messy and is not well suited for finish work.

White glue
The primary adhesive. Used to attach most paper materials. When applied properly, white glue dries quickly but allows for disassembly for experimentation.

Acetate adhesive
Used for Plexiglas. A drop on the end of a knife blade can be applied by dragging the blade along the edge of the Plexiglas.

Straight pins
Used to attach parts while glue is setting. Pins can be pulled, set for reinforcement, or cut off with side cutters.

Artist spray adhesive
Used for attaching paper surfaces that will buckle with white glue. A very light coat on plans allows them to be used as templates. Avoid hardware store adhesive sprays, as they are too strong for this use.

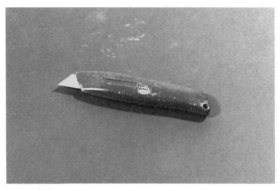

Matte knife
For cutting very thick materials. The blade thickness on this tool is not suited for fine work.

Small metal and plastic
Triangles can be used to align model parts for gluing and for making accurate modification cuts directly on the model.

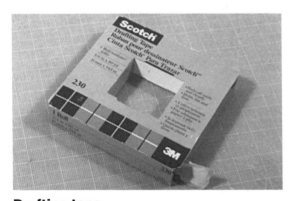

Drafting tape
Used to attach parts while glue is setting. Avoid masking tape, as it will tear paper surfaces.

Small-scale rule with end cut off
Used for taking measurements directly from the model. A scale can be drawn on a wooden stick to serve the same purpose.

Needle-nose pliers
Used for delicate work and as an inexpensive third hand.

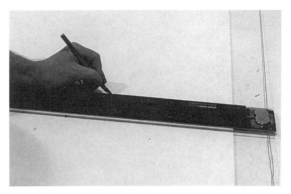

Steel-edge parallel bar
Makes cutting parts much faster. Useful for manufacturing multiple pieces of the same pattern.

Modeling saw and miter box
Used for clean cuts on small blocks and rods as well as angle cuts.

Rolling-style pizza cutter
Used for transferring drawing lines to modeling surfaces. Roll cutter along lines to leave traces in modeling material. Cutters with pointed edges work best.

Sandpaper
Sandpaper can be used to level and remove the burrs from cuts.

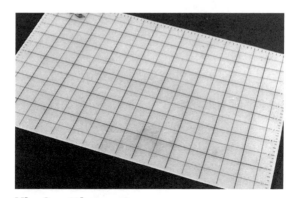

Vinyl cutting mat
Used to save drawing-board surfaces.

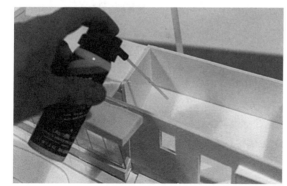

Canned compressed-air cleaner
Used for cleaning dust off models. Works well for hard-to-reach inside corners.

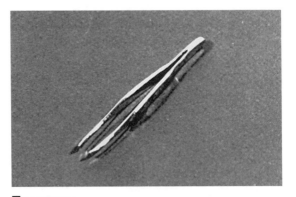

Tweezers
Used to handle delicate parts.

Electric drill and small bits
Used for gang-drilling multistory column holes in floor plates and other special holes.

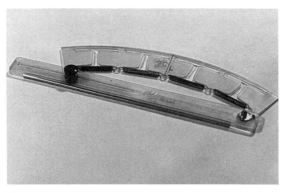

Acu arc
Used for drafting smooth, scaled curves.

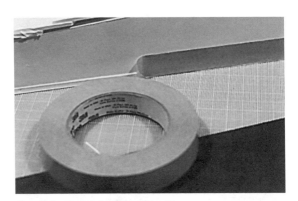

Double-faced transfer tape
Used to attach paper without the buckling tendencies of white glue.

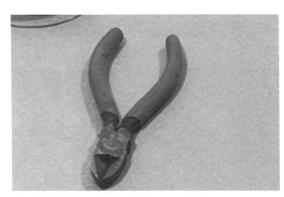

Side cutters
For cutting pins and wire.

Soldering gun
For soldering wire and metal. Guns offer high-heat power and quick heat-up. Heat wire near solder joint until wire is hot enough to melt solder when touched to joint. Use rosin core solder. Do not touch solder to gun tip.

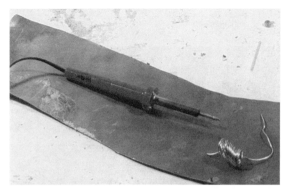

Soldering iron

Soldering irons like this one are low heat and can be used on wire but take longer to heat up. The cost is low and may be a good alternative to soldering guns.

Cutting dykes and tin snips

Dykes can be used to cut wire, and the tin snips are for cutting thin metal sheets. For very thin wire, metal scissors can be used.

Carving knives

For sculpting wood, an array of carving knives can be helpful. An inexpensive set can be used for small work on soft wood such as basswood. Larger professional knives are needed for any serious work.

Third hand

Helps hold parts for gluing, drying, and other tasks.

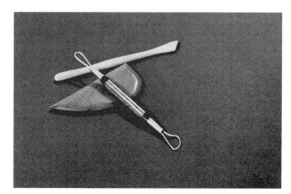

Sculpting loop and forming tools

The loop and paddles are used to work with clay and Plasticine.

Shurform

Shurforms are ideal for roughing out forms on Styrofoam blocks. They can be used on wood with limited success.

Materials

The following section describes the basic materials used for the majority of modeling tasks.

Many choices are available; however, for the purpose of this book, the primary focus is on inexpensive, easily manipulated paperboard materials.

Sculptural forms can be crafted from a variety of materials. In the case of platonic solids such as cones and spheres, conventional cardboard materials or metal sheets work well. For irregular and curvilinear forms, materials such as wood, foam, clay, wire, and plaster are more suited to the task. For additional information on working with wood, metal, and plastic, see the Appendix.

Material Considerations

- The speed with which the model is to be built

- The degree of modification and experimenting desired

- The ability of a material to hold its shape or span at scale modeling distances

- The thickness of the scaled component

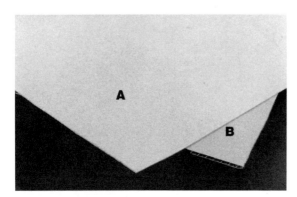

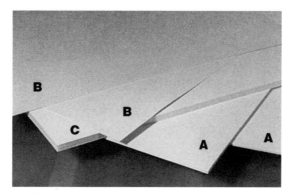

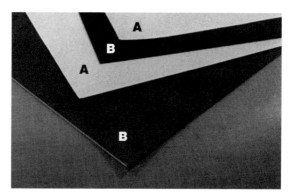

A: Gray chipboard

- Available in two- or four-ply
- Inexpensive
- Cuts easily
- Spans moderately
- Thicker plies hard to cut
- Rougher finish
- Interesting alternative to whiteboards

B: Corrugated cardboard

- Sheets are usually 1/8″ thick
- Rough finish
- Interesting alternative
- Inexpensive and cuts easily
- Spans larger spaces well
- Reflects material thickness of midsize to larger models
- Can mock textured surface if top layer is removed

A: Foam core

- Available in 1/16″, 1/8″, 3/16″, 1/2″ thicknesses
- Finished in appearance
- Cuts easily
- Suitable for large scales
- Can be matched to scale thickness

B: White museum board (Strathmore)

- Available in two-, four-, five- and six-ply thicknesses
- Finished in appearance
- Relatively expensive
- Easy to cut
- Thinner plies not suitable for large spans

C: Gatorboard

- A thick, tough board similar to foam core
- Used primarily for model bases
- Finished in appearance
- Very difficult to cut

A: Poster paper

- Similar to thin museum board
- Inexpensive
- Available at drug and office supply stores
- Reasonably finished in appearance
- Suitable for small models
- Easy to cut
- Spans poorly

B: Colored matte board

- Similar to four-ply chip board
- Takes several passes to cut
- Spans well
- Used for coding and contrast
- Edges should be mitered at 45 degrees on nonintegral color board

Note: With integral color board, the color goes all the way through and is a better alternative. The exposed white edges of nonintegral color board severely degrade model appearance.

Plastic and wood modeling sticks
Available in square and rectangular balsa or basswood shapes.

Plastic and wood dowels
Available in a variety of sizes and lengths.

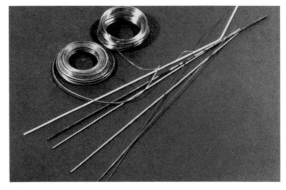

Wire

- White, plastic-coated wire
- Copper, steel, and aluminum rolls
- Straight modeling wire or "piano wire" preferred for cases where straight lines are desired

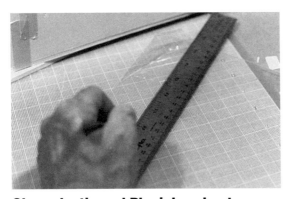

Clear plastic and Plexiglas sheets

- Used for glass simulation
- Available as thin Plexiglas from suppliers, at hobby shops, and/or as inexpensive picture framing sheets. Avoid thin acetate sheets.

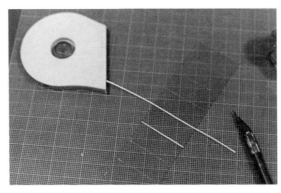

White graphic art tape

- Used for mullion simulation
- 1/32" wide and smaller

Sewing thread
Can be used to simulate cable lines or thin rods in tension.

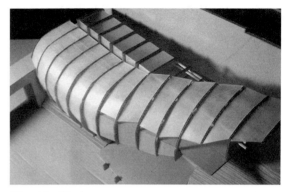

Plastic Mylar
Mylar drafting sheets can be easily cut and used for curved translucent panels.

Enamel spray paint
Spray paint can be used to paint models and wood rods. Automobile primer should be used as an undercoat on cardboard to prevent buckling.

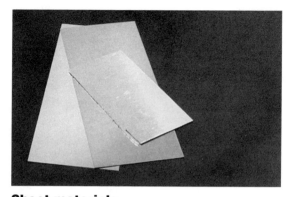

Sheet materials
Thin bronze and aluminum metal sheets can be used to make a number of special shapes.

Cloth and trace
Drawing trace or light cloth can be used to fill in planes and simulate translucent membranes. They can be curved and warped as needed.

Metal sheets
Thin metal sheets can be used to make planes and curving forms. See Appendix.

Metal screens
Metal hardware cloth and screen are useful in making compound curving shapes.

Wood modeling sheets

Wood modeling sheets come in balsa, basswood, and thin plywood. Irregular shapes can be cut from them.

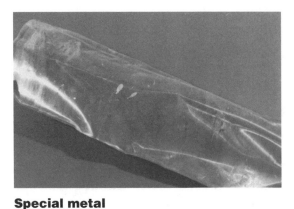

Special metal

Heavier sheets of metal can be used to form shapes. These can be obtained from aluminum and copper flashing rolls as well as from galvanized metal duct material.

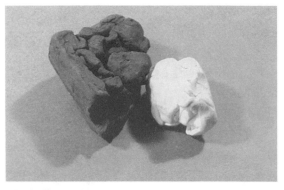

Modeling clays

Several types can be used to make sculptural forms or small massing studies. Lizella clay is the traditional clay, but Plasticine or plastic modeling clay is more useful. Sometimes Sculpey, an oven-fired clay, can serve well.

Metal rods

A variety of copper and aluminum rods can be soldered together for structural members. Aluminum wire is also useful at times, but piano wire is the most common type to be employed.

Poured and spread liquids

Several types of casting and liquid-based form-building materials are available. The most common is molding plaster. Papier-mâché made from diluted white glue is useful, as well as Rockite mix.

Cut and carved and shapes

Simple wood and Styrofoam blocks can provide the basic massing to cut and carve a variety of shapes from them.

Found objects

Found objects can be used as a basis to modify the forms. Drinking cups, cardboard tubes, and Styrofoam and rubber balls, as well as packing forms, are just a few of the things that can be used.

Found objects

Found objects can be used to combine with other objects. A partial list would include old tools and utensils, household items, and electronic parts.

Tree material

Round Styrofoam balls.

Tree material

Small dried flowering plants or yarrow trees.

Tree material

Lichen sold as modeling material or found in sandy areas.

Tree material

Paper and Styrofoam layers.

241

Tree material
Wood or plastic dowels.

Tree material
Dense foam used to make flower-arranging bases and also sold at model supply shops.

APPENDIX

Topics for Continuing Exploration

This appendix provides further information concerning alternative media, transferring model dimensions, photography, and detailed presentation models.

Alternative Media

Most of the models in this book have been made with paperboard materials. These materials are valued for being inexpensive, quick to assemble, and easy to modify. As such, they are ideal for the majority of study models; however, there are situations in which it is advantageous to use wood, metal, plastic, and plaster in model making.

These media can be combined as an expedient way to construct components or employed for expressive purpose. Although they may not completely reflect the behavior of full-scale components, they may provide a better understanding of material properties.

The use of these materials has been touched on in the previous chapters, and although a detailed treatment is beyond the scope of this book, the following sections augment earlier information on material choices and equipment used to work with them.

Plastic and Foam

For plastic materials such as Plexiglas, the tools applicable to working with wood can be used effectively. Plexiglas can be cut with table or band saws, and belt sanders can be used to smooth and shape edges. If clear, polished edges are desired, a strong electric wheel is required. Grit compounds for buffing can be purchased in gradated degrees of coarseness and applied to the wheel in three applications. Starting with coarse grit compound and moving from medium to fine, edges can be buffed to a clear, smooth finish.

Polystyrene is a dense foam suited to cutting and shaping to make quick sculptural forms. Blocks or sheets can be laminated together with contact cement or construction glue to create larger pieces. Although the material can be cut with hand or power saws and shaped with a Shurform tool, a hot wire cutter can make shaping more accurate. The wire cutter uses a tightly strung, heated wire to slice through the foam. The pieces can be guided by hand or held steady by mechanical guides similar to those found on a table saw. Some types of foam can then be sanded to even out surface variations.

Polystyrene model
The blocks of foam that make up this model have been cut with a hot wire and sanded smooth.

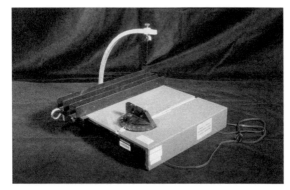

Hot cutting wire
Equipment heats a thin wire so foam can be pushed through it to cut like a band saw.

Wood

Constructions made from wood are often built as finely crafted presentation models. For this level of finish, books found at the end of this chapter are good sources of information. However, for study models and simple presentation constructions, there are many uses for wood. For massing models and sculptural shapes, wood blocks can be cut quickly with a band saw and sanded smooth with a belt sander (see "Cut and Carved Forms" in Chapter 8). Balsa sheets and sticks also can be used to produce finish constructions with simple equipment as shown to the right.

Materials

For simple models, wood sticks and soft wood scraps work well. Woods with an even grain structure and a degree of softness such as mahogany or basswood (ironically, classed as hardwoods) are the preferred materials for high-level finish models. Many of these materials can be found at hobby or modeling supply stores; however, for larger blocks of mahogany and basswood, a hardwood lumber supplier is the most likely source. Large blocks can also be made by glue-laminating smaller ones together.

Dimensional Modeling Sticks

- Balsa: Inexpensive and cuts easily

- Basswood: More expensive, but holds form better than balsa, and ends can be sanded with accuracy

- Mahogany: Often used for rich color with similar qualities to basswood

- Oak dowels: Must be sawn for clean cuts

Sheets

- Balsa wood sheets: Finished appearance, cuts easily, spans well, and reflects material thickness of smaller to midsized models

- Modeling plywood: Similar properties to balsa; can be cut with a power saw or can be rough cut with a mat knife and sanded smooth

Wood blocks

- Balsa

- Bass wood

- Mahogany

- Pine, spruce, cedar, fir: Common soft woods used in residential construction and entirely adequate for study models

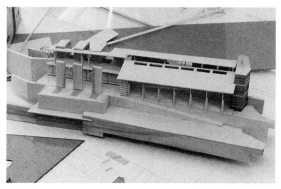

Wood model
The planes for these models are typical of what can be made from thin basswood sheets and modeling plywood.

Wood model
The curved planes of the model were made from thin plywood sheets. The sheets were bent by soaking them in hot water and then locking them into position with clamps until dry.

Woodworking Equipment

For balsa sheets and all sticks, simple X-ACTO knives and modeling hand saws can be used. All other wood materials (especially blocks) will require power tools or carving knives.

The basic power equipment needed to work with wood includes a table saw, band saw, and some form of belt sander. These can be inexpensive tools, as the wood is relatively soft and cuts will probably be small.

For sculptural shapes, power tools can be used to rough the shapes. Carving tools and power sanders can be used to finish the shapes.

Table saw
An inexpensive table saw with an 8-in. blade. On low-end saws such as this, the rip fence is inaccurate and must be checked with a square. *Note:* Avoid small modeling table saws, as they are very underpowered.

Belt sander
Hand-held home construction types or premounted units can be used for model sanding work. Shown is a hand-held type. It can be mounted with homemade clamps or with an aftermarket bracket.

Drill press and hand drill
In making inexpensive models, a drill press can be useful. Alternately, a hand drill can be mounted on an aftermarket stand and used as a substitute until use of a drill press is warranted.

Hand-held Jig Saw
This type of saw can be used for rough cuts and limited curved cuts. It is wise to compare the power ratings on jigsaws, as many inexpensive saws can cut only the thinnest of materials.

Band saw
Shown is a minimally sized, two-wheel saw. *Note:* Avoid inexpensive three-wheel band saws. Because of tight wheel radiuses, they break blades regularly.

Metal

Models are rarely constructed entirely from metal; however, rods, wire, and shaped planes can be very useful as component pieces.

Materials

Many of these materials can be found as common items in hardware stores. Small rods and tubes, as well as sheets of aluminum and bronze, are available at most hobby and modeling shops. Heavy-gauge metal can be purchased at a metal supply yard.

Thin Sheets

- Aluminum and galvanized flashing
- Galvanized metal
- Copper, bronze, and aluminum modeling sheets
- Screen wire aluminum, bronze, and fiberglass
- Hardware cloth with holes from 1/8" to 1/2"

Wire, Rods, and Tubes

- Copper, brass, and steel wire
- White plastic-coated wire
- Copper, brass rods and tubes
- Coat hangers
- Heavy-gauge steel and aluminum wire
- Reinforcing bars

Aluminum Shapes

- Rods
- Round and square tubes
- Angles

Heavier Gauge Metal

- Rods
- Square stock
- Plate steel
- Angles

Fabrication Equipment

Cutting, connecting, and bending heavier metal parts can be involved.

Connecting

For small rods and plates, joints can be soldered or, in some cases, hot glued. For larger pieces, bolted or welded connections are required.

Welding on thin metal with arc welding equipment tends to burn holes in the metal very quickly. For best results, use a small metal inert gas (MIG) welding unit (recently available at reasonable prices). These units feed a thin wire from a spool to serve as a constant welding rod and are easy to use. They are also surprisingly portable and have low power requirements. Thin metal can also be brazed with oxyacetylene torches and spot welded.

Note: Without more specialized equipment, aluminum cannot be welded.

Cutting

For small rods and plates, hacksaws and tin snips can be used. Cutting of thicker metals, other than those for which tin snips are applicable, can sometimes be accomplished with metal-cutting abrasive wheels used in a circular saw or in an electric miter box. Metal blades in a powerful jigsaw or Sawzall can be effective for cutting sheet metal up to 1/16".

For heavy cutting, equipment beyond what is common to most model shops is required. These include oxyacetylene torches, power hacksaws, nibblers, metal-cutting band saws, plasma torches, and shears.

Bending

Thin sheets and wire rods can be easily curved and bent by hand. Some pieces can be held in a vise and bent with pliers or hammers. Anything thicker will require special equipment and is usually not used.

However, for those interested in bending thick metal:

- It is necessary to heat large solid rods with an oxyacetylene torch before bending.
- Thick metal sheets require the use of a "bending brake."
- Structural shapes such as tubes and angles must be passed through a rolling mill.

Plaster

Material

Molding plaster, also referred to as *hydrocal,* is available in small cartons at hardware stores or in 100-lb. bags at Sheetrock supply stores. Be sure to specify "molding" plaster, as other varieties are prone to shrink excessively when drying.

Tools

Once plaster has cured, it can be sanded, cut, and carved similarly to wood with many of the same tools such as Shurforms, sandpaper, carving knives, chisels, and bandsaws.

Mixing Plaster

For small batches, one-gallon plastic buckets, plastic containers, and cut-down milk jugs make excellent mixing bowls. For larger batches, five-gallon paint and Sheetrock buckets serve well. Plaster is mixed in a ratio of about two parts plaster to one part water. This means, for any container, it should start just about one-third full of water. It is also helpful to leave some room in the container for adjusting the mix. Plaster is then shaken into the water in a sifting manner until an island of plaster begins to form on top of the water. At this point, the solution is mixed by hand until all lumps are smoothed out. The mix should be about the consistency of pudding or thinner for coating tasks. For papier mâché–like applications, the mix should be runny. With practice, you will be able to get the proportions right using this method, but until then, the mix can be thickened by adding plaster or thinned with more water.

The working time until plaster begins to set is about 10 to 20 minutes, so it is best to mix quickly to allow time for application. If you work fast enough, successive batches of plaster can be mixed in the same container without cleaning it. However, once a batch has begun to harden in the container, it can no longer be used, as lumps will be carried into the new mix.

Using cold water can retard the setting time, while warm water will speed it up. Plaster will set hard, if the mix is made correctly, in a matter of 30 to 40 minutes. Additional layers can be built on top of a first layer of plaster right away but must sit for a number of hours before water has evaporated sufficiently to allow sanding.

Clean Up

Containers must be cleaned of residual plaster before reusing. If left to dry in a flexible plastic container, plaster can be popped out. To wash containers, use a bucket of water so waste plaster can settle to the bottom and be thrown out later. All plaster should be put in trash cans and never down the sink, as it will settle and block plumbing drains.

Anchoring Cement

Anchoring cement is a good alternative to plaster and is commonly available. It is much stronger than plaster and in many cases will not require models to be internally reinforced with wire.

Transferring Model Data

Measuring Models to Locate Two-Dimensional Drawing Dimensions

Projects that have been executed completely in model form can be measured and translated into two-dimensional drawings by the following methods.

How to Measure

Points of intersection in space are measured with the scale rule as X, Y, and Z dimensions from a base plane and two 90-degree reference lines. It is helpful to buy or construct a small-scale rule suited to the delicacy of the work. Make sure that the base of the ruler begins at 0'0".

The triangle is used to mark the height of the intersection above the table plane. The triangle also helps locate the correct point on the measuring rod directly over (normal to) the edge of the reference grid below. See the section on Morrow Library in Chapter 4.

Alternately, designers increasingly employ digitizing equipment similar to that used for aerospace design. A digitizer is placed at the desired points on the model, and XYZ coordinate readings are automatically recorded to generate drawings (see Chapter 5).

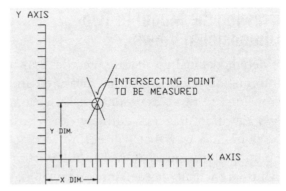

Measuring the model
The ruler is extended out 90 degrees from the reference grid to mark the X dimension of a point. The height is marked on the triangle, then the ruler is swung 90 degrees to record the Y dimension.

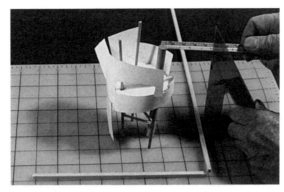

Plan view
This view is looking down on the point to be measured. The X and Y axes correspond to the edge of the grid. The X and Y dimensions would be transferred and noted for their height above the plane of the measuring surface.

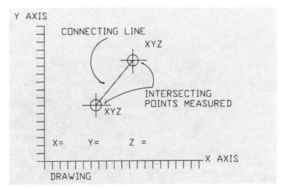

Drawing
The XYZ coordinates are located on the plan drawing. Lines between the points are connected to describe the form in plan. *Note:* Z coordinates can be shown only on elevations and sections but should be noted on plans.

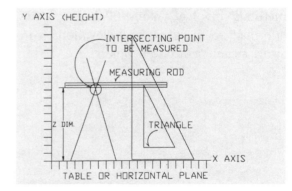

Elevation
The height (Z axis) of the point to be measured should be marked on the triangle. *Note:* The triangle also helps maintain a 90-degree relationship between the reference grid and the measuring rod.

Drawing the Model in Two-Dimensional Views

When modeling information precedes drawn information, models must be measured and converted to two-dimensional plan, section, and elevation drawings. Although this must be done in a way that will ensure accurate building dimensions, only key intersecting points are actually needed for construction.

Plotting every point needed to draw complex geometries can be a time-consuming process. Accurate numbers must be used for intersections, but shortcuts can be employed to draw reasonably accurate images of the model for visualization purposes and to show elevation details.

Two common low-tech methods for converting models to plan and sectional drawings are shown on the right. Both of these methods involve taking 90-degree views, "normal" to the plans and elevations, with either a camera or photocopier.

Photographing
Models can be photographed "face on" and traced from enlarged prints.

Copying
Models can be placed directly on the glass of a copy machine to make elevation images. See the Morrow Library in Chapter 4.

Photographed plan view
The warped planes of this model are difficult to fully measure. By reducing them to a plan view, they can be drawn with a degree of accuracy and ease.

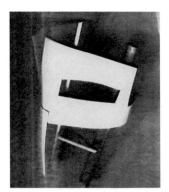

Photocopied image
The resultant photo copied images can be traced and scaled. They will be somewhat distorted, but the directly measured XYZ coordinates will ensure construction accuracy.

Model Photography
Photography Techniques

Although detailed information on quality digital shutter speeds and lens openings is limited, the following guidelines can produce acceptable results using a quality digital camera. It is highly advisable to photograph models as soon as they are finished, as time quickly takes its toll on these constructions. Automatic settings can be used, but with manual capability, understanding exposure options can be useful.

Exposure Openings

Images tend to remain focused in foreground and background areas (depth of field) at a smaller lens opening, about F8 to F16. White models can bounce so much light off of their surfaces that light meters often call for openings smaller than required. It is wise to test the meter reading with a neutral gray surface. Moreover, for the best insurance against the variables of artificial light sources, it is important to bracket your shots (take exposures above and below the meter readings).

Shutter Speeds

Fast shutter speeds are used to stop action. This is rarely needed with model photography. However, slow shutter speeds, about one-fifteenth of a second all the way to 1 second, allow models to be photographed in low light conditions including artificial lighting. Automatic settings may not slow down enough to work well with artificial lighting.

Outdoor Lighting

Shooting outdoors is the easiest solution to lighting. The camera will tend to read lighting conditions correctly, low-speed film can be used, and automatic cameras are effective. A calm, sunny day with the sun at a lower angle in the sky (early or late in the day) produces the best modeling shadows. Experiment by turning the model around and watching through the lens as different shadows are cast.

Day lighting
High-contrast lighting effects can be captured on very clear days with lower afternoon or morning sun angles.

Shaded day lighting
Even light can be obtained in outdoor settings on overcast days or in large shaded areas.

Day lighting
The sun can be used for medium contrast as well, by avoiding extremely clear conditions and working closer to midday. Models should be turned in the sun to find optimum shadow angles.

Indoor Lighting

Lighting can be accomplished by using a single photo flood lamp. The use of a single source of light will allow you to simulate the shadow-casting effects of the sun. Light can also be bounced off a white board to soften its effects and control the way it hits the model. For even lighting, two lights can be placed on opposite sides of the model. The light source must be out of the camera eye, preferably behind it to avoid hot spots.

You can also photograph the model indoors, using daylight from a north-facing bank of windows, with a tripod and very slow shutter speeds. The camera can be hand held down to shutter speeds of about one-fifteenth of a second using a steady hand or something to brace against. Shutter speeds cannot usually be controlled on inexpensive, automatic cameras.

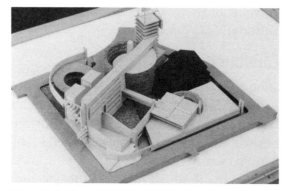

Day lighting
Models can be photographed indoors with sufficient daylight. North-facing clerestory windows work well to avoid unwanted mullion shadows and provide plenty of light. Slow shutter speeds are recommended.

Grazing light on the model
A single-source lamp can be used from below to graze light across the model. The light can be bounced off of white sheets or covered with cloth to soften harsh effects.

Even lighting
Using two light sources placed slightly in front and to either side of the model provides an evenly lighted surface.

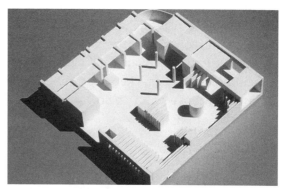

Single-source light
Strong shadow patterns that make the forms read as sculptural objects can be created by using a single light. For best results, turn the model and move the light to experiment with shadow angles.

Views

Models can be photographed from many angles, depending on what one wishes to communicate. Overall or bird's-eye views can convey a sense of the total building. Low views, shot up into the model, can give the effect of being on the site looking up at the building. A model scope (a special device like a small periscope that can be fitted to the camera) can be used to photograph interior views and help capture eye-level views. Special extension tubes and other lens devices can also be made to bring the camera eye down into the model at less expense.

Models can be photographed "straight on" to eliminate as much perspective as possible and to create images similar to elevation drawings. These views can be useful as tracing guides to produce orthographic drawings from models, as discussed in "Transferring Model Data" in the preceding section.

The sculptured or modeled view is probably the most common used for capturing the overall geometry of a model as a three-dimensional object.

At eye level
The eye-level view is taken at a height of a scaled figure to simulate the view of a person moving through the space.

Bird's-eye
The bird's-eye view is taken looking down on the model and provides an overall picture of a complex or object.

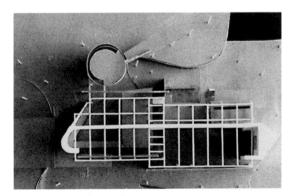

Plan/elevation view
This view is a frontal shot taken 90 degrees to the model plane. Images of this type simulate orthogonal drawing views and can be used to convert model views to plan drawings by tracing over them.

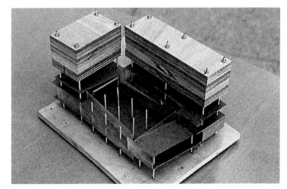

Sculptural view
The sculptural view is similar to the bird's-eye view but taken from lower angles to display the three-dimensional quality of the forms.

Backgrounds

A smooth, regular-textured background with some tonal contrast to the model such as chipboard, black cloth, or brown Kraft paper can work well. Clean, even surfaces such as concrete or carpet can serve as backgrounds out of doors, as long as there is enough area to keep the edges out of the camera frame.

Several ideas are shown to help illustrate how backgrounds can work, ranging from the natural sky to gray backdrop paper.

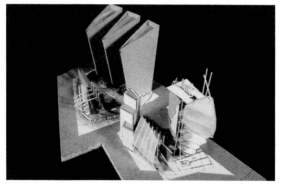

Black contrasting backdrop
For light-colored models, dark backdrops such as black cloth or backdrop paper can be used to highlight tones. For dark models, light paper can be used.

Blue paper
The outdoor sky can be easily simulated with blue paper placed behind the model.

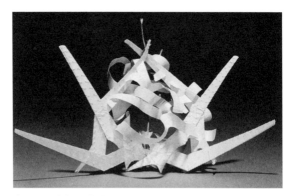

Curved backdrop
Although dark backdrop paper or cloth can completely negate the background, gray and white paper, placed under the model and rolled up the wall, will create a smooth gradation of tones.

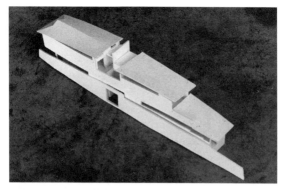

Natural, even surface
A concrete floor, sidewalk, carpet, or other even-toned surface can be used as a neutral background. Light surfaces should be sought for dark models and dark ones for light constructions.

Natural sky
The outdoor sky can be used by placing the model on a ledge and shooting into the model at an angle that will crop out all other background objects. This works best facing north in order to avoid glare from the sun.

Digital Media

Over the past 15 years, visual communication has employed digital media as an integral part of the design process. This has produced a quantum expansion in the way drawings, photographs, and graphics can be brought together.

It should be noted that with these new tools come drawbacks, but as a rule, the advantages are well worth the limitations.

Digital Cameras

The digital camera is an integral part of digital media.

Cameras range from snapshot models to high-end professional equipment, with prices starting around $100 and escalating to well over $2,000 for professional cameras and lenses. For best results, single-lens reflex (SLR) cameras with manual capability should be used. Canon and Nikon are common brands making high-quality SLR cameras. As of this writing, good-quality SLR cameras can be purchased for $500 to $1,000.

Model Documentation

Camera Settings

Resolution

The camera should be set to give the highest-quality image available. Lower-quality settings can save camera memory, but the trade-off will be very poor images when trying to enlarge work. Images for emailing and other low-resolution purposes can be reduced in size after downloading and copying.

Compression

Compression removes duplicate information and fills it in with similar information later. This produces a glossing over of the image. The lowest (or least) compression setting possible should be used. Most cameras can be set to take raw files (no compression), but the file will become inordinately large and translation software will have to be used to convert the image.

Manual Settings

Automatic settings may provide acceptable results, but the camera shutter speed will seldom slow down sufficiently for low-light conditions on automatic. Assuming your camera has the option of manual controls, they should be mastered and used.

Flash/Lighting

Using a direct camera flash as a light source produces poor images. Unless you are taking process documentation shots, such as study model records, the flash should be turned off. Day lighting or photo floods should be used as an alternate source. *Note:* An external flash can be used if it is bounced off the ceiling or a reflector, but this can be difficult to control and usually requires a high-end camera with a flash shoe.

Light Readings

A further refinement can be made by using a gray card when taking light readings. Alternately, the images can be bracketed with the manual control to ensure correct exposure.

Steadying the Camera

Low and artificial lighting conditions require the camera to be mounted on a tripod. Since most midrange models do not have a cable release adapter, care must be taken to depress the camera button with even pressure.

Viewing the Image

Non-SLR cameras suffer from the phenomenon referred to as parallax. That is, things seen through the view finder shift as you get closer to them, making it necessary to line up shots in the monitor. This technique can work well; however, out of doors, the monitor is hard to see.

Photo Montage

Illustration

The board below shows a presentation made by using layers created by software such as Photoshop or InDesign. The boards on the far right show some of the possibilities of montage techniques.

Image to be cut out

This image was taken in the studio setting and includes distracting background elements. Photoshop or other imaging software can be used to mask or remove the background entirely.

Photo montage

Computer renderings can be enhanced and combined with scanned images of figures and objects to convey a virtual image of space.

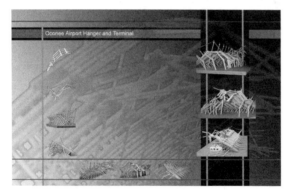

Layered images

Drawings and photographs can be cut out of backgrounds, imported, and scaled. Each type of information (text, graphics, images, etc.) is placed on a different layer. Each layer can be manipulated for color and transparency. Layered images can be moved on top of each other, and large background images can provide visual connections to relate all the elements. When completed, layers can be flattened to make a single file.

Image with background cut

The background of the image above has been replaced with black by cutting out everything around the model base. To produce the image on the right, the background has been removed around the outline of the building image.

Photo montage

Photographs of the physical models can be combined with photographs of the site to place buildings in their physical settings. Work must be done to make a convincing fit.

Resources
Modeling Books

The following books offer information concerning architectural models as a conceptual approach and the making of presentation models. Several of the ones listed are now out of print but usually can be found used on Amazon.com or other web sites.

Mark Morris, *Models: Architecture and the Miniature* (New York: John Wiley & Sons, 2006).

Wolfgang Knoll and Martin Hechinger, *Architectural Models, Construction Techniques,* 2nd ed. (New York: McGraw-Hill, 2007).

Fredrick Kurrent, *Scale Models: Houses of the 20th Century* (Translated from German into English: Gail Schamberger-Basel; Boston; Berlin: Birkhauser, 1999, out of print).

Akiko Busch, *The Art of the Architectural Model* (New York: Design Press, 1991, out of print).

Sanford Hohauser, *Architectural and Interior Models,* 2nd ed. (New York: Van Nostrand Reinhold, 1982, 1993, out of print).

Computer Modeling Books

For further research, the books listed below discuss computer modeling and various approaches to it. A few of these may be out of print at this writing but can also be found used on Amazon.com or other web sites.

Lisa Iwamoto, *Digital Fabrications: Architectural and Material Techniques* (New York, Princeton Architectural Press, 2009).

Kostas Terzidis, *Algorithmic Architecture* (Burlington, MA: Elsevier Ltd., 2006).

Greg Lynn, *Folds, Bodies and Blobs: Collected Essays* (Bruelles: La Lettre Vole, 1998).

Greg Lynn and Hani Rashid, *Architecture Laboratories* (New York: Distributed Art Publishers, 2002).

Greg Lynn, *Folding in Architecture* (New York: Academy Editions, 1993).

Computer Modeling Programs

3D Studio Max, Revit
Company: Autodesk
www.autodesk.com

Maya
Company: Autodesk
www.autodesk.com

TriForma
Company: Bentley
www.bentley.com

Form Z
Company: Autodessys
www.autodessys.com
www.formz.com

Rhinoceros
Company: RSI 3D systems and software
www.rhino3d.com

Google SketchUp
Company: Google SketchUp
www.sketchup.google.com

Rhino Rendering
Company: Rhinoceros
www.Rhino3d.com

Brazil
Company: Robert McNeel & Associates
www.brazil.mcneel.com

V-Ray
Company: Visual Dynamics
www.vray.com

MEL
Company: Audodesk
www.usa.autodesk.com

Generative Components GC
Company: Bentley
www.bentley.com

Grasshopper
Company: Grasshopper
www.grasshopper3d.com

Vectorworks
Company: Nemetschek
www.nemetschek.net

Flamingo
Company: Flamingo
www.flamingo3d.com

Penguin
Company: Penguin
www.penguin3d.com

Design Software

Photoshop and InDesign CS
www.adobe.com
1-800-833-6687

QuarkExpress
www.quark.com
1-800-676-4574

Digital Cameras

Nikon Cameras
www.nikonusa.com

Canon Cameras
www.powershot.com

Rapid Prototyping Services

ProtoCam
www.protocam.com
Services: Stereolithography (SLA)
Selective Laser Sintering (SLS)

Quickparts
www.quickparts.com
Services: Stereolithography (SLA),
Selective Laser Sintering (SLS),
Fused Deposition Modeling (FDM)

CTEK, LLC1402 Morgan Circle
Tustin, CA 92710
Services: 5 Axis Computer Numerically Controlled Milling, CNC Modeling

Rojac
www.rojac.com
Services: 5 Axis Computer Numerically Controlled Milling, CNC Modeling

Rapid Prototyping Equipment

Z Corporation
20 North Avenue Burlington, MA 01803
www.zcorp.com
Equipment: Powder printers

3D Systems
333 Three D Systems Circle Rockhill, SC 29730
www.3dsystems.com
Equipment: Multi-Jet Modeling (MJM),
5 Axis, Computer Numerically Controlled Milling, CNC Modeling
V-Flash Desktop Modeler

Stratasys Inc.
14950 Martin Dr., Eden Prairie, MN 55344-2019
www.stratasys.com
Equipment: Fused Deposition Modeler (FDM)
5 Axis, CNC Modeling

Sanders Prototype Inc.
P.O. Box 540 Pine Valley Mill, Wilton, NH 03086
www.sanders-prototype.com
Equipment: Stereolithography (SLA)

Supply Sources

Most of the basic modeling supplies can be purchased at local art supply stores or campus bookstores. If stores are not available in your area, several chain stores sell through the mail. Two well-known stores are Charrette and Dick Blick.

Charrette

31 Olympia Avenue
Box 4010
Woburn, MA 01888-9820
1-800-367-3729
Email Custserv@charrette.com

Dick Blick Art Materials

P.O. Box 1267695
US Highway 150 East
Galesburg, IL 61402
1-800-447-8192

Many of the materials used in model making can be found in hobby shops and hardware stores. These include lichen and model trees, wood and plastic sticks, balsa, basswood sheets, modeling plywood, metal rods, bronze and aluminum modeling sheets, small metal parts, sandpaper, molding plaster, Perma Scene, and spray paint.

Plastic sheets for windows can be found at Plexiglas suppliers. Thin plastic cover sheets or inexpensive picture frames can also be used. Sheets of acetate can be purchased at art supply stores and are usually available in several thicknesses.

Some of the more specialized drafting and cutting equipment, such as Acu-Arcs, can be found at architectural printing companies and through Charrette.

Common wood, such as pine, spruce, and plywood, can be purchased at building supply stores. Blocks of hardwood, such as basswood, poplar, and mahogany, can be found at hardwood building suppliers.

A range of metal components such as aluminum tubes and angle iron can be found at hardware stores. Steel supply yards will be the likely source for square stock, steel rods, and heavy-gauge sheets.

Sheet metal suppliers that stock metal ductwork, flashing, and gutter materials can be good sources for rolls of copper and galvanized sheets.

Large quantities of molding plaster in 90-lb. bags can be found at drywall supply houses.

The following people have contributed models and built work to the text and are credited for their contribution to the diversity and strength of its contents.

Academic Architecture Programs
The Catholic University, School of Architecture and Planning
Studio Critics: Christina Cole, Sophia Gruzdys

Francisco Lopez de Arenosa—page 7, top left; page 39, bottom left.

Studio Critic: Louis Boza

Page 34, top right; page 39, top left, top middle; page 48, top left; page 127, bottom left; page 129, bottom right; page 130, bottom middle, bottom right; page 131, bottom middle, bottom right; page 134, top middle, top right, bottom left, bottom middle, bottom right; page 135, bottom left, bottom right; page 136, top left.

Clemson University, College of Architecture, Arts & Humanities
Studio Critic: Robert Bruhns

Graduate 1 design: Nic Fonner, Will Wingfield—page 25, bottom left.

Studio Critic: Lynn Craig

Page 15, bottom left; page 43, top right.

Studio Critic: Ted Cavanagh

Heather Bachman—page 5, bottom right.

Studio Critic: Keith Green

Graduate 3 design: Jim Graham—page 133, top right.

March Thesis studio design: Steven Kendall Keutzer—page 203, bottom right.

Studio Critic: Harry Harritos

First-year studio: Michael Brown—page 22, bottom left.

Third-year studio: Kevin Kievit—page 12, top right.

Studio Critic: Douglas Hecker

Graduate 3 design: Gregory Swinton—page 125, bottom left.

Fourth-year design: Shannon Vermeulen—page 21, bottom right.

Studio Critics: Ulrike Hiene and Dan Harding

Graduate 1 design: Adam James, Jake DeMint—page 42, top left; page 136, bottom left.

Kyle Keaffaber, Jonathan Edens—page 190, bottom right; page 202, bottom right. Tara Walsh, Lindsay Waters—page 48, top right, bottom right; page 57, bottom left; page 69, top middle, top right, bottom left, bottom middle, bottom right.

Fourth-year design: Virginia Black, Adie Hailat—page 66, right; page 70, top middle, top right, bottom left, bottom middle, bottom right.

Studio Critic: Ray Huff

Grad-1: Shane Knight—page 12, top left; page 15, top left.

Studio Critic: David Lee

Second-year design: page 121, top middle, bottom left, bottom middle, bottom right; page 136, top right.

Studio Critic: Robert Miller

MARCH graduate thesis: Rob Moehring—page 245, bottom right. David Jones—page 49, top left. Joshua Allison, Brian Couch, Nikos Katsibas, Kim Kraft, Thomas Reidy—page 14, bottom right.

Grad 1: Kenneth Huggins, Sonia Alvarado, Trifon Dinkov, Bill D'Onofrio, Chris Karpus, Ansely Manuel, Bart Shorack, page 14, top left. Sallie Hambright—page 37, top left.

Studio Critic: Criss Mills

Second-year design: Jason Butz—page 191, bottom left; page 192, bottom right. Joseph Hall—page 191, bottom middle. Gloria Hamm—page 42, bottom middle. Trevor Jordan—page 34, bottom left. Sara Moore—page 52, top left, top right, bottom left, bottom right. Erica Morrison—page 186, top middle. Robert Neel—page 42, bottom left. Ryan Ramsey—page 122, top left, top right; page 189, bottom middle. Puja Vachhani—page 13, bottom right. Shannon Vermeulen—page 4, bottom left.

Graduate 2 design: Lauren Culp—page 62, top left; page 73, top left, top right, bottom left, bottom right; page 187, top left. Adie Hailat—page 4, top left; page 20, top left; page 49, top right, bottom right; page 53 top middle; page 59, top left, bottom left. Blake Hoffman—page 53, top left. Patrick Lee—page 9, bottom left, bottom middle; page 11, bottom right; page 20, bottom right; page 53 top right. Aaron Swiger—page 4, bottom right; page 9, top right; page 38, top left, top right, bottom left, bottom right; page 48, top middle, bottom middle; page 57, top left; page 192, top right. Aaron Swiger, Stephen Troutman—page 206, bottom right. Stephen Troutman—page 21, bottom middle. Barak Yaryan—page 20, bottom left; page 60, bottom middle. Lauren Culp, Adie Hailat, Blake Hoffman, Patrick Lee, Kaitlyn Mooney, Kyle Miller, Carson Nolan, Mililian Scott, Lori Sons, Aaron Swiger—page 74, top left, top right, bottom; page 75, top left, top middle, top right, bottom left, bottom middle, bottom right.

Building Technology: Nick Barrett—page 189, bottom left; page 201, bottom left. Carla Landa—page 25, top middle; page 189, top middle. Elizabeth Miraziz—page 25, top right. Sarah Woodard—page 191, top right.

Graduate 3 design: Katherine Dixon—page 4, bottom middle; top middle; page 72 top right, bottom left, bottom middle, bottom right; page 19, bottom left. Annette Himilick—page 13, bottom middle; page 42, top middle; page 71, top middle, top right, bottom left, bottom middle, bottom right. Kate Sedor—page 42, right; page 205, top right. Harrison Wallace—page 19, bottom right.

Third-year design: Gabriella Bumgartner—page 36, top right, bottom right. Clay Montgomery—page 9, bottom right; page 55, bottom left; page 190, top middle.

Second-year studio: Michael Brown—page 24, bottom right; page 26, top left. Joe McCoy—page 256, top right. Frayssee Lyle—page 46, top right, bottom right.

Studio Critics: Criss Mills and Harry Harritos

Third-year design: Jenny Schildecker—page 241, top left; Betty Prime—page 187, top middle; page 239, bottom middle.

Studio Critics: Criss Mills, Robert Hogan, and Martha Skinner

Third-year studio: Glen Timmons—page 51, top middle, bottom middle.

Liza Lewellan—page 51, top right, bottom right.

Studio Critic: Kemp Money

Grad 1 design: Thad Rhoden, Lindsey Sabo, Yuko Murata—page 24, top right.

Studio Critic: Ron Real

Second year design: Knox Jolly—page 190, bottom left.

Studio Critics: Kris Scheerlink and Jose Miguel Rolda'n

Third-year design: Joseph Tucker and team BAC—page 200, bottom left.

Studio Critic: Martha Skinner

Fourth-year design: Johanna McCrehan—page 54, bottom left. Clay Montgomery—page 55, top left.

Studio Critic: Franca Tribiano

Grad 1 design: Christopher Palkowitsch—page 54, top right.

Florida International University, School of Architecture
Studio Critic: Rene Gonzalez

Design 1: Marcus Centurion—page 206 bottom left; Angel Suarez—page 37, top right, bottom right. Desmond Gelman—page 50, top left, bottom left.

Design 7: Mark Marine—page 6, top left; David Boira—page 26, bottom left.

Georgia Institute of Technology, College of Architecture

Studio Critic: Bruce Lonnman

First-year design: page 14, bottom left. Josh Andrews—page 34, bottom right. John Sitton—page 188, bottom left; page 252, bottom right.

Studio Critic: Lee Kean

Second year design: Greg Sugano—page 5, bottom right; Brian Karlowitz—page 191, top left.

Studio Critic: Tahar Messadi

Third year design: Micah Hall—page 6, bottom left.

Studio Critic: Harris Dimitropoulos

Mike Piper—page 181, bottom left; page 43, top left; page 253, bottom right. Casper Voogt—page 46, top left. Bernard Gingras—page 46, bottom left. Sam Hoang—page 252, top right.

Studio Critic: Denise Dumais

Fourth year design: Cameron Beasley—page 63, top middle, bottom middle; page 181, top right.

Studio Critic: Michael Gamble

Graduate design studio: Rob Bartlett—page 7, bottom right; page 189, top right, page 196, bottom right; page 244, top right. Tim Black—page 15, top right. Meridith Colon—page 43, bottom left. Daniel Maas—page 202, bottom left. Jason Vetne—page 245, top right.

Studio Critic: Chris Jarrett

Graduate design studio: Lyle Woodall—page 62, top right. Garvin Smith—page 43, bottom right. David Guirdry—page 63, top right.

Studio Critic: Charles Rudolph

Graduate design studio: Troy Stenlez—page 5, top left; page 252, top left.

Studio Critic: Carlos Tardio

Page 5, top right; page 6, top right; page 55, top middle, top right, bottom middle, bottom right; page 193, top left. Mihir Patel—page 54, top middle, bottom middle.

Iowa State University, Architecture Department

Studio Critic: Karen Bermann

Pre-Architecture Studio: Michelle Swanson—page 36, top left, bottom left. Kate Podany,—page 254, bottom left.

Louisiana Tech University, School of Architecture

Studio Critic: Damon Caldwell

Christopher Anderson—page 133, bottom left. Benjamin Barker—page 133, bottom right. Jared Boudreaux—page 131, top middle. Lucas Bridges—page 132, top middle. Damon Caldwell—page 127, bottom right; page 131, top right, bottom left. Robyn Crumby—page 130, top middle, top right. Kyle Culver—page 134, top left. Darrell Foy—page 138, top middle, top right, bottom left, bottom middle, bottom right.

Group 3—page 122 bottom left. Emily Gullatt—page 128, bottom left. Cassidy Keim—page 135, top right. McCune Keim—page 137, top left, top right, bottom left, bottom right. Lance Mathews—page 129, top left. Frank Meyer—page 126, top left, top right, bottom left; page 132, bottom middle; page 203, top right. MMKK—page 135, top left.

The Ohio State University, Austin E. Knowlton, School of Architecture

Studio Critic: Bruce Lonnman

First year design: page 50, top right.

Southern California Institute of Architecture

Studio Critics: Tom Buresh, Annie Chu, Perry Kulper

Graduate design studio: Cameron Beasley—page 14, top right; page 254, bottom right.

Southern Polytechnic State University School of Architecture

Studio Critic: Frank Venning

Vertical design studio: Chris Crossman—page 185, top left. Clyde Clair—page 8, bottom left. Pual Deeley—page 8, bottom right. Ruben Aniekwu—page 239, bottom left. Chris Garrett—page 17, top left. Thad Truett—page 17, bottom left; page 180, bottom left. Scott Jeffries—page 185, bottom right; page 190, bottom middle. Don Son—page 189, bottom right. Karin Keuller—page 253, top left. Bart Stone—page 201, top right.

Studio Critics: Howard Itzkowitz and Jordan Williams

Second year design: Scott Fleming—page 17, bottom right; page 181, top right; page 64, bottom right. Steve Damico—page 63, bottom right.

Syracuse University, School of Architecture

Studio Critic: Bruce Lonnman

First year design:—page 18, top right; page 34, top left; page 37, top middle, bottom middle; page 63, top left.

Structures: page 24, top left.

Tuskegee University Department of Architecture

Studio Critics: Criss Mills, Patricia Kerlin, George Epolito

Second year design: Allen Pickstock—page 50, bottom middle; page 186, bottom middle. Grant Kolbe—page 50, bottom right. Dayton Schroeter—page 251, top right.

Studio Critic: Criss Mills

Fourth year design: Stephen Douglas—page 50, top middle; page 253, top right.

Studio Critics: Criss Mills, Jack Ames

Thesis studio: Leslie Musikavanhu—foreword; page 3, bottom left. Emilee Eide and Todd Niemiec—page 180, top left.

University of the Arab Emirates

Studio Critic: Bechir Kenzari

Salha Suliman Al Hassani—page 193, bottom left. Hanadi Rashed Al Zaabi—page 193, bottom right.

University of Arkansas, School of Architecture

Studio Critics: Tim DeNoble, Michael Bruno, Tad Gloeckler, Steven Miller

Second-year design: Juan Andrad—page 24, top left.

University of Auckland, School of Architecture

Studio Critic: Beshire Kenzari

Design 2 and design 3: Kenneth Sin—page 200, bottom right. Melanie Tonkin—page 186, bottom right.

University of North Carolina at Charlotte, College of Architecture

Studio Critic: Jose Gamez

Fourth year design: Zeb Smith—page 68, top left, bottom left, top right, bottom right.

University of Southwestern Louisiana, School of Architecture

Studio Critics: Hector Lasala, Ed Gaskin

Basic Design Studio: Jason Simeneaux—page 56, top left, top right, bottom left, bottom right.

Architecture Design III: Randy Damico—page 3, top right; page 67, top left, top right, bottom left, bottom middle, bottom right; page 254, top left.

University of Texas at San Antonio

Studio Critic: Candid Rogers

Cassandra Cantu, Bailey Porter, Claudio Resendiz—page 45, bottom left. Jaime Alfredo, Domingo Sanchez, Jose Terrazas—page 76, top middle, top right, bottom left, bottom middle, bottom right.

Wentworth Institute of Technology

Studio Critic: Professor Dr. Sigrun Prahl

Design V Housing, Fall 2003: David Noe, Erick Swenson—page 256, top middle, bottom middle.

Design Professionals
3XN

Liverpool

Page 4, top middle; page 18, bottom right; page 19, top middle, top right; page 21, top middle, top left; page 22, bottom right; page 26, bottom right; page 60, bottom right; page 61, top right; page 99, top middle, top right, bottom left, bottom middle, bottom right; page 100, top left, top middle, top right, bottom left, bottom middle, bottom right.

Renault Truckland

Page 97, top left, top right, bottom left, bottom right; page 98, top left, top middle, top right, bottom left, bottom middle, bottom right.

Jack Ames, Architect

Page 196, top right.

BIG—Bjarke Ingels Group

Slussen

Client: Stockholm Stad. Collaborators: AKT. Size 85.000 M2. Location: Stockholm, SE. Status: Ongoing. Team: Bjarke Ingels, Niels Lund Petersen, Jan Magasanik, Mark Jay, David Marek, Ole Schroder, Roberto Rosales Salazar, Maria Mavrikou, Kamil Szoltysek, Daniel Sundlin, Harry Wei, Christian Alvarez Wei, Teis Draiby, Ondrej Janku, Johan Cool—page 16, top right.

Shanghai Expo 2010 Danish Pavillion

Type: Commission. Size: 3,000M2. Client: Erhavers-og Byggestyrelsen. Collaborators: 2+1, Arup AGU. Location: Shanghai, China. Status: Ongoing. Team: Bjarke Ingels, Niels Lund Petersen, Henrick Villemoes Poulsen, Finn Norkjaer, Jan Magasanik, Kamil Szoltysek, Sonja Reisinger, Tobia Hjortdahl, Klaus Tversted, Jan Borgstrom, Pauline Lavie, Teis Draiby, Daniel Sundlin, Line Gericke, Armen Menendian, Karsten Hammer Hansen, Martin Mortensen—page 7, top right; page 11, top middle; page 13, top left; page 23, bottom left, bottom middle; page 33, top left, bottom left; page 39, bottom right; page 104, top middle,

top right, bottom left, bottom middle, bottom right; page 105, top left, top middle, top right, bottom left, bottom middle, bottom right; page 106, top left, top middle, top right, bottom left, bottom middle, bottom right.

Mountain Dwellings

Client: Hopfner A/S, Danish Oil Company A/S. Size: 33,000M2. Location: Copenhagen, DK. Status: Completed Summer 2008. Collaborator: JDS, Moe & Brodsgaard, Freddy Madsen, SLA. Team: Bjarke Ingels, Jakob Lange, Finn Norkjaer, Jan Borgstrom, Henrick Villemoes Poulsen, Julien De Smedt, Annette Jensen, Dariusz Bojarski, Dennis Rasmussen, Eva Hviid-Nielsen, Joao Vieira Costa, Jorn Jensen, Karsen V. Vestergaard, Karsten Hammer Hansen, Leon Rost, Louise Steffensen, Malte Rosenquist, Mia Frederiksen, Ole Elkjaer-Larsen, Olle Nannberg, Roberto Rosales Salazar, Rong Bin, Sophus Sobye, Soren Lambertsen, Wataru Tanaka—page 13, bottom left; page 23, top left, top middle; page 101, top middle, top right, bottom left, bottom middle, bottom right; page 102, top left, top middle, top right, bottom left, bottom middle, bottom right.

Scala Tower, Public Library, Hotel, Offices

Client: Centerplan. Collaborators: Adams Kara Taylor, The Municipality of Copenhagen. Size: 45,000M2. Height: 145M. Location: Copenhagen, DK. Status Ongoing: (Designed 2007). Team: Bjarke Ingels, Andreas Klok Pedersen, Camilla Hoel Eduardsen, Christian Bratz, Karsten Hammer Hansen, Simon Lyager

Poulsen, Ville Haimala, Sara Sosio, Julia Szierer, Daichi Takano—page 103, top middle, top right, bottom left, bottom middle, bottom right.

Robert Bruhns/Jack Ames

Page 186, top right.

Callas, Shortridge Architects—by Steven Shortridge

Page 87, top left, top right, bottom left, bottom right; page 88, top left, top right, bottom left, bottom middle, bottom right.

Charleston Civic Design Center

Page 180, bottom right; page 16, bottom left, bottom right; page 242 top right.

Coop Himmelb(l)au

Page 132, bottom left; page 154, top right, bottom right; page 155, top left, bottom left, bottom middle, top right, middle right, bottom right; page 156, top left, bottom left, top right; page 157, top, middle, bottom.

Courtesy of Eisenman Architects

Page 144, bottom right; page 145, top left, bottom left, top middle, top right, bottom right.

Enric Miralles and Benedetta Tagliabue Architects

Arcelor Pavilion

Pavilion for a centenary for the city of Esch-sur-Alzette in Luxembourg, Esch-sur-Azlette,

Luxembourg, 2005–2006. Project leader: Makoto Fukuda (Miralles Tagliabue EMBT). Collaborators: Nancy Chidiac, Morten Engel, Mariano Castillo, Gaele Cabessa, Gabriele Rotelli, Guile Amadeu, Aaron Beasley, Marco Orozco, José Angel Ramon, Michela Cicuta, Maria Chiara Ziliani, Andrea Pagliarulo, Seth Wilson, Verónica Valeros, Andrew J. Yalcin, Eulalia Marisma, Steven Fuhrman, Lythia Xynogala, Carlos Sarmiento, Catalina Montaña (Miralles Tagliabue EMBT). Architects on site: Stefano Moreno (Moreno Architeture). Engineer Structure General: Walter de Toffol (INCA Ingénieurs Conséils Associés). Tecnic Colaborator: Pierre Engel (Arcelor Building & Construction Support). Client: Arcelor. Contractor: Queck—page 3, top left; page 11, bottom left; page 33, top right, bottom right; page 92, top middle top right, bottom left, bottom middle, bottom right.

New Headquarters of Gas Natural

Barcelona, October 1999–2007. Client: Torremarenostrum S.L.: Gas Natural SDG S.A.

Competition Project Team Elena Rocchi. Collaborators Xavier Rodriguez, Tomoko Sakamoto, Javier Garcia German, Daniel Roselló, Marc de Rooij, Umberto Viotto, Torsten Skoetz, Sania Belli, Josep Mias, Marta Cases, Ezequiel Cattaneo.

Model Fabian Asunción, Leonardo Giovannozzi, Francesco Matucci, Rafael de Montard, Sonia Henriques, Jan Löcke, Cristiane Stauss, Barbara Oelbrandt, Mette Olsen, Jad Salhab, Akira Kita, Annie Marcela Henao.

Initial Design Phase: Project Director: Elena Rocchi, Lluís Cantallops. Project team: Roberto Sforza, Andrea Landell de Moura, Lluis Corbella. Collaborators: Leonardo Giovannozzi, Fabrizio Massoni, Umberto Viotto, Mònica Batalla. Model Fabian Asunción, Rafael de Montard.

Detailed Design Phase: Project Director: Josep Ustrell. Project Team: Andrea Salies Landell de Moura, Lluis Corbella, Roberto Sforza, Montse Galindo, Marco Dario Chirdel, Eugenio Cirulli, Adriana Ciocoletto, Liliana Sousa. Collaborators: Miguel del Olmo, Elena Nedelcu, Nagy Péter Sándor, Christian Kreifelts, Davin Robinson, Celine Carbes, Paulo Carneiro, Bernardo Figueirinhas, Katrin Wittman, Fabio Sgroi, Alexandra Spiegel, Federica Gozzi, Ludwig Godefroy, Laura Valentini, Massimo Chizzola, Santiago Crespi, , Adelaida Passeti. Model: Christian Molina, Stefan Geenen, Maria Pierres, Felipe Bernal, Abelardo Gómez, Daniel Erfeld, Jordi Rollan, Miguel Sánchez, Ana Stoppani, Dirk Mayer, Nuno Rodríguez, Gabriele Rotelli, Rocco Tenca. Structure: Julio Martinez Calzón, MC2 Estudio de Ingenieria, Madrid. Services: PGI Grup. Quantity Surveyor: CIC. M. Roig i Assoc. S.L.—page 10, bottom right; page 39, bottom middle; page 93, top middle, top right, bottom left, bottom middle, bottom right.

Public Library in Palafolls, Barecelona, Spain 1997–2007

Promotor: Town Hall of Palafolls. Construction Project; February 1999

Principals-in-charge: Josep Ustrell, Makoto Fukuda.

Collaborators: Tomoko Sakamoto, Sania Belli, Koichi Tono, Markus Lechelt, Jan Maurits Locke, Juan Carlos Mejía del Valle, Adrien Versuere, Richard Breit, FlorenciaVetcher, Jad Salhab, Nils Becker, Ezequiel Cattaneo, Manuela Schubert, Marco Orozco, Josep Mias, Daniele Baratelli, Daniele Romanelli, Catalina Montaña, Ornella Lazzari. Natalia Leone.

Basic Project: November 1998. Project Team: Makoto Fukuda, Hirotaka Koizumi.

Collaborators: Guillame Faraut, Angel Gaspar Casado.

Competition: First Prize, August 1997

Collaborators in the competition: Elena Rocchi, Michael Eichorn, Niels Martin Larsen, Nicolai Lund Overgaard, Isabel Sambeth, Ana Maria Romero, Germán Rojas, Carlos Alberto Ruiz, Alfonso Lopez, Marc de Rooij. Site Area: 1700 m^2, Building area: 714 m^2.

Client(s): Town Hall of Palafolls. Consultants: Engineering: STATIC, Gerardo Gonzalez, Barcelona, Nilo Lletjós (IOC). Mechanical engineer(s): Interior designer(s): Miralles Tagliabue–EMBT Landscape architect(s): Miralles Tagliabue–EMBT. Surveyor: Albert Ribera, Barcelona. Services: PGI, Instalaciones Arquitectónicas, Josep Massachs—page 13, top middle; page 58, top middle, bottom middle; page 91, top left, top right, bottom left, bottom right.

Rehabilitation of Santa Caterina Market

Barcelona, 1997–2005

Awards: Primer Premio en Concurso, Abril 1997 National Award of Generalitat de Catalunya 2001, Spanish Ceramic Awards ASCER 2005–Architectural Prize, Ciutat de Barcelona Award 2005. Saloni Award 2006

Client: Foment de Ciutat Vella S.A. Definitive Project 1999–2005. Project Director: Igor Peraza. Collaborators: Hirotaka Koizumi, Josep Miàs, Marta Cases, Constanza Chara, Fabián Asunción, Eugenio Cirulli, Santiago Crespi, Gianfranco Grondona, Lluis Corbella, Massimo Chizzola, Makoto Fukuda, Joan Poca, Alejandra Vazquez, Marco Dario Chirdel, Josep Belles. Alicia Bramon, Laura Valentini, Adelaide Passetti, Jorge Carvajal, Andrea Landell de Moura, Torsten Skoetz, Karl Unglaub, Adrien Verschuere, Loïc Gestin, Annie Marcela Henao Ezequiel Cattaneo, Leonardo Giovannozzi, Annette Hoëller, Sabine Bauchmann, Silke Techen, Barbara Oel Brandt, Mette Olsen, Florencia Vetcher, Nils Becker, Raphael de Montard, Montse Galindo, Barbara Appolloni, Jean François Vaudeville, Peter Sándor Nagy, Ignacio Quintana, Christian Molina, Stefan Geenen, Maarten Vermeiren, Torsten Schmid, Tobias Gottschalk, Stefan Eckert, Ute Grolz, Thomas Wuttke, Luca Tonella, Stephanie Le Draoullec, Monica Carrera, Mirko Sivestri, Beatriz Minguez de Molina.

Special collaboration: Ricardo Flores, Eva Prats. Basic Project 1998

Collaborators: Joan Callis, Makoto Fukuda, Hirotaka Kuizumi, Fabián Asunción, Ane Ebbeskov Olsen, Dani Rosselló, Francesco Mozzati, Francesco Jacques-Dias, Fernanda Hannah.

Competition: 18 April 1997. Collaborators: Elena Rocchi, Makoto Fukuda, Ricardo Flores, Fabian Asunción, German Zambrana, Lluis Cantallops, Anna Maria Tosi, Marc Forteza Parera, Anna Galmer, Liliana Bonforte, Tobias Gottschalk, Stefan Eckert, Ute Grölz, Thomas Wuttke, Luca Tonella, Stéphanie Le Draoullec, Monica Carrera.

Engineer Structure (General): Robert Brufau. Engineer (Roof): Jose Maria Velasco Engineer (Housing): Miquel Llorens. Installations: PGI. Ceramic manufacturer: Toni Cumella—page 94, top left, top right, bottom left, bottom right; page 95, top left, top middle, top right, bottom.

Spanish Pavilion for Shanghai World Expo 2010

First prize June 2007

Competition: Project Director: Makoto Fukuda, Arch, Salvador Gilabert, Arch

Project: Project Director: Salvador Gilabert, Arch

Construction: Project Director: Salvador Gilabert, Arch

Project Director on site: Igor Peraza, Arch

Collaboradors (Miralles Tagliabue EMBT): Makoto Fukuda. Arch., Mattia Cappelletti, Arch., Vaiva Simoliunaite, Arch, Arch., Jack O'Kelly, Arch., Qiwei Hu, Arch., Gabriele Rotelli, Arch. Guile Amadeu. Ailyn Alfaro, Alessandra Deidda, Alessandro Balbi, Alice Puleo, Armando Arteaga, Barbara Asnaghi, Carles Pastor, Carolina Carvalho, Cesar Trujillo, Christian Pamies, Clara Nubiola, Cristina Salvi, Daniela Bortz, Diego Parra, Ermanno Marota, Ewa Pic, Fernanda Riotto Fernandes, Francesca Ciprini, Françoise Lempereur, Gian Mario Tonossi, Giorgia Cetto, Giovanni Cetto, Gitte Kjaer, Giuseppe Maria Fanara, Gordon Tannhauser, Guillermo Marcondes Zambrano, Guto Santos, Jan Kokol, Johane Ronsholt, Jose Andrés Cantor, Jose Antonio Pavon, Judith Plas, Kazuya Morita, Kirsti Øygarden, Lee Shun Chieh, Lin Chia Ping, Logan Yuen, Luciana Cardoso, Luis Alejandro Vivas, Manuel Rearte, Marco Quagliatini, Maria Francesca Origa, Maria Loucaidou, Marta Martinez, Michael González, Michelangelo Pinto, Michele Buizza, Mireia Soriano, Natalia Leone, Noelia Pickard, Olivia Kostika, Paola Lodi, Paul Andrew Brogna, Phuoc Tan Huynh, Roberto Stefano Naboni, Sara Cuccu, Simona Covello, Stefan Geenen, Susana Oses, Travis McCarra, Verena Vogler, Virginia Chiappa Nunez, Xavier Ferrús, Rafael Loschiavo Miranda Client: SEEI (Sociedad Estatal para Exposiciones Internacionales). Date: 2007—in progress. Inauguration date: 1 May 2010. Place: Shanghai, China. Area: 8500 mq—page 61, bottom left; page 96, top middle, top right, bottom left, bottom middle, bottom right: page 120, top right; page 190, top right.

All Images Courtesy of Garofalo Architects and Inigo Manglano-Ovalie

Page 150, top right, bottom right; page 151, top left, bottom left, top middle, bottom middle, top right, bottom right.

Copyright Gehry Partners, LLP

Page 146, bottom right; page 147, top left, bottom left, top middle, bottom middle, top right, bottom right; page 148, top left, top middle, bottom middle, top right; page 149, bottom left, top left, top right.

Henning Larsen Architects

Page 127, top left, top right; page 128, top left, top right; page 129, top right, bottom left; page 130, bottom left; page 132, top right; page 186, bottom left; page 193, top right.

The Copenhagen Opera House

Page 11, top right; page 12, bottom left; page 15, bottom right; page 21, top right; page 57, top right, bottom right; page 107, top left, top right, bottom; page 108, top left, top middle, top right, bottom left, bottom middle.

Massar Children's Discovery Center

Page 4, top right; page 5, bottom left; page 9, top middle; page 11, top left; page 12, bottom

right; page 19, top left, bottom middle; page 23, right; page 35, top left, bottom left; page 60, top middle, top right; page 111, top middle, top right, bottom left, bottom middle, bottom right; page 112, top left, top middle, top right, bottom left, bottom middle, bottom right; page, 113 top left, top middle, top right, bottom left, bottom middle, bottom right; page 192, top left; page 254, top right.

The Scala Competition

Page 13, top right; page 53, bottom left, bottom middle, bottom right; page 58 top left, bottom left; page 110, top middle, top right, bottom left, bottom middle, bottom right; page 256, bottom right.

The Samba Bank Headquarters

Page 7, bottom left; page 58, top right, bottom right; page 61, bottom right; page 109, top middle, top right, bottom left, bottom middle, bottom right.

Bruce Lonnman

Page 17, top right.

MC2 Architects Inc.

Page 8, top left; page 10, top left; page 14, bottom middle; page 41, bottom right; page 181, bottom right; page 201, bottom right; page 202, top right; page 203, bottom left, top left; page 254, bottom middle.

Copyright Mithun, Juan Hernandez

Page 16, top left; page 25, bottom middle.

Morphosis

Rensselaer Electronic Media and Performing Arts Center Competition, 2001 Troy, New York

Team: Principal/Lead Designer: Thom Mayne; Project Designers: Edgar Hatcher and Chris Warren; Project Assistants: Hanjo Gelink, Carlos Gomez and Eghard Woeste—page 132, bottom right; page 141, top left, top right.

Antoine Predock

Page 152, bottom right; page 153, top left, bottom left, top right.

Roto Architects Inc.

Page 89, top left, top right, bottom left, bottom right; page 90, top left, top right, bottom left.

Rowhouse Architects Inc.

Page 24, top right; page 44, top right, bottom right; page 181, bottom middle.

Ryobi Technologies Inc.

Page 27, top left, top right.

Mack Scogin Merrill Elam Architects, Inc. (formerly Scogin, Elam and Bray Architects)

Buckhead Library

Page 78, top right, bottom left, bottom right.

Laban Dance Centre, BIS Competition, Reston Museum

Page 79, top left, top right, bottom left, bottom middle, bottom right.

Morrow Library

Page 80, top left, top right, bottom left, bottom middle, bottom right.

Turner Center Chapel

Page 81, top left, top right, bottom left.

Fine Arts Center, University of Connecticut at Storrs

Mack Scogin with Merrill Elam; Design team: David Yocum, Eulho Suh, Chris Hoxie, Cameron Wu, Cecilia Tham, Barnum Tiller, Brian Bell, Helen Han, Kenneth Cowart, Adam Stillman, Helen Chu, Katherine Bray. Stereolithography Consultant: American Precision Prototyping, Jason Dickman. Theater Planning and Design Consultant: Fisher Dachs Associates, Joshua Dachs. Performing and Visual Arts Construction Cost Management: Donnell Consultants, Sean Ryan. Landscape Architects: Michael Van Valkenburgh Associates, Mattew Urbanski. Engineers: Arup, Caroline Fitzgerald, Neil Woodger and Raj Patel. Associate Architect: Loyd Taft Archtiect, Loyd Taft. Lighting Consultant: Lam Partners, Bob Osten and Justin Brown—116, top left; page 143, top right, bottom middle, bottom right.

Gates Center for Computer Science

Design Team: Mack Scogin Merrill Elam Architects. Architect, Michael Van Valkenburgh Associates. Landscape Architect, EDGE Studio. Local Architect, Gensler Associate Architect. Civil and Environmental Consultants Civil and Geotechnical Engineer: Arup Structural Engineer, Arup Mechanical and Plumbing Engineer, Arup Lighting Design, Arup Electrical Engineer, Arup Fire Protection and Life Safety Consultant, Arup Communications and IT Consultant, Arup LEED Consultant, Arup Acoustical Engineer Arup Audiovisual Consultant, Arup Security Consultant, Collective Wisdom Specifications Consulting CHBH Digital Assets Manager, Heery International Cost Consultant, C & C Lighting Pausch Bridge Lighting Design, Tim Haahs Parking Consultant, Ingersoll Rand Security and Safety Hardware Consultant.

Wiss, Janny, Elstner Associates Façade Assessment, P. J. Dick, Incorporated Construction Manager Construction Engineering Consultants Geotechnical Engineer, Gateway Engineers Surveyor.

Mack Scogin Merrill Elam Architects: Mack Scogin Principal, Merrill Elam, Principal; Lloyd Bray, Senior Project Architect, Kimberly Shoemake-Medlock Senior Project Architect and Manager Alan Locke, Jared Serwer, Jason Hoeft, Clark Tate, B Vithayathawornwong, Dennis Sintic, Carrie Hunsicker, Misty Boykin, Barnum Tiller, Matt Weaver, John Trefry, Margaret Fletcher, Helen Han, Ben Arenberg, Brian Bell, Trey Lindsey, Francesco Giacobello, Daniel Cashen, Jeff Collins, Janna Kauss, Patrick Jones, Cayce Bean, Jeff Kemp, Anja Turowski , Bo Roberts, Matthew Leach, Gary McGaha, Ted Paxton, Britney Bagby, Jacob Coburn, Amanda Crawley—page 3, bottom right; page 21, bottom left; page 86, top left, top right, bottom left, bottom right.

Knowlton Hall, School of Architecture

Project Team: Architect: Mack Scogin Merrill Elam Architects, Mack Scogin with Merrill Elam, David Yocum, Brian Bell, John Trefry, Penn Ruderman, Barnum Tiller, Cecila Tham, Jeffrey Collins, Kevin Gotsch, Margaret Fletcher. Associate Architects: WSA Studio, formally Wandel and Schnell Architects, Inc. Robert Wandel, AIA, Principal. Cissy Wong, AIA, Project Architect. Alan Sulser, Ivan Amy, Lannetta Vader, Yanitza Brongers, Kristen Poldemann. Structural Engineer: Lantz, Jones & Nebraska, Inc. Mechanical/Electrical/Plumbing Engineer: H.A.W.A. Consulting Engineers. Civil Engineer: Bird & Bull, Inc. Landscape Architect: Michael Van Valkenburgh Associates. General Contractor: P. J. Dick, Inc. Photographer: Timothy Hursley, The Arkansas Office—page 5, bottom middle; page 10, bottom left; page 59, top right, bottom right; page 83, top middle, top right, bottom left, bottom middle, bottom right; page 84, top left, top middle, top right, bottom left, bottom middle, bottom right.

Pittsburgh Children's Museum

Mack Scogin with Merrill Elam, Design Team: Cecelia Tham, David Yocum, Briam Bell, Tim Harrison, Barnum Tiller, Ted Paxton,

Charlotte Henderson, Hillary Ingram, Penn Ruderman, Angela Pearce, Special Consultants (3D modeling preparation for translation into stereolithography) model: Kimo Griggs Architects, Kimo Griggs—page 142, top right, bottom right; page 143, top left, bottom left.

Wang Campus Center, Wellesley College

Project Team: Architects: Mack Scogin Merrill Elam Architects. Mack Scogin with Merrill Elam, Timothy Harrison, Christopher Agosta, David Yocum, Kimberly Shoemake-Medlock, Jeffrey Collins, Jennifer Pindyck, Barnum Tiller, Christian Rice, Michael Wirsching, Jennifer Hurst, John Trefry, Stephen Trimble, Kevin Gotsch, Andrea Korber, Jane Lee, Ashley Moore, Margaret Fletcher, Brian Bell, Trey Lindsey, Sophia Greenbaum, Helen Han, Ted Paxton, Landscape Architect: Michael Van Valkenburgh Associates, Structural Mechanical and Plumbing Engineer: Arup. Civil Engineer: Vanasse Hangen Brustlin, General Contractor: Richard White Sons, Project Managers: Genesis Partners, Lighting Consultant: LAM Partners, Photographer: Timothy Hursley—page 9, top left; page 11, bottom middle; page 39, top right; page 40, bottom right; page 82, top middle, top right, bottom left, bottom right.

Yale University Health Services Building

Design Team: Mack Scogin Merrill Elam Architects Architect. Perkins + Will Health

Services Design Consultant Michael Van Valkenburgh Associates Landscape Architect, HM White Site Architects Landscape Architect of Record, Nitsch Engineering Civil Engineer, DeSimone Consulting Engineers Structural Engineer, Arup Mechanical and Plumbing Engineer, Arup Lighting Design, Arup Electrical Engineer, Arup Fire Protection and Life Safety Consultant, Arup Communications and IT Consultant, Arup Acoustical Engineer, Arup Audiovisual Consultant, Arup Security Consultant.

Collective Wisdom Specifications Consulting, Atelier Ten Environmental Engineer

Front Façade Consultant: Ryan-Biggs Associates Façade Engineer, Vermuelens Cost Consultants Cost Consultant. Tighe & Bond Parking Consultant. Turner Construction Company Construction Manager, Haley & Aldrich Geotechnical Engineer, Stephen Bang Consultants Food Service Consultants.

Mack Scogin Merrill Elam Architects: Mack Scogin, Principal, Merrill Elam, Principal. Jennifer Pindyck, Bud Shenefelt, Michael Filisky, B Vithayathawornwong, Christopher Agosta David Karle, Anja Turowski, Clark Tate, Jason Hoeft, Christopher Almeida, Mack Cole-Edelsack, Trey Lindsey, Misty Boykin, Laura Edwards, Matt Weaver, Carrie Hunsicker, Rubi Xu, Jeff Kemp, Margaret Fletcher, Bo Roberts, Jonathon Baker, Tim Do—page 85, top middle, top right, bottom left, bottom middle, bottom right.

Jack Thalinious

Page 43, bottom middle; page 191, bottom right; page 251, bottom right.

Frank Venning Architect

Page 8, top right; page 251, bottom left.

Z Corporation

Page 27, bottom left; page 123, top left; page 125, top left.

Photography Credits
3XN

Page 4, top middle; page 18, bottom right; page 19, top middle, top right; page 21, top middle, top left; page 22, bottom right; page 26, bottom right; page 60, bottom right; page 61, top right; page 97, top left, top right, bottom left, bottom right; page 98, top left, top middle, top right, bottom left, bottom middle, bottom right; page 99, top middle, top right, bottom left, bottom middle, bottom right; page 100, top left, top middle, top right, bottom left, bottom middle, bottom right.

Christopher Agosta

Page 142, bottom right; page 143, bottom left.

Assassi/Productions

Page 90, top left, bottom left.

BIG—Bjarke Ingels Group

Page 7, top right; page 11, top middle; Page 13, top left, bottom left; page 16, top right;

page 23, top left, top middle, bottom left, bottom middle; page 33, top left, bottom left; page 39, bottom right; page 101, top middle, top right, bottom left, bottom middle, bottom right; page 102, top left, top middle, top right, bottom left, bottom middle, bottom right; page 103, top middle, top right, bottom left, bottom middle, bottom right; page 104, top middle, top right, bottom left, bottom middle, bottom right; page 105, top left, top middle, top right, bottom left, bottom middle, bottom right; page 106, top left, top middle, top right, bottom left, bottom middle, bottom right.

Tom Bonner

Page 155, bottom left.

Loyd Bray

Page 78, top right, bottom left; page 79, bottom left; page 80, top left, top right, bottom middle, bottom left; page 81, top left, top right.

Damon Caldwell

Page 122, bottom left; page 126, top left, top right, bottom left; page 128, bottom left, bottom right; page 129, top left; page 130, bottom left, top middle, top right; page 131, top middle, top right; page 132, top middle, bottom middle; page 133, bottom left, bottom right; page 134, top left; page 135, top left, top right; page 137, top left, top right, bottom left, bottom right; page 138, top middle, top right, bottom left, bottom middle, bottom right; page 203, top right.

Benny Chan\Fotoworks

Page 89, top right, bottom left, bottom right.

Coop Himmelb(l)au

Page 132, bottom left; page 154, top right; page 155, top right, middle right; page 157, top middle, bottom middle.

Susan Desko

Page 79, top right.

Courtesy of Eisenman Architects

Page 144, bottom right; page 145, top left, bottom left, top middle, top right, bottom right.

All Images Courtesy of Garofalo Architects and Inigo Manglano-Ovalle

Page 150, top right, bottom right; page 151, top left, bottom left, top middle, bottom middle, top right, bottom right.

Copyright Gehry Partners, LLP

Page 146, bottom right; page 147, top left, bottom left, top middle, bottom middle, top right, bottom right; page 148, top left, top middle, bottom middle, top right; page 149, bottom left, top left, top right.

Henning Larsen Architects

Page 5, bottom left; page 7, bottom left; page 9, top middle; page 11, top left, top right; page 12, bottom left, bottom right; page 13, top right; page 15, bottom right; page 19, top left, bottom middle; page 21, top right; page 23, right; page 35, top left, bottom left; page 53, bottom left, bottom middle, bottom right; page 57, top right, bottom right; page 58 top left, top right, bottom left, bottom right; page 60, top middle, top right; page 61, bottom right; page 107, top left, top right, bottom; page 108, top left, top middle, top right, bottom left, bottom middle; page 109, top middle, top right, bottom left, bottom middle, bottom right; page 110, top middle, top right, bottom left, bottom middle, bottom right; page 111, top middle, top right, bottom left, bottom middle, bottom right; page 112, top left, top middle, top right, bottom left, bottom middle, bottom right; page, 113 top left, top middle, top right, bottom left, bottom middle, bottom right; page 192, top left; page 254, top right; page 256, bottom right.

Armin Hess

Page 155, bottom right.

Timothy Hursley

Page 78, bottom right; page 80, bottom right; page 81, bottom left.

Enric Miralles and Benedetta Tagliabue Architects

Page 3, top left; page 10, bottom right; page 11, bottom left; page 13, top middle; page 33, top right, bottom right; page 39, bottom middle; page 58, top middle, bottom middle; page 61, bottom left; page 91, top left, top right, bottom left, bottom right; page 92, top middle, top right, bottom left, bottom middle, bottom right; page 93, top middle, top right, bottom left, bottom middle, bottom right; page 94, top left, top right, bottom left, bottom right; page 95, top left, top middle, top right, bottom; page 96, top middle, top right, bottom left, bottom middle, bottom right: page 120 top right; page 190, top right.

Copyright Mithun, Juan Hernandez

Page 16, top left; page 25, bottom middle.

Bumyken Na

Page 93, bottom left.

Photo Copyright Robert Reck

Page 152, bottom right; page 153, top left, bottom left, top right.

Roto Architects Inc.

Page 89, top left; page 90, top right.

Mack Scogin Merrill Elam Architects, Inc. (formerly Scogin, Elam and Bray Architects)

Page 3, bottom right; page 5, bottom middle; page 9, top left; page 10, bottom left; page 11, bottom middle; page 21, bottom left; page 39, top right; page 40, bottom right; page 59, top right, bottom right; page 82, top middle, top right, bottom left, bottom right; page 83, top middle, top right, bottom left, bottom middle, bottom right; page 84, top left, top middle, top right, bottom left, bottom middle, bottom right; page 85, top middle, top right, bottom

left, bottom middle, bottom right; page 86, top left, top right, bottom left, bottom right; page 116, top left; page 142, top right, bottom right; page 143, top left, bottom left, bottom middle

Steven Shortridge

Page 87, top left, top right; page 88, top left, top right, bottom left, bottom middle, bottom right.

Sigrun Prahl and Erick Swenson

Page 256, top middle, bottom middle.

Eulho Suh

Page 143, top right, bottom right.

Carlos Tardio

Page 5, top right; page 6, top right; page 54, top middle, bottom middle; page 55, top middle, top right, bottom middle, bottom right; page 193, top left.

David Yocum

Page 79, top left, bottom middle, bottom right.

Marcel Weber

Page 157, bottom middle.

Brandon Welling

Page 141, top right, top left.

Copyright by Gerald Zuggman

Page 154, bottom right; page 155, top left; page 156, top left, bottom left, top right.

Z—Corporation

Page 27, bottom left; page 123, top left; page 125, top left.

INDEX